European Observatory on Health Systems and Policies Series

Edited by Josep Figueras, Martin McKee, Elias Mossialos and Richard B. Saltman

Human resources for health in Europe

Edited by

**Carl-Ardy Dubois,
Martin McKee and
Ellen Nolte**

Open University Press

Open University Press
McGraw-Hill Education
McGraw-Hill House
Shoppenhangers Road
Maidenhead
Berkshire
England
SL6 2QL

email: enquiries@openup.co.uk
world wide web: www.openup.co.uk

and Two Penn Plaza, New York, NY 10121–2289, USA

First published 2006

A catalogue record of this book is available from the British Library

ISBN-10: 0 335 21855 5 (pb)   0 335 21856 3 (hb)
ISBN-13: 978 0335 21855 4 (pb)   978 0335 21856 1 (hb)

Library of Congress Cataloging-in-Publication Data
CIP data applied for

Typeset by RefineCatch Limited, Bungay, Suffolk
Printed in the UK by Bell & Bain, Ltd, Glasgow

European Observatory on Health Systems and Policies Series

The European Observatory on Health Systems and Policies is a unique project that builds on the commitment of all its partners to improving health care systems:

- World Health Organization Regional Office for Europe
- Government of Belgium
- Government of Finland
- Government of Greece
- Government of Norway
- Government of Spain
- Government of Sweden
- Veneto Region
- European Investment Bank
- Open Society Institute
- World Bank
- CRP-Santé Luxembourg
- London School of Economics and Political Science
- London School of Hygiene and Tropical Medicine

The series

The volumes in this series focus on key issues for health policy-making in Europe. Each study explores the conceptual background, outcomes and lessons learned about the development of more equitable, more efficient and more effective health systems in Europe. With this focus, the series seeks to contribute to the evolution of a more evidence-based approach to policy formulation in the health sector.

These studies will be important to all those involved in formulating or evaluating national health care policies and, in particular, will be of use to health policy-makers and advisers, who are under increasing pressure to rationalize the structure and funding of their health systems. Academics and students in the field of health policy will also find this series valuable in seeking to understand better the complex choices that confront the health systems of Europe.

The Observatory supports and promotes evidence-based health policy-making through comprehensive and rigorous analysis of the dynamics of health care systems in Europe.

Series Editors

Josep Figueras is Head of the Secretariat and Research Director of the European Observatory on Health Systems and Policies and Head of the European Centre for Health Policy, World Health Organization Regional Office for Europe.

Martin McKee is Research Director of the European Observatory on Health Systems and Policies and Professor of European Public Health at the London School of Hygiene and Tropical Medicine as well as a co-director of the School's European Centre on Health of Societies in Transition.

Elias Mossialos is Research Director of the European Observatory on Health Systems and Policies and Brian Abel-Smith Reader in Health Policy, Department of Social Policy, London School of Economics and Political Science and Co-Director of LSE Health and Social Care.

Richard B. Saltman is Research Director of the European Observatory on Health Systems and Policies and Professor of Health Policy and Management at the Rollins School of Public Health, Emory University in Atlanta, Georgia.

European Observatory on Health Systems and Policies Series

Series Editors: Josep Figueras, Martin McKee, Elias Mossialos and Richard B. Saltman

Published titles

Purchasing to improve health systems performance
Josep Figueras, Ray Robinson, Elke Jakubowski (eds)

Health policy and European Union enlargement
Martin McKee, Laura MacLehose and Ellen Nolte (eds)

Regulating entrepreneurial behaviour in European health care systems
Richard B. Saltman, Reinhard Busse and Elias Mossialos (eds)

Social health insurance systems in Western Europe
Richard B. Saltman, Reinhard Busse and Josep Figueras (eds)

Health care in Central Asia
Martin McKee, Judith Healy and Jane Falkingham (eds)

Hospitals in a changing Europe
Martin McKee and Judith Healy (eds)

Funding health care: options for Europe
Elias Mossialos, Anna Dixon, Josep Figueras and Joe Kutzin (eds)

Regulating pharmaceuticals in Europe: striving for efficiency, equity and quality
Elias Mossialos, Monique Mrazek and Tom Walley (eds)

Forthcoming titles

Mental health policy and practice across Europe
Martin Knapp, David McDaid, Elias Mossialos and Graham Thornicroft (eds)

Primary care in the driver's seat
Richard B. Saltman, Ana Rico and Wienke Boerma (eds)

Human resources for health in Europe

✓

The European Observatory on Health Systems and Policies is a partnership between the World Health Organization Regional Office for Europe, the Governments of Belgium, Finland, Greece, Norway, Spain and Sweden, the Veneto Region, the European Investment Bank, the Open Society Institute, the World Bank, CRP-Santé Luxembourg, the London School of Economics and Political Science and the London School of Hygiene and Tropical Medicine.

Contents

Acknowledgements

This volume is one of a series of books produced by the European Observatory on Health Systems and Policies. We are grateful to all the authors for their hard work and enthusiasm in this project and to Armin Fidler for writing the Foreword.

In addition to the work of the authors (see List of contributors), this work draws on a series of nine case studies provided by: Suzanne Wait (France); Susanne Weinbrenner and Reinhard Busse (Germany); Natasha Azzopardi Muscat and Kenneth Grech (Malta); Are-Harald Brenne (Norway); Monika Strózik (Poland); Kirill Danichevski (Russia); Beatriz González López-Valcárcel, Carmen Delia Dávila Quintana and Elena Rodríguez Socorro (Spain); James Buchan and Alan Maynard (UK); and Zilvinas Padaiga, Luidvika Lovkyte, Zeneta Logminiene and Jack Reamy (Lithuania). These case studies will be appearing in a companion volume, for which we are grateful to Bernd Rechel for editing.

We appreciate the contributions of those who participated in a workshop held in Berlin to discuss a draft of the volume. These were, in addition to the case study writers and the chapter authors: Walter Baer, Philip Berman, Auron Cara, Paul de Raeve, Tatul Hakobyan, Gulin Gedik, Galina Perfilieva, Pille Saar, Peter Scherer, Markus Schneider, Noah Simmons, Marjukka Vallimies Patomaki and Lud F. J. van der Velden. We are also grateful to Reinhard Busse and his assistant Patricia Meirelles for hosting and organizing the workshop.

We are especially grateful to the Canadian Health Services Research Foundation for their award of a post-doctoral fellowship to Dr Dubois, and to Jonathan Lomas, its Chief Executive Officer, for his support and encouragement.

We very much appreciated the time taken by the final reviewers, Nigel Edwards and Philip Berman, and we benefited from their helpful comments and suggestions.

Finally, this book would not have appeared without the hard work throughout the project of the production team led by Francine Raveney, with the able assistance of Sue Gammerman, Caroline White and Nicole Satterley.

List of tables

List of figures

List of contributors

Carl Afford is a consultant on employment and social affairs based in Brussels with particular interest in labour economics, health sector employment and the dissemination of good practice.

Rita Baeten is researcher at the Observatoire Social Européen in Brussels on issues related to health care and the European Union.

James Buchan is Professor in the Faculty of Health and Social Sciences at Queen Margaret University College, Edinburgh.

Anna Dixon is Lecturer in European Health Policy in the Department of Social Policy at the London School of Economics and Political Science.

Carl-Ardy Dubois is Assistant professor in the Faculty of Nursing Sciences at the University of Montreal.

Sigrún Gunnarsdóttir is a PhD candidate at LSHTM and a researcher and consultant in nursing human resource management at Landspitali University Hospital Reykjavík.

Yves Jorens is Professor of social security law (national and international), at the Faculty of Law of the Ghent and Antwerp University in Belgium. He holds responsible positions in different EU-Projects on European Social Issues. He is also a lawyer at the Brussels Bar.

Elizabeth K. Kachur is a medical education consultant with 22 years of experience in the field.

Karl Krajic is a senior scientist at the Ludwig Boltzmann Institute for the Sociology of Health and Medicine, director of the University Course on Teaching in Nursing and Midwifery Education and lecturer at the Sociology department of the University of Vienna.

Suszy Lessof is Project Manager at the European Observatory on Health Systems and Policies.

Ann Mahon is Senior Fellow and Director of Postgraduate Programmes at the Centre for Public Policy and Management, Manchester Business School, University of Manchester.

Alan Maynard is Professor of Health Economics and Director of the York Health Policy Group in the Department of Health Sciences at the University of York.

Martin McKee is Research Director at the European Observatory on Health systems and Policies and Professor of European Public Health at the London School of Hygiene and Tropical Medicine.

Ellen Nolte is a Senior Lecturer at the London School of Hygiene and Tropical Medicine and a Research Fellow at the European Observatory on Health Systems and Policies.

Anne Marie Rafferty is Professor of Nursing Policy and Dean of the Florence Nightingale School of Nursing and Midwifery, King's College, London.

Charles Shaw is an independent adviser to WHO, World Bank, national aid agencies and ministries of health on quality in health care systems.

Bonnie Sibbald is Professor of Health Services Research at the National Primary Care Research and Development Centre and Chair of the University of Manchester Institute of Health Sciences.

Ruth Young is Reader in Health Policy Evaluation at the Florence Nightingale School of Nursing and Midwifery, King's College, London.

Series editors' introduction

European national policy-makers broadly agree on the core objectives that their health care systems should pursue. The list is strikingly straightforward: universal access for all citizens, effective care for better health outcomes, efficient use of resources, high-quality services and responsiveness to patient concerns. It is a formula that resonates across the political spectrum and which, in various, sometimes inventive, configurations, has played a role in most recent European national election campaigns.

Yet this clear consensus can only be observed at the abstract policy level. Once decision-makers seek to translate their objectives into the nuts and bolts of health system organization, common principles rapidly devolve into divergent, occasionally contradictory, approaches. This is, of course, not a new phenomenon in the health sector. Different nations, with different histories, cultures and political experiences, have long since constructed quite different institutional arrangements for funding and delivering health care services.

The diversity of health system configurations that has developed in response to broadly common objectives leads quite naturally to questions about the advantages and disadvantages inherent in different arrangements, and which approach is 'better' or even 'best' given a particular context and set of policy priorities. These concerns have intensified over the last decade as policy-makers have sought to improve health system performance through what has become a Europe-wide wave of health system reforms. The search for comparative advantage has triggered – in health policy as in clinical medicine – increased attention to its knowledge base, and to the possibility of overcoming at least part of existing institutional divergence through more evidence-based health policy-making.

The volumes published in the European Observatory on Health Systems and Policies series are intended to provide precisely this kind of cross-national health policy analysis. Drawing on an extensive network of experts and policy-makers working in a variety of academic and administrative capacities, these studies seek to synthesize the available evidence on key health sector topics using a systematic methodology. Each volume explores the conceptual background, outcomes and lessons learned about the development of more equitable, more efficient and more effective health care systems in Europe. With this focus, the series seeks to contribute to the evolution of a more evidence-based approach to policy formulation in the health sector. While remaining sensitive to cultural, social and normative differences among countries, the studies explore a range of policy alternatives available for future decision-making. By examining closely both the advantages and disadvantages of different policy approaches, these volumes fulfil central mandates of the Observatory: to serve as a bridge between pure academic research and the needs of policy-makers, and to stimulate the development of strategic responses suited to the real political world in which health sector reform must be implemented.

The European Observatory on Health Systems and Policies is a partnership that brings together three international agencies, six national governments, a region of Italy, three research institutions, and an international non-governmental organization. The partners are as follows: the World Health Organization Regional Office for Europe, which provides the Observatory secretariat; the governments of Belgium, Finland, Greece, Norway, Spain and Sweden; the Veneto Region; the European Investment Bank; the Open Society Institute; the World Bank; CRP-Santé Luxembourg; the London School of Hygiene and Tropical Medicine; and the London School of Economics and Political Science.

In addition to the analytical and cross-national comparative studies published in this Open University Press series, the Observatory produces Health Care Systems in Transition (HiTs) profiles for the countries of Europe, the journal *EuroHealth* and the newsletter *EuroObserver*. Further information about Observatory publications and activities can be found on its web site, www.euro.who.int.observatory

Josep Figueras, Martin McKee, Elias Mossialos and Richard B. Saltman

Foreword

It is a truism that human resources are critical for health systems. Yet despite this, only very recently has there been more of a substantive debate about this issue internationally. Europe and the countries of the former Soviet Union (FSU) pose a particular challenge, due to the profound transformation that is taking place in society, as well as the far-reaching changes in political and economic systems over the past 15 years (the enlargement of the European Union (EU) and the dissolution of the Soviet Union). In order to cope with the parallel changes in health systems, many policy-makers believe that the human resources aspect of health must be addressed more effectively within health and public sector reform.

This book is one of the first to address comprehensively many of the key issues for human resources development across Europe, in the EU, the new EU member states and the countries of the former Soviet Union. The authors also take a look at the action required at strategic, regional and local levels in Europe to strengthen skills, expertise and analysis of human resources for health and to strengthen the health professions' integration into health policy-making. The authors argue that new human resources systems, improved management and evidence-based training institutions are needed at regional and local levels in order to address new demands from patients as well as changing epidemiological and demographic contexts.

European integration in many countries has been characterized by public sector reforms and legal adjustments in order to achieve compliance with all aspects of the Acquis Communautaire. In parallel, health systems in many countries have experienced a considerable transformation, requiring their workforce to hone new skills for new technologies, and adopt new behaviours in the market economy that has established new relationships with employers and clients. Staff in ministries of health and health insurance agencies as well as in public and private provider institutions will experience ever more competition for fewer lower-skilled jobs. At the same time there will be increased demand for new specialties, new skills and high-performing staff. Many of the health sector reform efforts in the Europe and Central Asia (ECA) region (the countries of central and eastern Europe and the former Soviet Union) contain the paradox of aiming to reward performance and empower staff while at the same time implementing downsizing and redundancy, as many FSU countries inherited substantial overcapacities and an inadequate human resource skill mix. The negative sides of these changes imply the loss of institutional memory and the use of downsizing as a way of achieving financial savings rather than adminis-trative reform. This results in a substantial development challenge for the region. Doctors and nurses, managers and fiduciary analysts need to be equipped to carry out their responsibilities in a rapidly evolving environment – the challenge of hospital restructuring in the region is testimony to that. An added difficulty is how to retain qualified staff in the lower-income countries in the region. The brain drain of health professionals is a real issue for many coun-tries in the region, further hastened by European integration and freedom of movement within the EU.

This book makes the case that health workers need to have access to con-tinuous professional development that includes skills for performance manage-ment, management of contracts and other new ways of operating in reformed systems. While there is a young generation of highly trained economists and policy specialists emerging from the ECA region, the region still suffers from a lack of public health specialists, managers and fiduciary specialists, as well as doctors trained in modern, evidence-based medicine. In many countries social workers have become available for the first time, but only in very small num-bers. The role of central government in setting standards for professional prac-tice and legal requirements for registration need to be strengthened so that human resources policies, registration and regulation are mutually supportive. Registration requirements that include experience in rural or remote areas would help to address the uneven distribution of health workers.

Finally, it remains to be seen what the rapidly changing political environment in Europe will entail for the health professions. Until now changes have been mostly good: consumers have access to more and better information; there is better dissemination of international best practice; and there are more inter-national training opportunities available. These are all elements that, in the end, should benefit the consumer/patient. However, there are also concerns looming large: the risks associated with greater mobility of patients and health professionals and the need to synchronize standards across very diverse health systems in even more diverse economies. We remain hopeful that this book will contribute to a substantive policy debate in Europe and the countries of the former USSR on how to tackle this challenge.

Armin Fidler
Health Sector Manager
Europe and Central Asia Region
The World Bank

chapter one

Human resources for health in Europe

Carl-Ardy Dubois, Ellen Nolte and Martin McKee

Introduction

In many countries the elusive quest for a perfect model of health care has led to an almost constant series of proposals for reform. Often reflecting swings of the political pendulum, there seems to be an endless sequence of proposals for fundamental and often complex transformations of the ways in which health care is paid for and delivered (Saltman and Figueras 1997). Yet this intensive attention to financing and structural transformation is less often accompanied by consideration of those who must adapt in order to deliver care in this changing environment. The ways in which the health care workforce is recruited, trained, rewarded, regulated and managed have often failed to keep pace with the changing demands facing health care systems (Healy and McKee 1997; Buchan 2000; Filmer et al. 2000; McKee and Healy 2001). Yet health care is a highly labour-intensive enterprise; more than in most other sectors of society. Successful reform depends upon a concomitant transformation in the operating conditions of the health care workforce (Martineau and Martínez 1997; Dussault 1999).

Attention to this topic is especially timely. Policy-makers show increasing interest in the comparative performance of health care systems, with growing recognition that this is intimately linked to the skills, motivation and commitment of the staff. As part of this debate, the concept of stewardship has emerged as a primary function contributing to the performance of health care systems. Effective use of health care workers can be considered a key element of effective stewardship and a sine qua non for attainment of the health system goals of improving health and responding to the legitimate expectations of the population (World Health Organization 2000). At the same time, there health care system reform therefore must be linked to effective management of this workforce, with a focus on how it impacts on the quality, accessibility and cost of health service delivery (Ozcan et al. 1995; Bennett and Franco 2000; Pan American Health Organization (PAHO) 2001). Specifically, many groups require much higher levels of skills, coupled with a system that ensures lifelong learning. There is also a need for systems that encourage (rather than inhibit) teamwork, with coordination across sectoral boundaries and between specialties and professions. Quality of care is assured by providing everyone with the opportunity to maximize their own potential; those who fall below acceptable standards will be identified and helped to improve, wherever possible.

Despite the clear importance of this workforce, many influential reports have suggested that existing systems to optimize its contribution are out of step with developments in health care systems (Kohn et al. 1999; NHS 2000). One area where this is seen as important is the management of quality of care. While professional freedom continues to be the hallmark of medical practice in many countries, increasingly this independence has been stigmatized as a source of runaway costs and lack of responsiveness to consumers and purchasers of care (Light 1997). Several reports of high-profile cases of medical mismanagement have raised concerns that the regulatory system may not protect the public effectively or guarantee continuing competence (Ozcan et al. 1995; Wilson et al. 1995; Smith 1998; Beecham 2000).

There are concerns about the systems of basic education of health professionals, particularly their ability to foster a culture of critical analysis that can form the basis for evidence-based practice and lifelong learning (Sackett et al. 1996, 1997). Many of the mechanisms for dealing with potentially poor professional performance are based on either outdated or inappropriate legislation and are ad hoc, fragmented and procedurally tortuous (Donaldson 1998). Even where the opportunities for change are identified and accepted, inappropriately designed health care legislation and regulation can create unreasonable barriers to policies that promote interdisciplinary work, optimal use of competencies and the efficient provision of care (Pong et al. 1995).

In summary, there is extensive evidence of shortcomings in the management and regulation of the health care workforce that impede the ability to respond positively to the opportunities offered by the changes taking place in health care systems. Fostering new policies and practices of management of the workforce that are fit for their purpose is thus a critical aspect of health care reform. This can contribute to improved health care delivery, enhanced public protection and the creation of a flexible and cost-effective health care system, optimizing health care outcomes and facilitating coordination between providers, consumers and purchasers.

The approach taken in this book

Drawing on previous Observatory studies, such as those on the role of the hospital or on EU enlargement, this book has emerged from a process of analysis at two levels. On one level, a series of common issues are examined, based on an analysis of relevant theories and of empirical evidence from a wide range of industrialized and middle-income countries. On the second level, there is detailed examination of specific themes by means of case studies in individual countries, selected to illustrate particular issues. These are being published separately. The countries have been chosen to provide a range of approaches to the governance of health workers, including some with particularly challenging health care workforce issues that demand policy attention and some whose health care systems and/or health care workforces have experienced recent explicit reforms. Those selected were France, Germany, Lithuania, Malta, Norway, Poland, the Russian Federation, Spain and the United Kingdom.

In France there is growing evidence of dissatisfaction among doctors and increasing difficulty in concluding agreements with health care professionals (Sandier et al. 2002). The demography of the medical profession is also a critical issue. While the prevailing situation of oversupply continues to guarantee relatively easy accessibility to care, many fear a shortage of doctors as a result of past decisions to impose quotas on medical schools.

In Germany the political system is characterized by a strong corporatism that is reflected in the governance of the health care system, which is self-regulated by tightly knit structures that bring together sickness funds, hospitals and physicians' associations. There are many rigidities that make it difficult to change patterns of care, most obviously the rigid separation of ambulatory and hospital care, the former provided almost exclusively by office-based physicians (Busse 2000).

Lithuania offers an example of a country that faces the double challenge of emerging from the USSR and acceding to the EU. One of the poorer countries in the enlarged EU, it faces a particular threat of losing health professionals who now have much greater opportunities for international mobility (Krosnar 2004).

Norway has a highly dispersed population. It has faced major challenges in ensuring a supply of health professionals to its rural northern areas, as well as ensuring that those individuals do not become professionally isolated.

Poland provides another example of a country that has just acceded to the EU. As a consequence the training of health professionals has undergone a major process of reform (Zajac 2002). However, there are real concerns about the potential impact of greater workforce mobility and the risk that key staff will be attracted to better-paid jobs in other Member States.

The Russian Federation is undergoing a transition from the Soviet model of professional training, with undergraduate specialization in medicine and only basic training for nurses. Although it has seen the birth of independent professional associations, these have yet to develop clearly focused roles. There remain major imbalances in staffing and skill mix, with regulatory and financial barriers to necessary change.

In Spain the majority of medical staff are considered to be civil servants. Centrally negotiated working conditions leave managers with an extremely limited capacity to offer incentives and enforce professionals' commitment to the objectives of a particular institution (Rico and Sabes 1996). Oversupply of doctors is a critical issue and engenders a legacy of difficulties including unemployment among physicians.

Malta's health care system faces particular issues associated with duplication of public and private care, lack of continuity between the various provider settings, poor salaries, excessive working hours and a shortage of doctors in the junior and middle grades as most doctors move overseas for higher training. Within the highly centralized and regulated health system, the process of staff recruitment is centrally controlled and rigid working conditions prevail. Further challenges, associated with the accession to the EU, include compliance with the WTD, retention of health care professionals and updating the professional legislation.

In the United Kingdom the National Health Service (NHS) has been especially innovative in several key areas. One such is performance management, with a complex system to promote continuing professional development and to implement wide-ranging performance management. This has given rise to initiatives such as the revalidation of professionals and publication of league tables. The NHS Plan sets out a series of ambitious targets for strengthening the health care workforce and modernizing the regulation of health care professionals (NHS 2000). In addition, the United Kingdom has responded to a shortage of health professionals by being particularly innovative in changing professional boundaries and skill mixes, as well as recruiting from other countries. It provides many examples of both the opportunities and challenges of increasing international mobility.

Inevitably the issues related to human resources in health are potentially almost boundless. In the World Health Report 2000, human resources for health (HRH) were defined as the stock of all individuals engaged in promoting, protecting or improving the health of populations. Such a definition encompasses not only health professionals but also a range of other occupational groups, such as drivers, cleaners, cooks, accountants, managers and economists, who are contributing to different domains of health systems. Such a definition also departs from a traditional view that has tended to focus only on formal caregivers with extensive formal training. It also encompasses the informal health care sector: self-care providers, traditional healers and volunteer and community carers.

Given this broad scope of human resources and the large number of professions and occupations that make up the formal health care workforce (several hundred according to some classifications), it would be unrealistic to plan a detailed examination of the overall scope of HRH within a single study. Some explicit boundaries are required. Pragmatically, this project focuses primarily on the two main health care professions: physicians and nurses. There are many reasons for this. Doctors' primacy in the hierarchy of health care workers, their role in the allocation and use of resources and their influence in shaping the organization of health care make them a centrepiece of health care delivery and the overall health policy. Nursing professionals with other closely related occupations (midwives, nurse assistants, etc.) account numerically for the most significant group in any health care system and undertake tasks in all areas of health services. Nursing has been one of the occupational groups that has been most affected by recent developments in health care systems and provides a good opportunity to examine the processes associated with the changing organization of work and the problems resulting from poor human resource management in health care.

Health professions are characterized by strong interdependence between professional groups. As a consequence, the practice of physicians and nurses and the outcomes of their services are influenced by the work of many other professions and occupations that fulfil important functions in the delivery of health services. Often, issues such as skill substitution are put forward as a means of optimizing care and responding to physician and nurse shortages; this makes it necessary to examine the roles of other professional groups. Thus, while focusing on physicians and nurses, this research has also sought to document relevant issues related to other health occupations that have emerged. In addition, special attention has been paid to health care managers (including physician and nurse managers), who play a critical role in the smooth running of services and the implementation of many policies that impact on the health care workforce.

Addressing the key issues

Human resources is a broad topic that encompasses a wide variety of issues. This book seeks to move away from the traditional fragmented approach of human resource management, which fails to take full account of the synergy of the interventions associated with discrete aspects of human resources (Martínez and Martineau 1998). It explores the contribution that the health care workforce can make to achieve the goals of the health care system, examining in turn a series of functions that relate to the production, development, regulation and management of HRH in Europe.

Beginning in Chapter 2, it explores in more detail the current developments affecting health care systems and their implications for the health care workforce. It highlights the shared challenges and policy responses but also cautions about the scope for policy transfer between settings that may be quite different.

Chapter 3 examines migration, an issue that has been seen as both a problem and a solution. International recruitment is seen increasingly as a solution to shortages in some countries, the active recruitment of nurses, doctors and other professionals increasing any natural migration flows in which individuals move across borders for a range of personal reasons. At the same time this can create shortages for others. For these reasons, the issue of migration of health professionals has risen high on the policy agenda in recent years.

Chapter 4 explores the work undertaken by health professionals and, specifically, the division of tasks between different groups. These divisions reflect many considerations but evidence about who would be best is rarely one of them. There may be regulations specifying which tasks are restricted to one professional group, such as the right to prescribe, or there may be cultural norms, which, although unwritten, have just as great an effect. Underlying these factors is a set of issues that includes a difference in the power of different professions, itself often a reflection of gender relationships in society: a predominantly male medical profession controlling a predominantly female nursing profession. However, there is increasing evidence that traditional demarcations do not support the optimal ways to provide care and there is considerable scope for changing the mix of skills involved in delivering many aspects of health care, moving from an individual model of practice to one that is based on multiprofessional teamwork.

If health care reform is to achieve its goals, there must be an adequate supply of appropriate categories of personnel with the requisite skills. Chapter 5 explores how the evolving challenges that face health care systems place pressure on education programmes to deliver training that will offer packages of skills that differ from those traditionally offered. For instance, health professionals require enhanced communication skills if they are to respond adequately to changing public expectations about shared decision-making. The dynamic expansion of the scientific basis of health care requires health professionals to obtain new skills in managing knowledge and using effective tools that can support clinical decision-making. As more care is provided by multiprofessional teams, health professionals will need the skills to create and sustain teams in ways that optimize the opportunities offered by joint working. The growing complexity of health care means that clinically trained staff will require enhanced managerial skills to ensure that inputs are brought together in the right place at the right time. The development of these skills will involve changes in the way in which training is delivered, in curricula, in educational funding and in the governance of health professions, with implications that go beyond the health care system to affect higher education and research.

Ensuring the creation of a trained workforce and identifying who should be doing what are only the first steps. It is necessary to ensure that these key resources are used to achieve optimal health care outcomes. Chapter 6 examines what enables health professionals to achieve the best possible outcomes in the most efficient way. It draws on evidence about the effects of different types of performance monitoring. It shows how performance management encompasses a broad set of issues, including the organization and division of work, practice standards, payment methods, circulation of information, management practices and tools, evaluation and accountability mechanisms.

While much of this book focuses on health care professionals, it is important to recognize the key role played by health managers, some, but not many, of whom will also be health professionals. Chapter 7 sets out the crucial role of health care managers (including physician and nurse managers) who are responsible for the smooth running of health services. It assesses the recent development of the health management workforce in Europe, investigates the impact of recent reforms on this element of the workforce and examines challenges that must be addressed to ensure appropriate levels of managerial oversight and leadership of the health care system. Recent developments associated with new public management across Europe, the emergence of new forms of professional organization and the hybrid mix of managerial and clinical roles are examined in order to assess their contribution to a reordering of professions and management in the health sector and raise new challenges for the health care workforce.

The health policy-maker can draw on a variety of tools to achieve the goals of the health care system. A key issue is to ensure alignment of the incentives contained within this system so that the health care workforce is encouraged rather than inhibited from making decisions that facilitate achievement of the system's goals. Chapter 8 examines the evidence in relation to different

Related books from Open University Press

Purchase from www.openup.co.uk or order through your local bookseller

PURCHASING TO IMPROVE HEALTH SYSTEMS PERFORMANCE

Edited by Josep Figueras, Ray Robinson and Elke Jakubowski

Purchasing is championed as key to improving health systems performance. However, despite the central role the purchasing function plays in many health system reforms, there is very little evidence about its development or its real impact on societal objectives. This book addresses this gap and provides:

- A comprehensive account of the theory and practice of purchasing for health services across Europe
- An up-to-date analysis of the evidence on different approaches to purchasing
- Support for policy-makers and practitioners as they formulate purchasing strategies so that they can increase effectiveness and improve performance in their own national context
- An assessment of the intersecting roles of citizens, the government and the providers

Written by leading health policy analysts, this book is essential reading for health policy makers, planners and managers as well as researchers and students in the field of health studies.

Contributors
Toni Ashton, Philip Berman, Michael Borowitz, Helmut Brand, Reinhard Busse, Andrea Donatini, Martin Dlouhy, Antonio Duran, Tamás Evetovits, André P. van den Exter, Josep Figueras, Nick Freemantle, Julian Forder, Péter Gaál, Chris Ham, Brian Hardy, Petr Hava, David Hunter, Danguole Jankauskiene, Maris Jesse, Ninel Kadyrova, Joe Kutzin, John Langenbrunner, Donald W. Light, Hans Maarse, Nicholas Mays, Martin McKee, Eva Orosz, John Øvretveit, Dominique Polton, Alexander S. Preker, Thomas A. Rathwell, Sabine Richard, Ray Robinson, Andrei Rys, Constantino Sakellarides, Sergey Shishkin, Peter C. Smith, Markus Schneider, Francesco Taroni, Marcial Velasco-Garrido, Miriam Wiley.

Contents
List of tables – List of boxes – List of figures – List of contributors – Series Editors' introduction – Foreword – Acknowledgements – *Part One* – Introduction – Organization of purchasing in Europe – Purchasing to improve health systems – *Part Two* – Theories of purchasing – Role of markets and competition – Purchasers as the public's agent – Purchasing to promote population health – Steering the purchaser: Stewardship and government – Purchasers, providers and contracts – Purchasing for quality of care – Purchasing and paying providers – Responding to purchasing: Provider perspectives – Index.

320pp   0 335 21367 7 (Paperback)   0 335 21368 5 (Hardback)

EDITOR   Philip Davis

DEPUTY EDITOR   Sarah Coley
CO-EDITORS   Elizabeth Cain
                            Angela Macmillan
                            Eleanor McCann
                            Brian Nellist

ADDRESS   The Reader Magazine
                            The Reader Organisation
                            The Friary Centre
                            Bute Street
                            Liverpool
                            L5 3LA

EMAIL   magazine@thereader.org.uk
WEBSITE   www.thereader.org.uk
BLOG   www.thereaderonline.co.uk

DISTRIBUTION   See p. 128

COVER IMAGE   Michael Troy, Artist and Illustrator,
                            'Jurassic Coast', Oils

ISBN 978-0-9567862-8-9

SUBMISSIONS

The Reader genuinely welcomes submissions of poetry, fiction, essays, readings and thought. We publish professional writers and absolute beginners. Send your manuscript with SAE please to:

The Reader Organisation, The Friary Centre, Bute Street, Liverpool, L5 3LA

Printed and bound in the European Union by Bell and Bain Ltd, Glasgow

THE READER

No. 49 SPRING 2013

Published by The Reader Organisation

the reader
organisation

Kohn, L., Corrigan, J.M. and Donaldson, M.S. (1999) *To err is human: building a safer health care system*. Washington, DC, Institute of Medicine, National Academy Press.

Krause, E. (1996) *Death of the guilds: professions, states and the advance of capitalism, 1930 to the present*. New Haven, CT, Yale University Press.

Krosnar, K. (2004) Could joining the EU club spell disaster for the new members? *British Medical Journal*, **328**: 310.

Light, D.W. (1997) The rhetorics and realities of community health care: the limits of countervailing powers to meet the health care needs of the twenty-first century. *Journal of Health Politics, Policy and Law*, **22**(1):105–45.

McKee, M. and Healy, J. (2001) The changing role of the hospital in Europe: causes and consequences. *Clinical Medicine*, **1**: 299–304.

McKee, M., Mossialos, E. and Baeten, R. (2002) *The impact of EU law on health care systems*. Brussels, Peter Lang.

McKinlay, J. and Stoekle, J. (1988) Corporatization and the social transformation of doctoring. *International Journal of Health Services*, **18**: 191–205.

Martineau, T. and Martínez, J. (1997) *Human resources in the health sector: guidelines for appraisal and strategic development*. Brussels, European Commission.

Martínez, J. and Martineau, T. (1998) Rethinking human resources: an agenda for the millennium. *Health Policy and Planning*, **13**: 345–58.

Narasimhan, V. et al. (2004) Responding to the global human resources crisis. *Lancet*, **363**: 1469–72.

National Health Service (2000) *The NHS Plan. A plan for investment. A plan for reform*. London, NHS.

Nicholas, S. (2002) Movement of professionals: trends and enlargement. *Eurohealth*, **8**(4): 11–12.

Ozcan, S., Taranto, Y. and Hornby, P. (1995) Shaping the health future in Turkey – a new role for human resource planning. *International Journal of Health Planning and Management*, **10**(4): 305–19.

Pan American Health Organization (PAHO) (2001) *Development and strengthening of human resources management in the health sector. 128th Session of the Executive Committee*. Washington, DC, PAHO.

Pong, R.W. et al. (1995) *Health human resources in community-based health care: a review of the literature*. Health Canada on Line, Health Promotion and Programs Branch (www.hcsc.gc.ca/hppb/healthcare/pubs/foundation/component1.htm).

Rico, A. and Sabes, R. (1996) *Health care systems in transition: Spain*. Copenhagen, WHO Regional Office for Europe.

Sackett, D.L. et al. (1996) Evidence-based medicine: what it is and what it isn't. *British Medical Journal*, **312**: 71–2.

Sackett, D.L. et al. (1997) *Evidence-based medicine: how to practice and teach EBM*. New York, Churchill Livingstone.

Saltman, R.B. and Figueras, J. (1997) *European health care reform: analysis of current strategies*. Copenhagen, WHO Regional Office for Europe.

Sandier, S. et al. (2002) France. In: Dixon, A. and Mossialos, E., eds, *Health care systems in 8 countries: trends and challenges*. Copenhagen, European Observatory on Health Care Systems.

Schneider, E.C. et al. (1999) Enhancing performance measurement – NCQA's road map for a health information framework. *Journal of the American Medical Association*, **282**(12): 1184–90.

Smith, R. (1998) All changed, changed utterly. British medicine will be transformed by the Bristol case. *British Medical Journal*, **316**: 1917–18.

Sochalski, J. and Aiken, L. (1999) Accounting for variation in hospital outcomes: a cross-national study. *Health Affairs*, **18**(3): 256–9.

Street, A. (2002) The resurrection of hospital mortality statistics in England. *Journal of Health Services Research and Policy*, **7**: 104–10.

Sullivan, W. (1995) *Work and integrity: the crisis and promise of professionalism in North America*. New York, Harper Collins.

West, M.A., Borrill, C. and Dawson, J. (2002) The link between the management of employees and patient mortality in acute hospitals. *International Journal of Human Resource Management*, **13**(8): 1299–310.

Wilson, R.M., Runciman, W.B. and Gibberd, R.W. (1995) The quality in Australian health care study. *Medical Journal of Australia*, **163**: 458–71.

World Health Organization (2000) What resources are needed? *In: World Health Report 2000. Health systems: improving performance*. Geneva, WHO.

Zajac, M. (2002) EU accession: implications for Poland's health care personnel. *Eurohealth*, **8**(4): 13–14.

possible and plausible futures. The methods remain largely descriptive but the aim is to build various images of the future, including those that may be considered highly improbable or reflect a discontinuity with current trends. This approach recognizes that current trends in need, demand, supply, composition and distribution of health services and HRH cannot be assumed to remain constant; therefore extrapolation from past and present trends is not sufficient to provide an adequate projection (Steering Committee on Future Health Scenarios 1995; Bezold and Mayer 1996; Fackelmann 1997; Coile and Brett 1999). Here, scenario analysis is still driven by an interest in the future but has moved beyond merely fulfilling a forecasting function to supporting a more open form of exploration, providing a warning of the range of potential threats and opportunities and suggesting areas for capacity development.

Finally, the **future as preferences and choice** approach represents an attempt to develop and implement a vision of a preferable future through effective stewardship. For health care and HRH, the focus is on ideological, institutional and social-cultural factors as drivers for change, rather than the more traditional technological and economic drivers. The future is perceived as a social construct resulting from diverse and conflicting views of various stakeholders seeking to direct health systems towards a set of commonly agreed and desired outcomes. This approach favours normative and participatory methods as a means both to prescribe strategies consistent with the desirable future and to mobilize key stakeholders to choose their own future and participate in its implementation (WHO 2000). As exemplified by a series of foresight exercises, this is driven primarily by a transformational interest and goes beyond the traditional small circle of technical experts, using processes designed to foster participation of a range of stakeholders in thinking about and creating a vision of the future of health care (Dunning 1992; Honingsbaum et al. 1995; Swedish Parliamentary Priorities Commission 1995; Department of Health 2003; Romanow 2002).

Examination of the future of HRH in Europe may thus profit from different perspectives (Table 2.1). Using different methods and emphasizing diverse sets of factors allow policy-makers to: (a) predict the most probable future profile of HRH on the basis of past, current and emerging trends; (b) explore alternative scenarios for trends in HRH, taking account of unexpected changes in the health care environment; and (c) identify societal expectations with regard to HRH and take appropriate steps to translate these into practice.

This single chapter realistically could not make full use of the multiple opportunities offered by these three perspectives in terms of prediction, scenario development and participative action. Focusing on those factors that have an indisputable influence on recent developments in European health systems, it examines their implications for the future of the health care workforce and highlights situations and circumstances in which scenario developments and consensus building may contribute to a better vision of the future workforce.

Table 2.1 Approaches to analysing future trends

	Future as prediction	*Future as exploration*	*Future as preferences and choice*
Main drivers of change	Megatrends: technology, demography, markets	Major unexpected events	Ideological, institutional and sociocultural factors
Types of future	Most probable futures	All possible and plausible futures	Desirable futures
Methods	Descriptive methods, forecasting techniques	Descriptive methods with emphasis on scenario developments	Normative and participatory methods
Interest in analysing the future	Prospective interest: extrapolate the most probable future	Prospective interest: paint a range of pictures of the future	Transformational interest: create a preferable future

Mapping the future of HRH in Europe: analysing the factors affecting the health care workforce

While the different approaches to analysing trends in health and HRH explored in the previous section may contribute usefully to exploring future trends in Europe, it is clear that no single discipline can address all aspects of human resources using these three perspectives simultaneously. Instead, a multidisciplinary approach is required to examine the full array of forces affecting HRH and to gain insights about how and why they are changing.

Figure 2.1 sets out a framework that we will use to analyse trends in the health care workforce. It builds on four closely related components of the health care production cycle and is adapted from the work of the US National Research Council (1999).

1 The *workforce* relates to health workers' profiles and their division into occupations.
2 The *work content* refers to the broad range of techniques, technologies and skills employed by health workers in order to provide health services.
3 The *workplace* includes the organizational, social and institutional contexts within which health care takes place.
4 *Work outcomes* comprise the quantity and quality of health services produced, the performance of health care providers, health outcomes and the various forms of rewards health care workers achieve through their work.

These key components are subject to a variety of influences. Demographic, technological, economic, political and institutional forces are factors that, at a

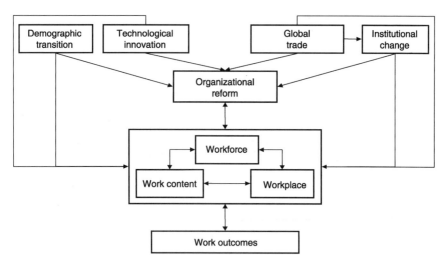

Figure 2.1 A framework for analysing future trends in HRH.

macro-level, shape the production of health care. However, these determinants usually operate through a range of strategies, structures and processes that prevail in organizations that employ health workers. Consequently, full exploration of future trends in health and HRH will also require analyses of the impact of organizational reforms. These different elements are examined in detail in the following sections.

Demographic trends

Demographic trends pose one of the most fundamental challenges to optimizing HRH, shaping the future health labour market directly, by impacting on the supply and composition of the health care workforce, and indirectly, by influencing the demand for products and services.

Direct effects

Across Europe, the ageing of populations – a consequence of persistently low fertility rates coupled with substantial gains in life expectancy – has emerged as a critical policy issue with important implications for both the nature of health care and the workforce that will provide it. The United Nations predicts that the population of Europe (including the Russian Federation) will fall from 726 million in 2003 to 696 million in 2025, resulting in a decline of the European share of the world's population from 11.5% to 9% (United Nations 2003). Within the 15 countries belonging to the EU before May 2004, the average age of the population is predicted to rise from 38.3 years in 1995 to 41.8 in 2015, with consequences for the available labour force. Thus, the working-age population, which increased consistently until the early 1990s, is estimated to decline over the next 25 years (European Commission 2000).

The impact of these trends can be seen already in the health sector. Countries such as Denmark, Iceland, Norway, Sweden and France are witnessing a greying of the nursing workforce: the average age of employed nurses is 41–45 years (DREES 2002; International Council of Nurses 2002a). In the United Kingdom, one in five nurses is aged 50 or older (Buchan 1999) and nearly half are over 40 (Finlayson et al. 2002). A major concern is the decline in the numbers of younger nurses. In the United Kingdom between 1988 and 1998 the proportion of nurses aged under 30 fell from 30% to 15% (UKCC 1998). Similar trends were observed in the medical profession. Thus, in 1985, 55% of French doctors were aged under 40, while by 2000 this had fallen to only 23% (DREES 2002). A United Kingdom census indicated that, in 2001, only 19% of the consultant (medical specialist) workforce was under the age of 40, while about 40% of those over 50 are likely to retire during the next 10–15 years (RCP 2002). These figures suggest that previous policies, such as restrictions on intake for medical and nurse training, alongside ageing populations and declining prospects for recruitment in the European labour market, will generate serious imbalances between the demand and supply of health care labour.

While much attention has been focused on the age structure of populations, other demographic changes will also impact on the composition of the work-force. These include changes in the gender balance, the participation of older workers and migration. Thus, female participation in the workforce is projected to increase further. Within the EU, labour force participation[1] by women aged 25–49 rose sharply from under 40% in the 1970s to over 70% by 2000 (Commission of the European Communities 2002). In the European OECD countries, labour force participation by women aged 15–64 years increased on average from 55% in 1990 to 60% in 2001, and male participation declined from 80% to 78% during the same period (OECD 2002b). This suggests that the gender gap in employment is declining and that women may provide the main source of labour supply growth in Europe.

Health care by its very nature is highly gendered. Women account for up to 77% of the health care workforce in Europe, with other estimates revealing that in all countries women account for at least 60% of HRH (Gupta et al. 2003). However, with the exception of Germany, this situation has been rather static, with no further feminization of the overall health labour force (Figure 2.2).

Importantly, the gender balance is becoming more favourable for women in even traditionally male-dominated health care roles such as medicine. In most European countries the proportion of female physicians (including general practitioners (GPs) and specialists) rose steadily during the 1990s (Figure 2.3). Similarly, the percentage of women enrolling in medical schools continues to increase in most countries and, in some cases, women entrants now outnumber men. For instance, in the United Kingdom women now take up 60% of medical school places and comprise 75% of GPs under the age of 30 (Department of Health 2003). In contrast, nursing was viewed historically as a female occupation and remains female-dominated (International Council of Nurses 2002a). Despite nurse shortages there is no clear indication that men will assume a greater share of the nursing workforce in Europe.

The increasing feminization of the medical profession has important consequences for workforce planning. The combination of physical constraints

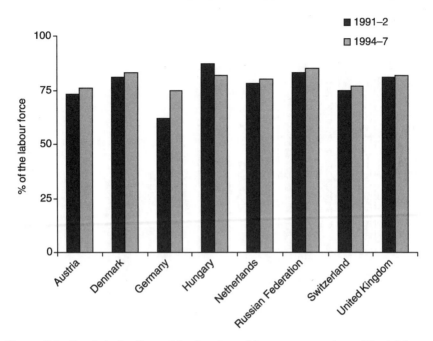

Figure 2.2   Trends in the share of the female workforce as a percentage of the total health workforce in selected countries in the 1990s (Germany 1989–1994) (adapted from Gupta et al. 2003).

imposed by pregnancy and childbirth and the cultural constraints arising from the conventional role of the mother as the dominant carer in a family means that women are more likely to take career breaks or to work part-time. Furthermore, in many countries, structural rigidities inhibit the flexible work patterns that would allow women to continue to participate in the workforce. These constraints often hinder career progression as women approach a 'glass ceiling' – their previous careers may have offered fewer opportunities to accumulate the same breadth of experience as their male counterparts. This is not a universal phenomenon, however, and some countries have seen substantial increases in the proportion of women becoming medical specialists, although often concentrated in certain specialties, such as paediatrics and obstetrics (Gjerberg 2001).

However, in many countries traditional gender roles, such as responsibility for child care, are changing (Clearihan 1999). As a consequence, men in the health care workforce may reject the traditional culture of long and often antisocial hours, seeking a more acceptable work–leisure balance. These factors need to be taken into account in order to provide realistic estimates for the number of physicians needed.

Another important trend impacting on the composition of the health care workforce is directly related to ageing populations. The employability of the workforce throughout the whole working life has received considerable attention and prompted various policy initiatives, particularly within the EU, to promote active ageing and limit early exit from the labour force. Building on the

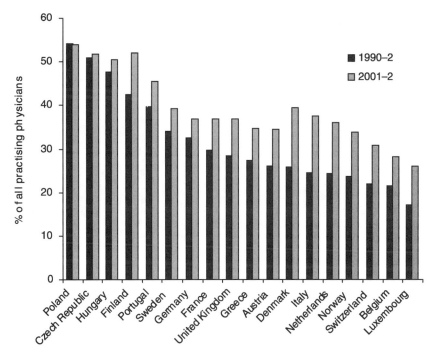

Figure 2.3 Female practising physicians as a percentage of all practising physicians in selected countries in the 1990s (Belgium 1990–1998, Sweden 1990–1999) (from OECD 2003).

Lisbon Strategy set out in 2000, the Stockholm European Council in 2001 recommended that Member States increase significantly the number of older people (aged 55–64) remaining in the workforce and the Barcelona European Council in 2002 proposed increasing the age of retirement by five years by 2010 (currently it averages 58 years). Yet, in 2001, the employment rate of older workers was only 38% in the 15 Member States of the EU pre-2004 and 37% in the enlarged EU (European Commission 2002). This figure is substantially lower in, for example, France, Italy, Belgium and Luxembourg, mainly because of advantageous early-retirement schemes that contrast with the lack of employment opportunities in CEE. In general, there seems to be a trend towards early retirement (Figure 2.4). As a result, the length of retirement compared to the duration of working life has increased in all parts of Europe (Table 2.2). It seems increasingly obvious that any increase in workforce participation by older workers will thus require fundamental changes in pension schemes and in employers' policies on recruitment and retention, including organizational practices and working conditions.

In health care, where the challenges are especially great, there are attempts to reverse the trend towards early retirement and retain older workers within the workforce. Although the medical workforce is ageing, several studies have shown that the proportion of physicians working beyond the age of 60 years has

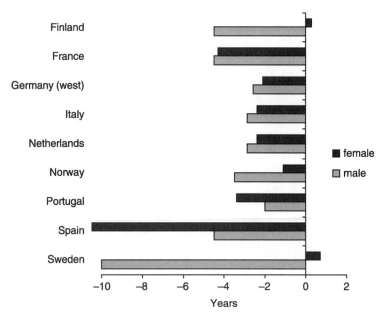

Figure 2.4   Changes in estimated average age of withdrawal from the labour force in selected European countries between 1970–1975 and 1993/4–1998/9 (adapted from OECD 2002a).

Table 2.2   Ratio of the duration of retirement compared to working life in Europe, 1950 and 1990

	1950	*1990*
Northern Europe	0.24	0.43
Southern Europe	0.19	0.49
Western Europe	0.26	0.53
CEE	0.27	0.48

Source: Observatoire des retraites (2000).

fallen in most European countries over the past decade (Royal College of Radiologists 2001; Audit Commission 2002; Gupta et al. 2003; OECD 2003; Sibbald et al. 2003).

This is also observed in nursing. In some countries there is the option to withdraw from employment as early as 55 years of age. The number of nurses taking advantage of this has been increasing since the early 1990s (International Council of Nurses 2002b). As a consequence, workforce participation rates among nurses over 55 have declined (Lader 1995; Buchan 1999; RCN 2003), a trend accelerated by other factors such as family demands, increasing workload in increasingly 'efficient' health care systems and the physical demands of nursing.

Finally, migration is also having a noticeable impact on both the overall demographic situation and the labour force in Europe. As fertility rates have dropped in most EU Member States, any increase in the EU population during the next decade is expected to result, largely, from net migration inflows. For example, in 2001 over 70% of the increase in the EU population was attributable to cross-border migration (Eurostat 2001c). In contrast, emigration has led to falling population numbers in CEE, with several countries, including Bulgaria, Romania, Slovenia, Poland and the Baltic states, having experienced negative net migration flows throughout the past ten years (European Commission 2002).

The promotion of labour mobility is a key feature of EU policies, based on the principle of free movement of people required by the single European market. Increased labour mobility also means that national workforces will become increasingly ethnically diversified. Thus, organizations must adapt in order to accommodate people from different cultural backgrounds and ensure that social interaction, communication and teamwork proceed smoothly within the workplace.

In health care, although cross-border migration has long played a part in health policy, the establishment of a regional labour market and imminent crisis in the supply of health professionals have given further impetus to professional mobility towards, between and within the regions of Europe, bringing both opportunities and threats. This is explored further in Chapter 3.

Indirect effects

Generational changes influence both who is available for health care employment and the nature of work that is required. While increasing longevity has been regarded as one of the greatest achievements of economic and social policy in Europe in the past century, it also creates considerable pressures for health systems. The traditional view that health care costs increase as a consequence of increasing age is now challenged as too simplistic, with evidence for compression of morbidity as successive generations reach old age in better health (Fries 1980, 1993; Fries et al. 1989; Hubert et al. 2002). At the same time, greater longevity poses new challenges owing to the increasing complexity of health problems with age, with more people suffering from multiple chronic conditions. Importantly, the association between cognitive decline and ageing has implications for the demand for social care at a time when traditional family support structures are weakening. Recent estimates suggest that the proportion of those aged 65 years and older could account for about 20% of the population in the EU by 2015, with the proportion of those aged 80 years and over estimated to rise from 3.9% in 1995 to 5.2% in 2015 (European Commission 2000). Thus, demand for and employment in health care are expected to increase, especially among those who work on the interface between health and social care, such as home-care workers, nurses, community health nurses and physiotherapists. In addition, sociodemographic trends, such as the growing proportion of women in paid employment, the increased likelihood that elderly people will live alone and the falling ratio of the middle-aged compared to elderly people, will mean that fewer people are available for

unpaid care, placing further strain on institutional and professional health care (OECD 1996).

In summary, the expected impact of demographic changes on the future health workforce in Europe appears paradoxical. While these changes lead to increasing demand for health services, ageing populations and demographic contraction reduce the size of the working-age population, with negative effects on the supply of the health care workforce. Thus, innovative policies are ever more necessary to increase participation by potential workers, especially women, older workers and migrants, to narrow the gap between the supply and demand for HRH.

Technology

Technological innovations act as another strong influence on HRH. Of course, technology and work are linked in all sectors of the economy. While work comprises a set of processes by which humans transform resources into outputs, technologies provide the means for this transformation (National Research Council 1999). The several ways in which technologies will shape the future of the workforce in health care are examined in turn below.

Mix of jobs and occupations

Advances in science and technology, new procedures and appliances continuously expand the knowledge and technical potential of health care, broadening the scope of diagnoses and treatable illnesses and altering the range and nature of health care provision. As a consequence, the demand for some existing occupations is likely to change as others emerge. For example, advances in biotechnology have increased the demand for health care workers with skills in bioengineering and genetics, while new information technologies have reduced the demand for some types of clerical staff. One Danish study found that pharmacies were able to reduce their staff by 6.3%, largely owing to new means of electronic communication (Silber 2003). At the same time, exploitation of new information technologies has created opportunities for new careers such as computer scientists, database managers and programmers. Technological innovation does not yet seem to herald the demise of any of the major categories of health professionals. However, it does call into question many traditional professional roles, leading to a move towards role substitution and expansion.

Health care settings

Increasingly sophisticated technological developments in areas such as surgery, imaging, invasive cardiology, transplantation, oncology and genetics will lead to a move to greater specialization in such areas, with expertise concentrated in a few centres (Goldsmith 1986; Robert 1999). At the same time developments in telematics, particularly in western Europe, offer the prospect of moving care away from hospitals. New generation intelligent systems and portable equipment for diagnosis and treatment are increasingly blurring the distinction

between primary and secondary care. These enable the provision of many services closer to the patient, with small units linked through telematics to specialist centres where necessary (Silber 2003). Advances in endoscopic and intravascular interventions, as well as the use of fast acting intravenous anaesthetics, are transforming entire surgical disciplines such as ophthalmology, urology and gynaecology; diagnostic or therapeutic interventions that have required a hospital environment can now be carried out in ambulatory settings. As exemplified by some recent initiatives in Norway, telemedicine and the related advances that connect health professionals and patients have the potential to enhance access to care by extending the range of professional services and access to specialized equipment in remote rural areas.

The nature and scope of work practice and skills

Advances in technology and the growing specialization of services have also increased the demand for knowledge in many areas of health care. With continuing debate as to whether recent technological developments increase skills or deskill the labour force, available evidence suggests that health workers, most notably clinicians, are increasingly required to acquire new competencies in order to perform their tasks. Knowledge management has thus become an integral part of the clinical decision-making process and health professionals are challenged to make appropriate use of information so as to base their practice on the best available evidence.

Effective electronic medical record systems require health care providers to participate directly in their development, maintenance and interpretation. The use of information processing systems for both administrative and clinical purposes has become increasingly important in many countries in Europe; for example, 80% of GPs in the EU reported using a computer in their practice (Table 2.3). In six European countries at least 55% of GPs use electronic records and, in 2001, 60% of all GPs in the EU were equipped with an Internet connection.

Provider–patient relationship

Information asymmetry remains a key feature of health care, although the growth of the consumer society, coupled with an explosion in information available via the Internet, is creating a more empowered group of patients who are no longer willing to accept uncritically the model of care provided for them. In the EU in 2002, the number of households with Internet access was reported at 40%, with the number of web users estimated at around 150 million, similar to the United States and compared to a total of 404 million users worldwide (European Commission 2004). There is also increasing usage in CEE, with an estimated rise to 27% by 2006 (Silber 2003). At the same time, the Internet is becoming an increasingly popular source of information on health (Larner 2002; Panes et al. 2002; Tuffrey and Finlay 2002). A better-informed public may elicit enhanced responsiveness from health service providers as individuals demand packages of care that are more suited to their perceived needs.

In summary, technological change is having an important impact on HRH by

Table 2.3 GPs' use of electronic technology (%)

	Use of computer in practice	Use of PDA[a] in practice	Use of Internet or GP network	Use of electronic medical records	Practices with a web site
Finland	100	4	100	56	63
Netherlands	100	31	100	88	47
Sweden	98	3	93	90	42
Germany	95	10	53	48	26
UK	95	18	87	58	27
France	89	11	80	6	11
Austria	82	2	64	55	18
Ireland	72	6	48	28	6
Spain	71	17	43	9	6
Denmark	70	1	62	62	13
Luxembourg	68	0	46	30	12
Italy	66	0	48	37	6
Belgium	66	7	51	42	9
Greece	52	3	27	17	4
Portugal	37	3	19	5	2
EU average	77	8	61	42	19

Source: Eurobarometer (2001), Taylor and Leitman (2002).
[a] Personal digital assistant

determining the types of services that health workers can perform, the settings in which they deliver them and their practice structures. However, technology is not a monolithic force and its influence is complex. It may reduce or increase costs, promote or inhibit coordination of care, enhance or diminish access to care and improve or worsen patient outcomes.

Globalization and trade liberalization

Intensification of the interdependence of global processes and markets emerges as an almost universal feature of economies in contemporary societies. These developments have an important impact on health care and the human resources that deliver it.

Let us look first at human resource generation and certification. One major development related to globalization is the growth of common international standards in many areas, including the health professions. International agreements designed to reduce barriers to trade across borders have provided new legal frameworks governing production and the international movement of health professionals. The development of common educational standards, harmonization or mutual recognition of qualifications between countries and liberalization of processes permitting professionals to practise have emerged as prerequisites for establishing effective regional markets, as, for example, in the EU. This is examined in detail by Baeten and Jorens in Chapter 12.

The emergent telecommunication infrastructure, a cornerstone of globalization, is shaping new modalities for basic and continuing education of people in the health professions. Digital libraries, tele-education, distance learning curricula and online educational programmes exemplify new forms of knowledge transmission and education in the global age.

Globalization has also prompted major reforms of health systems, with consequences for the size and mix of the health care workforce, as well as the nature and scope of their work. Market globalization requires the reduction of costs and improved efficiency in order to enhance competitiveness, with consequences for the labour-intensive health sector. Market-driven health care reforms in the United Kingdom resulted in substantial reductions of ancillary staff but increased the recruitment of administrative and managerial staff by 25%; precise figures are difficult to assess, however, because some jobs were redesignated. The integration of CEE economies with the single European job market and the global market requires a series of structural adjustments with far-reaching implications for the health care workforce. These include shifting the balance of health care from hospitals to primary care, creating new roles for certain professional groups such as nurses and retraining hospital specialists in general practice.

Finally, globalization is shaping new forms of regulation of health professions. Traditionally, the medical profession has been self-regulated and national professional associations have safeguarded their privileges of monitoring professional education and licensing, controlling and disciplining their members. Yet in the context of global economies and free movement of health care workers, professional jurisdictions and health labour markets now extend beyond state boundaries. As a result, internal forms of regulation and bargaining no longer appear sufficient, whether to ensure effective control of professional standards or to guarantee the protection of professional interests (Evetts 1998). There is an increasing move towards organizing professional bodies at a European level, driven by concerns about the absence of a voice in the European legislative process and the need for a better understanding of others' roles and responsibilities (Evetts 1999).

Globalization is also influencing professional power by challenging the trade union role of associations. Increased competition, deregulation, internationalization of the labour market, the quest for flexibility, fragmentation of working environments and a move away from collective bargaining processes can potentially erode trade unions' capacity to coordinate their bargaining power at national levels. With the singular exception of Scandinavia, trade unions in both western Europe (especially the United Kingdom, France and Germany) and CEE have recorded significant falls in their memberships during the past decade (International Labour Organization 1998b).

In summary, globalization and trade liberalization are having a substantial impact on HRH, affecting several aspects of production (education, licensing, continuous education), global, regional and national distribution, practices and organization of health professions. Thus, many key issues facing the future health care workforce will have a global dimension that must be taken into consideration by policy-makers at both the national and international levels.

Institutional changes

The future of the health care workforce cannot be dissociated from the institutional factors that determine the choices available to social actors and decision-makers. Social institutions shape the balance of power between key parts of the health care workforce and their relationship to other actors in the health system, namely the state, purchasers of care, consumers and citizens. Institutional features include, for example, the level of centralization of the health policy process, the state's degree of autonomy vis-à-vis competing interest groups and the distribution of responsibilities between various actors and sectors. These institutional features have an inevitable influence on the relationships between employers and employees, the structures of accountability, the roles of different occupations in the health policy process, the forms of interaction between different occupational groups and the relationship between health professions and the state.

Comparative analysis of labour relations has demonstrated how different models of corporatism and different structures of governance of labour markets in Europe are deep-rooted in different institutional traditions (Poole 1986; Crouch 1993; Ebbinghaus 1999, 2001a; Thelen 2001). For example, evolving from a centralist state tradition, the structural balance prevailing in many southern European countries, including France, Italy and Spain, is characterized by state control over key aspects of policy-making and adversarial relations between the state and social partners. The state operates as the main steward of HRH and has the tactical ability to influence important matters relating to their management (Wilsford 1995).

In contrast, the German type of legal corporatism is characterized by dispersion of power and influence between statutory public and private organizations. The state is responsible for defining the general framework for health care; however, the nongovernmental corporatist bodies perform crucial aspects of governance. A characteristic feature of governance in the Scandinavian institutional tradition is the high level of integration of organized groups within the state and a high degree of cooperation between the social partners. As the main steward of health care resources, the state benefits from the contribution of different groups coopted in its institutional machinery (Erichsen 1995; Blom-Hansen 2000).

Okma (2002) looked specifically at the relationship between the type of health care funding and the social partners' degree of involvement in health policy-making. She highlighted the typically strong role played by trade unions and health policy employers' associations in the countries of western Europe that have social health insurance systems. In contrast, these groups are often involved only indirectly in decision-making in countries with tax-based systems. Different traditions of administrative (de)centralization were also identified as important in shaping the structural balance of decision-making. For example, countries such as Germany, the Nordic countries and the Netherlands share a tradition of local self-government that creates opportunities to involve a range of actors at different levels in the governance of the health system. In contrast, countries such as France, the Mediterranean countries and the United Kingdom have a history of centralized governance that confers on the state

a high degree of autonomy in health policy and provides the structural levers needed to influence and even transform key aspects of health care production.

Other authors have shown how countries with different legal traditions are likely to adopt different regulatory styles, reflected in the scope and nature of regulatory activities, employment regimes and industrial relations systems (La Porta et al. 1997, 1998; Djankov et al. 2002, 2003; Botero et al. 2003). Common law countries such as the United Kingdom typically follow an institutional tradition that emphasizes judicial discretion (as opposed to codification of rules) and protection of individual rights, especially against government encroachment. In contrast, civil law systems that have followed distinct pathways in France and Germany evolve from an institutional tradition that typically relies on hierarchies and emphasizes codification of rules. Compared to those of common law, civil law countries tend to be more reluctant to deploy regulatory agencies that are independent of government.

Recent experiences in Europe suggest that the institutional framework that defines the boundaries of governance in developed democracies remains rather stable in the longer term. However, institutions have been subject to continuous adjustment and reform designed to accommodate the changing context of public policies. Institutional changes have been advocated as a prerequisite for addressing many inefficiencies in the delivery of health services and use of resources, increasing health care providers' accountability and creating a more flexible and responsive decision-making system.

Following the collapse of the Soviet Union, CEE countries have sought to reform their political institutions by moving away from highly centralized structures, devolving more responsibilities to lower tiers of government and to nongovernmental organizations. In the EU, the criteria for economic and monetary union prompted a series of institutional reforms that, beyond their economic implications, have also had a significant impact on health care and HRH (Ullrich 1997).

Since 1990, in an attempt to streamline and accelerate the decision-making process, successive Dutch governments have taken steps to alter existing corporatist arrangements and to eliminate the direct representation of organized stakeholders in shaping social policies (Okma 2002). Similar initiatives in various countries explicitly aim to remodel the structural balance in the health sector and to replace traditional corporate organizations with more open and more responsive structures (see Chapter 10).

The traditional model of centralized collective bargaining has come under increasing pressure, with calls for decentralization and greater flexibility. The introduction of market-based mechanisms into newly established internal markets has altered substantially the mix of governing instruments used in some health care systems.

Thus, although the institutional framework that defines the options for the future of the health care workforce is enduring, it is not immutable. While institutional pressures to maintain existing practices make it difficult to introduce radical changes, in many countries the steps taken to reform the social institutions will have far-reaching implications for the workforce.

Organizational reforms

As illustrated in Figure 2.2, demographic change, technological innovations and market and institutional changes will have a direct influence on HRH. However, the arguments developed in the previous sections indicate that, in many cases, these factors operate through strategies, structures and processes of the organizations that employ health care workers. This section shows how systematic efforts to reform health care systems have also exerted significant and independent effects on the health workforce and its working practices. It will examine four types of change associated with organizational reform: organization of work and division of labour, employment conditions, health and safety of health care workers and payment of providers.

Changes in the organization of work and division of labour

The reorganization of working practices features as a critical component of health care reforms. In Europe, many policies have emphasized cost-containment measures, the introduction of models of care promoting home care and the development of primary care services. Each has implications for the organization of work, the division of labour and particularly the boundaries between occupational groups. Thus, the introduction of various types of nurse practitioner in some countries strengthens the role of the nurse as an independent health professional with increasing responsibility for diagnosis and treatment in emergency care, preventive care and chronic disease management, often achieving better results than doctors (Vrijhoef et al. 2000, 2003; Sharples 2002). This is examined in detail by McKee et al. in Chapter 4.

The changing nature of health care is also reflected in the way that health professionals interact. Changes include the creation of multidisciplinary teams, group practices replacing solo practices and professional practices being decompartmentalized. The need to respond to upward pressure on health care costs by means of more efficient health services requires greater managerial accountability and presents a direct challenge to traditional professional discretion.

Changes in employment conditions

Perhaps one of the most telling changes arising from health care's organizational reforms has been the development of more flexible employment arrangements. While there has always been the problem of providing 24-hour cover, the task is becoming more acute because of the increasing opportunities to intervene with complex treatments. For example, 20 years ago a patient suffering a heart attack would have been put to bed and monitored while nature took its course; now this patient undergoes intensive investigations, potentially hazardous thrombolysis and possibly angioplasty. The care of low-birth weight babies has been similarly transformed by technological progress.

Shift work stands out as a key feature of health care: 83% of Belgian nurses, 75% of British nurses and 48% of hospital workers in Germany work shift systems (Verschuren et al. 1995). Overtime and extended unpaid hours of work

make a significant contribution to working time across Europe and have been regarded as vital elements of health care staffing if flexibility and continuity of services are to be achieved. In a survey commissioned in the United Kingdom in 1999, 59% of nurses reported that they had worked more than their contracted hours in the previous week (Robinson et al. 1999). The search for organizational flexibility has created new models of employment based on flexible contracts and transferring staff to alternative employers. As a result, job stability and security are no longer the rule in public services; instead, the lifetime career within a single organization is increasingly replaced by a series of non-standard working arrangements, including part-time employment, short-term contracts, on-call work, multiple employment, independent contracting and many other forms of employment. It has thus been demonstrated that in several EU countries (Belgium, Denmark, the Netherlands, Sweden, the United Kingdom) more than 40% of workers in public medical and social services work part-time. Only four countries (Greece, Italy, Portugal, Spain) have fewer than 10% part-time workers (De Troyer 2000). In the United Kingdom there is also evidence that an increasing number of GPs combine several part-time jobs, even though the work of doctors traditionally has been associated with full-time or self-employment (Allen 1992). Likewise, contracting out of ancillary services in hospitals, primary care and social services has become more common in many countries, particularly in the United Kingdom and the Scandinavian countries.

In general it appears that the search for more flexibility, a key component of restructuring health care organizations, is based largely on new approaches to working time and contracting. These approaches will be challenged by some of the sociodemographic changes outlined earlier, in particular the changing gender balance in many health professions, pressures to improve the balance between work and family and the reduction of junior doctors' hours under the WTD (Chapter 12). If a high level of quality and continuity of care is to be achieved and maintained then more innovative models are required in order to overcome the traditional division of labour, skill mix and incentives.

Threats to the health of health care workers

Organizational reforms combined with changes in demographics, technology and markets also raise important issues relating to the health of those working in the health sector. As indicated in previous sections, ageing of the workforce requires organizational conditions that enable older workers to cope with the demands of working in the modern health care sector.

Intensification of work due to technological advances and management methods, along with specific features such as shift work, antisocial and unpredictable hours, has increased levels of occupational stress, adding to the traditional physical risks associated with working in health care (International Labour Organization 1998a). Recent data indicate that work-related injuries in the health care sector are 34% higher than the EU average; work-related musculoskeletal disorders are highest in the health sector (Eurostat 2001a, b). Rising levels of dissatisfaction, work-related stress, reduced employee morale, absenteeism, and perceived loss of professional autonomy are other issues examined in Chapter 9.

Changing approaches to provider payment

Payment methods affect the performance of health workers and generate powerful incentives that have the potential to improve or reduce efficiency, equity, quality and patient satisfaction. Thus payment methods play a central role in restructuring health services. Many countries in Europe are exploring new ways to pay professionals: increasing diversity and flexibility, linking pay to performance, decentralizing responsibility for payment, balancing payment methods, separating health care purchasing and provision and increasing providers' accountability for the use of health care resources. Designing payment schemes does, however, pose considerable challenges related to adjustment of pay scales and differentials. It is important to avoid inconsistencies in payment systems that may distort the behaviour of providers or users, balancing the benefits of incentives with the potential for undesirable responses. These issues are examined in detail in Chapter 8.

In summary, this section shows how multiple drivers of change related to demography, technology, trade and markets, institutional context and organizational reforms will be shaping the future of HRH in Europe, with the following main changes.

- **Attributes of the workforce that delivers care.** Prevailing socio-demographic trends suggest that future HRH will depend increasingly on high participation of women, older workers and migrants to match supply with increasing demands. Removal of barriers to mobility for health care workers through the single European market will impact on both the formation of a more ethnically diversified workforce and its geographical distribution. Technological innovations and organizational reforms are changing the characteristics of the workforce: removing some occupations, creating opportunities for others and changing the knowledge, skills and ability required to perform some jobs. Changing population needs associated with ageing, rising expectations, family structures and living arrangements require substantial adjustments in the composition of the workforce, skill mix and distribution between regions, occupations and settings of care.
- **Content of health care.** Population ageing increasingly requires multidisciplinary forms of practice for the growing proportion of patients with debilitating and chronic conditions. This requires the provision of a mix of services over time and across settings. Technological innovations expand the range of choices for structuring health care but also require health workers to use available means consistent with the evidence base and constantly to revise their skills. Information technology is becoming an integral component in the delivery of care either as a tool to support the storage and retrieval of patient information or as an aid to clinical decision-making. In the context of organizational reforms, the traditional division of labour in health care is also challenged and many health occupations are taking on new roles and responsibilities that require the development of new skills. New approaches to working obscure traditional demarcations between occupations and challenge the traditional hierarchical structure of health care. Changing relationships between clinicians and patients also demand changes in communication skills.

- **Characteristics of the workplace.** As in many other industries, health care organizations have been subject to workplace redesign and changing working relationships as a means to increase flexibility, efficiency and productivity. Employment relationships, defined as a set of mutual obligations and expectations between employees and employers, have become increasingly uncertain and have moved towards more transient forms. Increasingly, career paths are built around a series of non-standard employment arrangements ('portfolio careers'). New forms of work practices such as shift work, temporary, part-time and on-call work, the impact of new technologies and increased intensification of work create new health hazards in the workplace and change the nature of working life in the health care sector. Some professional groups, such as nursing, voice growing concern about the increase in occupational stress, declining job satisfaction and growing problems with morale.

Ultimately, since HRH are the most important strategic assets in health care, identifying problems and determining which services will be provided, when, where, how and by whom, the performance of health systems will depend on the performance of their health workers (Dussault 1999). Imbalances in human resource systems created by the range of influences mentioned above may impact negatively on the outcomes of health workers and subsequently on the performance of the health system itself.

Building alternative scenarios for a diverse and changing Europe

The general trends set out in the previous sections are clearly discernible at European level; however, it is obvious that they will not affect each country to the same extent. Further, the trends described do not encompass the complete set of possibilities that a changing Europe will face. In reality, there is still a strong argument that HRH in Europe exist within a collection of national labour forces, each with specific features. Although it can be expected that the European workforce will become older and increasingly diverse, significant differences will remain between countries regarding the age structure of the populations, female labour participation rates and proportions of migrant workers. At European level, although EU legislation has an increasing impact on health care, at least in its 25 Member States and any candidate countries, health services in Europe remain primarily a matter of national competence.

European health care systems differ in terms of funding, organization and forms of governance. Each creates a different context for the management of HRH and generates specific structures and practices for a series of issues such as provider payments, performance management, working conditions and working relations. Despite pressures for convergence, major differences in economic conditions and policy choices are and remain reflected in the varying levels of resources allocated to health care, with differential impacts on the workforce. These are reflected, for example, in the diverse forms of labour market regulation and industrial relations structures. Over the past 20 years the United

Kingdom has pursued labour market deregulation, while the Swedish model has involved more subtle changes that have led to fundamental renegotiation of the national bargaining system to create a more flexible system of coordinated multi-industry bargaining (Thelen 2001). More systematically, Crouch (1993) and Ebbinghaus (2001a) distinguished various modes of interest mediation in industrial relations in Europe. It was also shown that the multiple models of the European welfare state exert a differential effect on the retention of older workers and are associated with different retirement patterns (Ebbinghaus 2001b). Such differences will continue and may drive national workforces in diverse directions.

Existing trends and their determinants will not necessarily remain constant. The further such trends are extrapolated, the greater the uncertainty. It remains difficult to predict how far the current vectors of change will reach and the extent of their resistance to emerging opposing forces. For instance, new forms of resistance to globalized markets and the historical experience of fragmentation of the global economy following the First World War suggest that a reversal of processes of globalization cannot be ruled out, if economic and political shocks are strong enough (Bertrand et al. 1999). It is often forgotten that international trade held a greater share of total global trade in the 1890s than it does now.

Although technological development and expansion of the knowledge base in health care appear to be irreversible trends, there are areas of great uncertainty, notably with regard to the moral and ethical dilemmas inherent in using these technologies to alter the future of human beings (Goldsmith 1986). This means that, in the highly complex and uncertain environment of health systems, it is very difficult to predict the future of the health care workforce and so devise a perfect strategy. A more sensible approach is to develop a range of possible scenarios taking account not only of the diversity within Europe but also of the political, economic, technological, institutional and social dimensions of uncertainty in a changing Europe. This also means that effective responses to the challenges to human resources depend not only on predictions based on past and current trends but also on developing human resource systems' ability to adapt to changing circumstances. Key factors to consider in developing alternative scenarios for the workforce include: women's level of participation in the workforce; the evolution of health workers' attitudes to working time and work–family balance; societal attitudes towards early retirement; older workers' level of participation in the labour force; evolution in migration flux; diffusion and adoption of emerging technologies; evolution in scopes of practice and role substitution; and variations in health care needs and health policy contexts in various European regions.

Towards a desirable future

In conclusion, this chapter has highlighted the importance of preparing the health workforce for the future of health care delivery. The trends identified suggest that significant and continuous changes will continue to affect health care systems across Europe in the foreseeable future. HRH's specific position in

the production of health care places them at the crossroads of all major changes. Consequently, a key challenge for health policy-makers is constantly to adjust the health labour market to the changing imperatives of health care delivery and to build a workforce that is consistent with the objectives of health systems. In view of the multiple challenges facing health care, a workforce that is appropriately trained, fairly compensated, adequately resourced and located in a high-quality workplace would appear to be an essential component to achieve the changes that are needed if health systems are to optimize their performance.

Yet defining what is appropriate, right and fair in a diverse set of possibilities is also a normative issue that requires agreement on what is desired. Beyond the influences exerted by the multiple forces for change described here, HRH requirements will also be determined by the wider societal dimension and policy choices about, for instance, the resources committed to health care, the adoption of new and expensive technologies, arbitration between competing priorities and the resolution of ethical dilemmas associated with emerging technologies in health care. Thus, the challenge for policy-makers is not only to be prepared to face what might happen but also to act proactively so as to reconcile the possible with the desirable. Each country needs to build a realistic vision of health (care) and HRH and to take appropriate steps to implement this. In many cases, current trends and the most probable futures may appear incompatible with this vision and will require policy interventions. In other cases, much uncertainty will remain and robust strategies will be required to keep to the desired objectives and promote changes that are likely to generate the most benefits.

But there is a paradox in health care. Although change is a dominant theme promoted by multiple forces questioning current systems, the implementation of new policies often elicits strong resistance from competing interests and structural inertia. Again this emphasizes human resources' critical role in health care – the workforce is key to achieving the desired changes in the health system and therefore it must be fully engaged in the process of change.

Finally, this analysis has demonstrated the multifaceted scope of issues around HRH. Weaknesses and imbalances in the health workforce may arise from multiple sources, impact on various aspects of health care production and alter multiple outcomes. Consequently, building and implementing a vision of a desirable health care workforce necessitates a comprehensive agenda that must take account of the broader system in which health services are provided and the impact of the many contextual factors outlined above. As these influences are largely outside the immediate control of the health sector, a further challenge will be to extend alliances beyond its own boundaries and engage a broad range of stakeholders in designing and implementing HRH policies.

Note

1   The labour force participation rate is the number of people in any group in the labour force (employed or unemployed; excluding those not working, unable to work, not seeking work) expressed as a percentage of the population aged 15 years and over in that group.

References

Allen, I. (1992) *Part-time working in general practice*. London, Policy Studies Institute.

Audit Commission (2002) *A focus on general practice in England*. Portsmouth, Holbrooks Printers.

Bell, W. (1997) *The foundations of futures studies, Volumes 1 and 2*. New Jersey, Transaction Publications.

Berkhout, F. and Hertin, J. (2002) Foresight futures scenarios: developing and applying a participative strategic. *Journal of Corporate Environmental Strategy and Practice*, **37**: 37–52.

Bertrand, G., Michalsski, A. and Pench, L.R. (1999) *Scenarios Europe 2010. Five possible futures for Europe*. Brussels, European Commission, Forward Studies Unit.

Bezold, C. and Mayer, E. (1996) *Future care: responding to the demand for change*. New York, Faulkner and Gray.

Blom-Hansen, J. (2000) Still corporatism in Scandinavia? A survey of recent empirical finding. *Scandinavian Political Studies*, **23**(2): 157–81.

Botero, J. et al. (2003) *The regulation of labor*. Working Paper Series 9756. Cambridge, MA, National Bureau of Economic Research.

Buchan, J. (1999) The greying of the United Kingdom nursing workforce: implications for employment policy and practice. *Journal of Advanced Nursing*, **30**(4): 818–26.

Clearihan, L. (1999) Feminisation of the medical workforce. Is it just a gender issue? *Australian Family Physician*, **28**(6): 529.

Coile, R.C.J. and Brett, E.T. (1999) Health care 2020: technology in the new millennium. *Health Management Technology*, **20**(11): 44–8.

Commission of the European Communities (2002) *Report from the Commission to the Council, the European Parliament, the Economic and Social Committee and the Committee of the Regions. Report requested by Stockholm European Council: 'Increasing labour force participation and promoting active ageing'*. Brussels, Commission of the European Communities.

Crouch, C. (1993) *Industrial relations and European state traditions*. Oxford, Clarendon Press.

Department of Health (2003) *Statistics for general medical practitioners in England: 1991–2001*. Bulletin, 2002/03 (February).

De Troyer, M. (2000) The hospital sector in Europe. Introductory report. TUTB-SALTSA Conference, Brussels, 25–27 September.

Djankov, S. et al. (2002) The regulation of entry. *Quarterly Journal of Economics*, **111**: 1–37.

Djankov, S. et al. (2003) Courts. *Quarterly Journal of Economics*, **118**: 457–522.

DREES (Direction de la recherche, des études, de l'évaluation et des statistiques) (2002) Les acteurs et les structures. *In: Données sur la situation sanitaire et sociale*. Paris, La Documentation française.

Dunning, A.J. (1992) *Choices in health care: a report by the Government Committee on Choices in Health Care*. Rijswijk, the Netherlands, Ministry of Health, Welfare and Cultural Affairs.

Dussault, G. (1999) *Human resources development: the challenge of health sector reform*. Prepared for the Latin America and the Caribbean Department, Human Development Division, World Bank.

Ebbinghaus, B. (1999) Does a European social model exist and can it survive? *In*: Huemer, G., Mesch, M. and Traxler, F., eds, *The role of employer associations and labour unions in the EMU*. Aldershot, Ashgate.

Ebbinghaus, B. (2001a) European labour relations and welfare-state regimes: a comparative analysis of their elective affinities. *In*: Ebbinghaus, B. and Manow, P., eds, *Comparing welfare capitalism: social policy and political economy in Europe, Japan and the USA*. London, Routledge.

Ebbinghaus, B. (2001b) When labour and capital collude: the political economy of early retirement. *In*: Ebbinghaus, B. and Manow, P., eds, *Comparing welfare capitalism: social policy and political economy in Europe, Japan and the USA*. London, Routledge.

Erichsen, V. (1995) Health care reform in Norway: the end of the profession state? *Journal of Health Politics, Policy and Law*, **20**: 719–37.

Eurobarometer (2001) *Flash eurobarometre 126 'Les médecins généralistes et l'Internet'*. Réalisé par Eos Gallup Europe à la demande de la Commission Européenne Direction Générale 'Société de l'Information'. Brussels, European Commission.

European Commission (2000) *People in Europe: Demographic change: the regional dimension. Trends and policy issues*. Brussels, European Commission.

European Commission (2002) *Employment in Europe 2002: recent trends and prospects*. Brussels, European Commission, Directorate-General for Employment and Social Affairs, Unit EMPL/A.1.

European Commission (2004) *Committee of senior officials on public health. Statistical tables in relation to the migration of nurses responsible for general care in the Community from 1977 to 2000. DGXV*. Brussels, European Commission.

Eurostat (2001a) *Statistics in focus. Theme 3, population and social conditions, 16/2001. Accidents at work in the EU 1998–1999*. Luxembourg, Office for Official Publications of the European Communities.

Eurostat (2001b) *Statistics in focus. Theme 3, population and social conditions, 17/2001. Work-related health problems in the EU 1998–1999*. Luxembourg, Office for Official Publications of the European Communities.

Eurostat (2001c) *Statistics in focus. Theme 3, population and social conditions, 19/2001. First demographic estimates for 2001*. Luxembourg, Office for Official Publications of the European Communities.

Evetts, J. (1998) Professions beyond the nation-state: international systems of professional regulation in Europe. *International Journal of Sociology and Social Policy*, **18**(11/12): 47–64.

Evetts, J. (1999) Regulation of professions in global economies: dimensions of acquired regulation. SASE, 11th Annual Meeting on Socio-economics, Globalization and the Good Society. Joint session of professions and knowledge, economy and society networks, Madison, Wisconsin, 8–11 July.

Fackelmann, K. (1997) Future health, future choices. *Science News Online 75th Anniversary Essay*, **151**(9): S17.

Finlayson, B. et al. (2002) Mind the gap: the extent of the NHS nursing shortage. *British Medical Journal*, **325**: 538–41.

Fries, J.F. (1980) Aging, natural death and the compression of morbidity. *New England Journal of Medicine*, **303**: 130–5.

Fries, J.F. (1993) Compression of morbidity 1993: life span, disability, and health care costs. *Facts and Research in Gerontology*, **7**: 183–90.

Fries, J.F., Green, L. and Levine, S. (1989) Health promotion and the compression of morbidity. *Lancet*, **1**: 481–3.

Garrett, M.J. (1994) An introduction to national futures studies for policymakers in the health sector. *World Health Statistics Quarterly*, **47**(3/4): 101–17.

Gjerberg, E. (2001) Medical women – towards full integration? An analysis of the speciality choices made by two cohorts of Norwegian doctors. *Social Science and Medicine*, **52**(3): 331–43.

Godet, M. (1987) *Scenarios and strategic management*. London, Butterworth.

Goldsmith, J.C. (1986) 2036: a health care odyssey. *Hospitals*, **60**(9): 68–9, 74–6.

Gupta, N. et al. (2003) Assessing human resources for health: what can be learned from labour force surveys? *Human Resources for Health*, **1**(1): 5.

Henchey, N. (1978) Making sense of future studies. *Alternatives*, **7**: 24–9.

Honingsbaum, F. et al. (1995) *Priority setting processes for health care in Oregon, USA; New Zealand; the Netherlands; Sweden and the United Kingdom.* Oxford, Radcliffe Medical Press.

Hubert, H.B. et al. (2002) Lifestyle habits and compression of morbidity. *Journal of Gerontology Series A: Biological Sciences and Medical Sciences,* **57**: M347–M351.

International Council of Nurses (2002a) *Nursing workforce profile 2002* (www.icn.ch/SewDatasheet02.pdf).

International Council of Nurses (2002b) *Overview paper.* ICN Workforce Forum, Reykjavik.

International Labour Organization (1998a) *Terms of employment and working conditions in health sector reforms.* Geneva, ILO.

International Labour Organization (1998b) *World Labour Report 1998–9. Industrial relations, democracy and social stability.* Geneva, ILO.

Lader, D. (1995) *Qualified nurses, midwives and health visitors.* London, HMSO.

La Porta, R. et al. (1997) Legal determinants of external finance. *Journal of Finance,* **52**: 1131–50.

La Porta, R. et al. (1998) Law and finance. *Journal of Political Economy,* **106**: 1113–55.

Larner, A. (2002) Use of Internet medical websites and NHS Direct by neurology outpatients before consultation. *International Journal of Clinical Practice,* **56**(3): 219–21.

National Research Council (1999) *The changing nature of work: implications for occupational analysis.* Washington, DC, National Academy Press.

Observatoire des retraites (2000) Retirement pensions: a statistical analysis. *La Lettre de l'Observatoire des Retraites,* May, No. 2.

OECD (1996) *Caring for frail elderly people: policies in evolution.* Paris, Organisation for Economic Co-operation and Development (Social Policy Studies No. 19).

OECD (2002a) *Age of withdrawal from the labour force in OECD countries.* Paris, Organisation for Economic Co-operation and Development (Labour Market and Social Policy Occasional Papers No. 49).

OECD (2002b) *OECD employment outlook 2002: statistical annex.* Paris, Organisation for Economic Co-operation and Development (www.oecd.org/dataoecd/29/42/1939233.-pdf).

OECD (2003) *Factors shaping the medical workforce.* Paris, Organisation for Economic Co-operation and Development.

Okma, K.G.H. (2002) What is the best public–private model for Canadian health care? *Policy Matters,* **3**: 2.

Panes, J. et al. (2002) Frequent Internet use among Catalan patients with inflammatory bowel disease. *Gastroenterología y Hepatología,* **25**(5): 306–9.

Poole, M. (1986) *Industrial relations: origins and patterns of national diversity.* London, Routledge and Kegan Paul.

RCN (2003) *More nurses, working differently? A review of the UK nursing labour market 2002–2003.* London, Royal College of Nursing.

RCP (2002) *Census of consultant physicians in the UK, 2001. Data and commentary.* London, Royal College of Physicians.

Robert, G. (1999) *Science and technology: trends and issues. Forward to 2015.* London, Nuffield Trust.

Robinson, D., Buchan, J. and Hayday, S. (1999) *On the agenda: changing nurses' careers in 1999.* Warwick, Institute of Employment Studies, Warwick University.

Romanow, R. (2002) *Building on values: the future of health care in Canada.* Ottawa, Commission on the Future of Health Care in Canada.

Royal College of Radiologists (2001) *Clinical radiology: a workforce in crisis. Board of Faculty of Clinical Radiology.* London, Royal College of Radiologists.

Sharples, L.D. (2002) A randomised controlled crossover trial of nurse practitioner versus doctor led outpatient care in a bronchiectasis clinic. *Thorax,* **57**(8): 661–6.

Sibbald, B., Bojke, C. and Gravelle, H. (2003) National survey of job satisfaction and retirement intentions among general practitioners in England. *British Medical Journal,* **326**: 22–4.

Silber, D. (2003) The case for eHealth. Presented at the European Commission's first high-level conference on eHealth, Brussels, 22–23 May.

Steering Committee on Future Health Scenarios (1995) *The Hemingford scenarios: alternative futures for health and health care.* Dordrecht, Kluwer Academic Publishers.

Swedish Parliamentary Priorities Commission (1995) *Priorities in health care: ethics, economy, implementation.* Stockholm, Ministry of Health and Social Affairs.

Taylor, H. and Leitman, R. (2002) European physicians, especially in Sweden, Netherlands and Denmark, lead US in use of electronic medical records. *Harris Interactive Health Care News,* 2: 16 (www.harrisinteractive.com/news/newsletters/healthnews/HI_HealthCareNews2002Vol2_Iss16.pdf).

Thelen, K. (2001) Varieties of labor politics in the developed democracies. *In*: Hall, P.A. and Soskice D., eds, *Varieties of capitalism: the institutional foundations of comparative advantage.* Oxford, Oxford University Press.

Tuffrey, C. and Finlay, F. (2002) Use of the Internet by parents of paediatric outpatients. *Archives of Disease in Childhood,* **87**(6): 534–6.

Ullrich, G. (1997) *Labour and social dimensions of privatization and restructuring: health care services.* Geneva, ILO.

United Kingdom Central Council for Nursing Midwifery and Health Visiting (1998) *Annual Report.* London, UKMCC.

United Nations (2003) *World Population 2002.* New York, United Nations Population Division, Department of Economic and Social Affairs.

Verschuren, R., de Groot, B. and Nossent, S. (1995) *Working conditions in hospitals in the European Union.* Dublin, European Foundation for the Improvement of Living and Working Conditions.

Vrijhoef, H.J., Diederiks, J.P. and Spreeuwenberg, C. (2000) Effects on quality of care for patients with NIDDM or COPD when the specialised nurse has a central role: a literature review. *Patient Education and Counselling,* **41**: 243–50.

Vrijhoef, H.J. et al. (2003) Undiagnosed patients and patients at risk for COPD in primary health care: early detection with the support of non-physicians. *Journal of Clinical Nursing,* **12**: 366–73.

Wehrmeyer, W., Clayton, A. and Lum, K. (2002) Foresighting for development. *Journal of Corporate Environmental Strategy and Practice,* **37**: 24–36.

WHO (2000) *Health futures: scenarios based development guidelines.* Report commissioned by WHO Regional Office for Africa.

Wilsford, D. (1995) States facing interests: struggles over health care policy in advanced, industrial democracies. *Journal of Health Politics, Policy and Law,* **20**(3): 571–613.

chapter three

Migration of health workers in Europe: policy problem or policy solution?

James Buchan

Introduction

International recruitment has become a solution to health professional skill shortages in some countries. This active cross-border recruitment of nurses, doctors and other professionals is in addition to any natural migration flows of individuals moving across borders for a range of personal reasons.

International migration and recruitment can have positive aspects: they can be a solution to staff shortages in some countries; they can assist source countries that have an oversupply of staff; and they can be a method for individual health workers to improve their skills and standard of living. However, it can exacerbate problems in countries that are understaffed and have a negative impact on the effectiveness of their health systems. This was highlighted in the World Health Assembly resolution in May 2004 (WHO 2004).

The migration of health professionals has therefore become a more significant feature of international health policy debate in the past few years (Buchan 2001; Chanda 2002; Pang et al. 2002; Tjadens 2002; Stilwell et al. 2003), and achieved additional prominence in the EU with the accession of the new Member States in 2004 (Krieger 2004). Some European countries, such as the United Kingdom, are recruiting staff from other countries. Others, such as Poland, were concerned about out-migration of health workers following accession although, by early 2005, this had not seemed to have become a significant issue.

This chapter assesses the implications of health worker migration in Europe: to what extent is it a problem or a solution to staffing requirements? It focuses on international migration: the movement of health workers across national borders. Although internal migration (i.e. movement within national

boundaries) is also a major factor for some countries, often compounding existing problems of geographical distribution, it is not examined here.

The chapter is divided into three sections, examining: (a) general issues related to migration and active international recruitment of health workers; (b) the current situation of health worker migration in Europe, looking at the migration of workers within, to and from Europe; and (c) the policy implications of migration, particularly health worker migration in an enlarged EU.

General trends in international migration

Recent research findings indicate five main trends in general migration.

- An increasing rate of international migration (Castles 2000; OECD 2000): the number of people migrating doubled from 75 million in 1965 to an estimated 150 million in 2000 (International Organization for Migration (IOM) 2000) when international migrants are defined as 'those who reside in countries other than those of their birth for more than one year'. Of these, about 80–97 million were migrant workers and members of their families (IOM 2000).
- A growth in migration of skilled and qualified workers (International Labour Organization (ILO) 2000; OECD 2000, 2002).
- More complex migration flows owing to greater information exchange, global awareness (Stalker 2000) and better transportation links (Castles 2000). Thus, between 1970 and 1990, the numbers of countries that qualified as major receivers of migrant workers rose from 39 to 67 and those that qualified as major senders rose from 29 to 55 (ILO 2000).
- Less distinct categories of migrant, e.g. planned migration for employment or asylum seekers (Stalker 1997). There has been an increasing mix of temporary/ permanent migrants and legal/illegal immigrants (Timur 2000) and a recent reported switch from permanent to temporary migration (Findlay and Lowell 2002).
- Increasing numbers of females migrating independently of partners or families (Timur 2000).

Krieger (2004) reported on countries of the EU, and EU enlargement, in an overview for the European Foundation for the Improvement of Living and Working Conditions, completed before the accession of new Member States in 2004.

- Thirteen million non-national citizens were living in the 15 EU Member States in 2000, half being nationals of other EU countries.
- The net inflow of migrants to the EU in 2000 was 680 000 people (2.2 per 1000 population).
- There is an income gap of 60% between central and eastern acceding countries and existing Member States, much higher than in the previous enlargement of the EU.
- The number of migrants from the new Member States and candidate countries will increase from one to four million by 2030, and the EU 'should not expect a tidal wave of emigrants from eastern and Mediterranean acceding and candidate countries'.

- Migrants from the new Member States are likely to be relatively young and educationally well qualified. Women will make up 40–45% of the total, creating a potential 'youth drain' in the source countries.
- The main target destination countries for these migrants will be Germany and Austria.

Stilwell et al. (2003) summarized the different types of migration.

- **Permanent settlers** are legally admitted immigrants who are expected to settle in the country, including persons admitted to reunite families.
- **Documented labour migrants** include both temporary contract workers and temporary professional transients: *temporary migrant workers* are skilled, semi-skilled or untrained workers who remain in the receiving country for finite periods as set out in an individual work contract or service contract made with an agency; *temporary professional transients* are professional or skilled workers who move from one country to another, often with international firms.
- **Undocumented labour migrants** are those who have no legal status in the receiving country because of illegal entry or overstay.
- **Asylum seekers** are those who appeal for refugee status because they fear persecution in their country of origin.
- **Recognized refugees** are those deemed at risk of persecution if they return to their own country. Decisions on asylum status and refugee status are based on the United Nations Convention Relating to the Status of Refugees, 1951.
- **Externally displaced persons** are those not recognized as refugees but who have valid reasons for fleeing their country of origin (such as famine or war).

Most health professionals moving *within* the EU will fall into one of the first two categories in the typology. Some coming from *outside* the EU, from other parts of the world, will be refugees, asylum seekers and displaced persons.

With the data available it is not possible to develop either a detailed Europe-wide or an international picture of the trends in flows of doctors, nurses and other health workers, or to assess the balance between temporary and permanent migrants. There is little international standardization of migration-related documentation so it is difficult to compare levels of general migration between countries (Auriol and Sexton 2002). The general lack of specific data related to health professionals requires primary research coordinated across all relevant source and destination countries (Mejia et al. 1979).

However, it is possible to illustrate country-level examples of the in- and out-flow of health professionals, enabling the dynamics of international recruitment and migration to be examined and the policy considerations to be illuminated.

The drivers of migration

The drivers for individuals to consider migrating are often characterized as push and pull factors. Table 3.1 summarizes some of the possible main factors related

Table 3.1 Main push and pull factors in migration and international recruitment of health workers

Push factors	Pull factors
Low pay (absolute and/or relative)	Higher pay
	Opportunities for remittances
Poor working conditions	Better working conditions
Lack of resources to work effectively	Better resourced health systems
Limited career opportunities	Career opportunities
Limited educational opportunities	Provision of post-basic education
Impact of HIV/AIDS	Political stability
Unstable/dangerous work environment	Travel opportunities
Economic instability	Aid work

Source: adapted from Buchan et al. (2003).

to health workers. To a certain extent, these present a mirror image on the issues of relative pay, career prospects, working conditions and environment available in the source and destination countries. Where the relative (or perceived) gap is significant, the pull of the destination country will be felt.

However, other factors may also act as significant push factors in specific countries at specific times, such as the impact of HIV/AIDS on health systems and health workers, concerns about personal security in areas of conflict and economic instability. Other pull factors, such as the opportunity to travel or to assist in aid work, will also be a consideration for some individuals.

Taking account of push and pull factors and individual circumstances, a typology of different categories of international overseas nurses has been developed (Buchan et al. 1997) (Table 3.2). This typology helps to delineate different push and pull factors, and could be applied to the type(s) of health workers' mobility to any European country. Different individuals will be motivated to move for different reasons and the mix of different types of migrant health workers may be different in different countries and at different times. Some temporary moves will become permanent, while some planned permanent moves will be short-lived in practice.

Other factors, such as geographical proximity and shared language, customs and educational curricula, may affect the choice of destination country. Postcolonial ties (often where source countries continue to share similar educational curricula and language) may also be a factor for some EU countries, such as the United Kingdom and Portugal.

Issues of professional and cultural adaptation must be considered. Doctors and nurses moving from one country to another may speak the language and possess recognized qualifications but it is likely that there will still be a period of adapting to the specific clinical processes and procedures and the broader organizational culture. This issue is underresearched (but see Yi and Jezewski 2000; Daniel et al. 2001; Buchan 2003).

Table 3.2 Typology of migrant health workers

Permanent move	
Economic migrant	Attracted by better standard of living
Career move	Attracted by enhanced career opportunities
Migrant partner	Unplanned move, result of spouse or partner moving
Temporary move	
Working holiday	Health professional qualification used to finance travel
Study tour	Acquisition of new knowledge and techniques for use in home country
Student	Acquisition of post-basic qualifications for use in home country
Contract worker	Employed on fixed-term contract; often awaiting improved job prospects in home country

Health worker migration in Europe

This section assesses the flows of some categories of health worker within Europe and the inflow of health workers to European countries from elsewhere. The latter, in particular, has been the focus of much of the recent policy attention. This section draws from information and data reported in the country case studies and reports mainly on doctors and nurses.

Three issues are examined in this section, each using different data sources: (a) cross-border migration of health professionals within EU countries, using data compiled by Directorate General XV of the European Commission (DGXV); (b) the findings from the country case studies; and (c) additional data from selected EU countries, providing illustrative examples of the dynamics of health workers' flows between countries.

There are two main indicators of the relative importance of migration and international recruitment to a country: the inflow of workers into the country from other source countries (and/or the outflow to other countries), and the actual stock of international health workers in the country at a certain time. Some of the recent policy documents and reports on the international migration of health professionals have highlighted the need to improve monitoring of cross-border flows. Currently, even the best available data are incomplete for any one country and not compatible between countries, constraining any attempt to develop a clear international or global picture of the overall flows of health workers. However, it is possible to take a national focus and use available data to fix any one country within the international dynamic and also to assess the connections with other countries in terms of the flows of workers.

Cross-border flows within the EU

DGXV collates statistics on the migration of doctors and general nurses within the EU, presented annually between 1977 and 2000 (European Commission

2004a, b). Unfortunately, no data are available for many EU countries and those data that are available are incomplete. Table 3.3 shows data on the numbers of doctors and general nurses authorized to practise in another EU country in 2000, by virtue of EU directives. This is the most recent year for which data are available. However, these cannot be used as a matrix to assess cross-border flows of doctors and nurses in the EU.

Country case studies

The limited data on internal migration of health professionals raise important questions in relation to EU accession. Some new Member States, such as Poland and Lithuania, are reporting that significant numbers of their health professionals are considering moving to longer established EU countries following enlargement. In the absence of improved monitoring capacity, it will be difficult to assess the actual flows in a systematic and comparable manner.

The country case studies highlight that some countries, such as the United Kingdom, hold more data on the inflow and outflow of health professionals than have been available to DGXV. At least in part, improved monitoring could be based on better access to and compilation of current country-level data rather than the generation of new data. Data and information presented in the

Table 3.3 Doctors and nurses of EU Member States obtaining authorization to practise in other EU countries in 2000

	Total no. authorized to practise in (country) in 2000		
	Doctors by virtue of basic qualification	Doctors by virtue of specific training in general medical practice	General nurses by virtue of EU Directive
Germany	a	4019	88
France	a	a	a
Italy	72	12	138
Netherlands	215	a	126
Belgium	a	a	a
Luxembourg	a	a	a
United Kingdom	a	a	a
Ireland	a	a	1097
Denmark	50	68?	17
Greece	a	a	a
Spain	257	61–63	128–133
Portugal	a	a	1611
Austria	72	5	99
Finland	29	22	4
Sweden	174	9	231

Source: European Commission (2004a, b).
[a] No data

country case studies can be used to highlight current stocks of health professionals in each of the countries and to identify current main source countries. Table 3.4 reports on country information from EU Member States and the Russian Federation.

These data present a mixed picture of current EU Member States. The United Kingdom reports a significant inflow of doctors and nurses, mainly from non-EU countries. Norway also reports some active recruitment, while migration has a negligible impact in France. Spain reports some outflow of nurses, including via a 'country to country agreement' with the United Kingdom. In some new Member States (Malta, Poland, Lithuania) there is an expectation that accession may lead to an increase in outflow of doctors and nurses. Poland and Lithuania report on surveys suggesting that many young doctors and nurses are considering moving westward.

Dynamics of flows of health workers in Europe: examples from Ireland, Norway and the United Kingdom

A source country becomes a destination country: nurses in Ireland

In the past, Ireland has been a major source of nurses for other English-speaking countries, particularly the United Kingdom, the United States and Saudi Arabia. Some Irish nationals travelled to the United Kingdom to work as nurses or to train there, staying on after qualification. This traditional outflow of nurses changed dramatically from the mid-1990s when the Irish economy began a sustained period of rapid growth, the health sector expanded and there was a growing nursing shortage, particularly in the capital city of Dublin (Department of Health and Children 2002).

Having been a country of emigrants, Ireland has become an active recruiter of nurses from elsewhere, encouraging Irish nurses to return home and actively recruiting in other English-speaking countries such as the United Kingdom and South Africa, as well as the Philippines (Figure 3.1). Thus, in 1990 approximately three of every four new registrations on the nursing register in Ireland (An Bord Altranais) had trained in Ireland; only 27% were from other sources. However, while numbers registering from Ireland remained constant at around 1500–1700 per year during the following decade, the numbers registering from non-Irish sources rose threefold. By 2000 non-Irish sources accounted for more than half of all new registrations, the United Kingdom being the main source country.

A measure of the outflow of nurses from Ireland to the United Kingdom, and vice versa, can be assessed using registration data in each country (Figure 3.2), highlighting the changing dynamics over the period. In the mid-1990s the net exchange of nurses, measured by registration data, was slightly in favour of the United Kingdom. However, by the end of the decade the situation had changed dramatically, with many more nurses now moving from the United Kingdom to Ireland.

Registration data can never give a complete and accurate picture but the trend

Table 3.4 Key indicators of migration and international recruitment of health workers

Country	Stock of international workers in country (% of total stock)	International inflow (% of total inflow)	Major source/destination countries	General comments
France	Doctors: 7000–8000 (3%).		Inflow from Belgium (nurses).	In-migration from EU 'not yet significant'. 'Very few' French physicians do their training in another EU country. 'No country in EU contributes more than 1 in 1000 health professionals working in France' – other than in nursing, where Belgium contributes 2 in 1000. Impact of migration is 'minimal'.
Germany	Doctors: 15 143. 'No data' on nurses.		Former Soviet Union, Iran, Greece, Turkey.	'Negligible' outflow of doctors.
Norway	2623 physicians (15% of stock, but includes Norwegian nationals trained in other countries).	32 physicians (active recruitment by Labour administration, 2002). 260 nurses (active recruitment by Labour administration, 2002).	Inflow from other Nordic countries, Germany, some Baltic states, Poland.	'Historically a large percentage of Norwegian physicians have received their education abroad'.
Spain			Inflow of physicians from Argentina. Outflow to Portugal, Sweden, France. Outflow of nurses to United Kingdom.	Agreement between Spain and United Kingdom for active recruitment of nurses by United Kingdom.

United Kingdom	8% of registered nurses (2002). Approx. one-third of the total of 70 000 NHS hospital medical staff were from other countries (2002).	12 000 nurses in 2002/3 (43% of new inflow). Over 10 000 doctors in 2003 (70% of total inflow of new full registrants).	*Nurses* Inflow: the Philippines, South Africa, Australia, India. Outflow: Australia, Ireland, United States. *Doctors* Inflow: e.g. India, South Africa, Australia, EU (e.g. Germany).	International recruitment an explicit policy to assist in increasing NHS workforce. Targeted recruitment of physicians and nurses. 'Ethical' recruitment code for NHS – no active recruitment from specified developing countries.
Lithuania			Doctors' outflow: Nordic countries, United Kingdom, Germany. Nurses' outflow: Nordic countries, Germany, United Kingdom, Ireland.	60% of medical residents and 27% of physicians intend to leave for other EU countries.
Malta			Physicians' outflow to United Kingdom and USA; inflow from eastern Europe. Nurses' inflow from Serbia and Montenegro and 'developing countries'.	'Large proportion of physicians migrate in 3–5 years following qualification . . . 70–80%'. 'Negligible' number of nurses migrating. 'Post accession brain drain . . . could seriously affect the local health care sector'. Seven-year period negotiated with EU to halt inflow if oversupply occurring.

Continued overleaf

Table 3.4 *Continued*

Country	Stock of international workers in country (% of total stock)	International inflow (% of total inflow)	Major source/destination countries	General comments
Poland	16 000 physicians have left to work abroad since 1995. 50 nurses to Netherlands (2002); 100 nurses to Sweden (2002).		Germany, Italy. Offers also reported from Netherlands, Spain, Norway, Sweden and Denmark (physicians). USA, Italy, United Kingdom, Saudi Arabia (nurses).	40% of first-year nursing students thinking of working abroad; language a barrier to mobility. Agreement signed in 2001 between Labour Offices of Poland and Norway, for Polish health workers to work in Norway.
The Russian Federation				No report of doctors recruited from other countries.

Source: country case-studies (see Chapter 1).

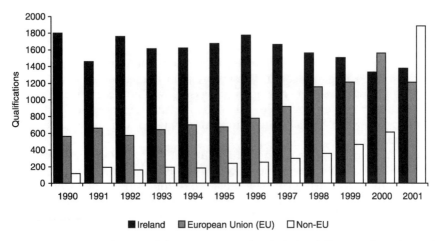

Figure 3.1 Origin of new qualifications registered with An Bord Altranais (from An Bord Altranais and Buchan et al. 2003).

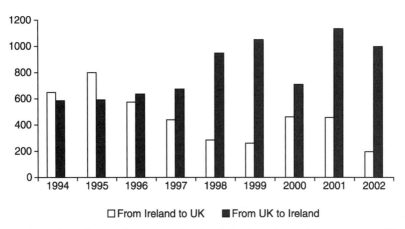

Figure 3.2 Flow of nurses between Ireland and the United Kingdom, as measured by number of requests for verification, 1994–2002.

is clear. The main point highlighted in the inflow data from Ireland is that in recent years it has been very dependent on international recruitment. Indeed, currently it appears to be significantly more reliant on international nursing labour markets than other developed countries. It is also apparent that the United Kingdom has become a main source of nurses to Ireland. Correspondingly, the United Kingdom has become less important as a potential destination for Irish nurses.

This dynamic has two major implications. First, the data suggest that many Irish nationals who travelled to the United Kingdom for nurse education have been returning to Ireland. Some may return soon after qualification but others do so after working in the United Kingdom or elsewhere after qualification. As a

result, the United Kingdom is experiencing a significant increase in the net outflow of registered nurses to Ireland, just as it attempts to redouble efforts to stimulate inflow.

A similar example of this changing dynamic is the recruitment of Finnish nurses to the United Kingdom. This was a significant feature for a few years in the late 1990s as a result of a temporary oversupply of nurses in Finland. Several hundred nurses were recruited but when nursing jobs became available in Finland, migration to the United Kingdom dropped and many Finnish nurses returned home.

This also illustrates the second main point. If there is no expectation that the employment situation in the home country will improve over time, it is likely that health workers will plan their moves to be long term or permanent. Conversely, migration is likely to be considered a temporary solution if there is an expectation of improvement in the home situation, with the view of returning when attractive career opportunities become available.

Broadening the sources of recruitment: Filipino nurses in Norway

Norway is not a member of the EU but has close ties to other Scandinavian countries. There has been an agreement for free movement of nurses within the Nordic countries for about 20 years. Nurses from other countries applying to work in Norway are recorded by a state registration organization (SAFH). Figure 3.3 illustrates the recent trend in the number of nurses registered by SAFH.

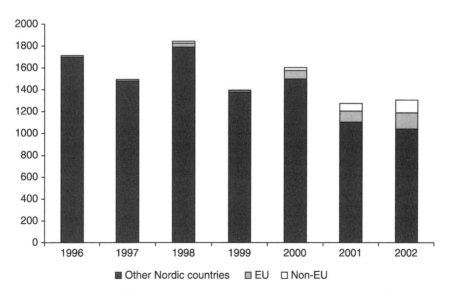

Figure 3.3 Number of international nurse registrants to Norway as recorded by SAFH 1996–2002 (2002 data are provisional). Other Nordic countries: Denmark, Finland and Sweden (from SAFH statistics on overseas recruitment and Buchan et al. 2003).

This suggests that there has been a relatively stable inflow of nurses annually to Norway since 1996 compared to the rapid increase recorded in Ireland. However, there appears to have been a broadening of source countries, with fewer nurses recruited from other Nordic countries and more from other European countries and elsewhere. Data for 2002 indicate that Sweden, Denmark, Finland, Germany and the Philippines were the five main sources of recruits.

Aetat, the Norwegian Public Employment Service, has been recruiting nurses from other countries on behalf of Norwegian employers since 1998. It is set a specific annual target limit for the number of recruits: 228 in 2001 and 260 in 2002. Aetat targets specific countries for active recruitment, conducts interviews and screening and arranges language training etc. Initially, the focus was within the EU, Finland and Germany being the two main 'cooperating countries' for the recruitment of nurses and a signed agreement between Aetat and a country counterpart. More recently, recruitment activity has spread to other countries, such as Poland and the Philippines. While Aetat is the main state-sponsored source, private sector recruitment agencies also recruit nurses on behalf of Norwegian employers.

Aetat's target-setting means that overseas recruitment to Norway is more regulated compared to that in many other countries. Norway also has the additional issue of having to provide language training to virtually all nurses from other countries. This has become more important with the shift from reliance on recruiting from other Nordic countries (where entry is easy and language differences are less pronounced) towards recruitment from a broader range of countries.

This example highlights several factors that any country will have to consider if it is actively to recruit health workers from elsewhere. Which countries should be targeted? Should there be an 'ethical' approach to international recruitment? How should it facilitate the adaptation of health professionals from other countries? Will it have to provide language training? Should it rely on recruitment agencies? These policy questions are discussed in the final section of this chapter.

International recruitment as an explicit policy: the United Kingdom's active recruitment of doctors

The United Kingdom is one example of a country that has used international recruitment as a deliberate policy to assist in meeting staffing growth targets in the NHS. Estimates of health professionals' inflow derived from registration records and work permits confirm that there has been a substantial increase in recent years.

In 2003, more than two-thirds of the 15 000 new full registrants on the United Kingdom's medical register were from other countries. The Department of Health (DoH) reports that about one in three of the 71 000 hospital medical staff working in the NHS in 2002 had obtained their primary medical qualification in another country (DoH 2003). The main sources of recruits were not from within the EU but from non-EEA countries, such as South Africa and India. Figure 3.4 shows the annual percentage of new doctor registrants from within the United

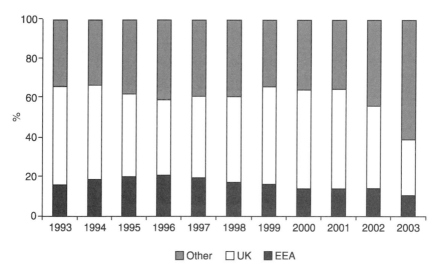

Figure 3.4 Doctors: number of new full entrants to GMC (United Kingdom) register from EEA countries, United Kingdom training and other countries, 1993–2003.

Kingdom, the EEA and non-EEA countries. This highlights a rapid upswing in the proportion of doctors registering from other (non-EEA) countries in the past two years.

This upward trend is, at least in part, a direct consequence of policy intervention. The Department of Health in England has been explicit in its support for international recruitment: 'International recruitment is a sound and legitimate contribution to the development of the NHS workforce' (DoH 2001). This support stems from the need to supplement home-based recruitment and 'return' initiatives if the NHS Plan targets for staffing growth are to be met. However, having recognized the potential consequences of such a strategy, it issued a Code of Practice on International Recruitment in October (DoH 2001), which requires that NHS employers do not recruit actively from developing countries, unless there is a bilateral agreement (Buchan 2004). A full list of proscribed countries and approved recruitment agencies was made available in early 2003.

This has important general implications. Recruitment agencies often play a key role as intermediaries in the international recruitment process. Some are based in the home country of recruits and act as an agent on their behalf to identify employment opportunities in other countries; others are based in destination countries, or are multinational, and act primarily as agents of the employer who is seeking specific types of health workers. Some agencies came under criticism in the United Kingdom as they were charging high fees to potential recruits or issuing misleading information about employment opportunities in a destination country. For this reason the Code was extended to provide a list of approved recruitment agencies that had agreed to comply with all aspects of its ethical approach.

The United Kingdom has become reliant on international recruitment, mostly from other English-speaking countries. Despite the provision of free

movement of health professionals within the EU, much of the recent international recruitment activity has been with Commonwealth countries. One exception is the recruitment of German doctors, which has continued for a number of years, despite the ending of oversupply in Germany (Simmgen 2004).

The relatively low level of migration of doctors from other EU countries to the United Kingdom highlights another general point about migration. As noted previously, many factors determine the direction and amount of migration of health workers. Entering the EU means entering a free mobility zone but factors such as language, similarity in professional education, historical (postcolonial) links and the balance of push and pull factors will also play a major role in shaping the dynamic, direction and net balance of the in- and outflows of health workers.

The impact of accession: will doctors move west?

In the lead up to EU enlargement in May 2004, there was debate about how many doctors and other health professionals from the new Member States might move west to established EU countries and to Scandinavia. At the time of writing it is too early to assess in detail the likely flows. However, it is clear that some of the outlined push–pull imbalances that will stimulate migration are present. Doctors can expect significantly higher salaries if they move west; they can also look to educational and career opportunities that are less prevalent in the new Member States.

A survey of physicians in the Czech Republic, Hungary, Lithuania and Poland, conducted in 2002, showed that between one-quarter and one-half of the respondents were thinking about migrating to other EU countries, while between 4% and 10% were definitely going to move (Open Society Institute 2003) (Figure 3.5). In Lithuania, the main reasons were higher salaries, better professional opportunities and better quality of life. The Nordic countries, the United Kingdom and Germany were reported to be the first choice countries (Open Society Institute 2003).

An intention to move is not the same as actually moving, however. It remains to be seen how many physicians will migrate. It is clear that the motivation to move, in terms of aspirations of better opportunities, does exist; membership of the EU will facilitate the movement of physicians from these countries to other parts of the Union.

Health worker mobility: general policy implications

This section discusses in more detail some of the more general policy questions that are raised by health worker migration and highlights key current knowledge gaps. The flow of health workers across national boundaries within the EU and into the EU from other sources, partly as a result of the growth of active recruitment by some countries, creates a series of challenges for national governments and international agencies.

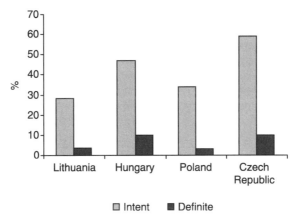

Figure 3.5 Percentage of physicians intending to migrate to EU countries, 2002 (from Open Society Institute 2003).

'Source' countries

Countries that are experiencing a net outflow of health workers need to be able to assess the underlying causes and evaluate the impact on health care provision. It is important that the available information base enables policy-makers to assess the relative loss of staff owing to outflow to other countries relative to internal flows, such as health workers leaving to work in the private sector or to take up other forms of employment. In some cases international outflow may be a very visible but only relatively small numerical loss of workers compared with flows of workers leaving the public sector for other sources of employment within the country.

In some countries, out-migration may be encouraged to reduce oversupplies of specific types of worker, or to encourage workers to acquire additional skills or qualifications. This managed flow has to be contrasted with any unmanaged outflow of health workers, which may threaten the sustainability of the health system, undermine planning and erode the current and future skills base. The creation of monetary or regulatory barriers that prevent health workers from leaving is one policy response, but this is unlikely to alleviate the push factors that motivate workers to leave in the first place and also cuts across notions of the free movement of individuals. Other policy responses to reducing outflow may aim directly at reducing push factors by, for example, addressing insufficient payment and career prospects, poor working conditions and high workloads and concerns about security or improving educational opportunities.

Another policy response is based on the recognition that outflow may not be hindered where principles of individual freedom are to be upheld, but that interventions can be developed to ensure that such outflow is managed and moderated. The 'managed migration' initiative in the Caribbean is an example of a coordinated regional intervention that aims to minimize the negative impacts of outflow while hoping to secure at least some benefit from the process (Yan 2002; Buchan and Dovlo 2004).

There is a need to place the level and impact of health workers' international

out-migration in the broader labour market context. For example, in many countries there is a need for a more detailed assessment of the actual impact of health workers moving to other countries compared to that caused by health workers leaving the health sector in-country. There is a need for more detailed evaluation of the various attempts to constrain outflow or encourage returners. Case study research would provide more evidence of 'what works' (and is appropriate) and could be linked to broader-based studies examining interventions to improve the recruitment and retention of health workers. This in turn is related to issues of capacity, governance and planning within the country.

An important related aspect is that of gender within the health care workforce, in terms not only of patterns of migration (or migration experiences) for male and female health workers but also of whether particular staff groups receive differential treatment because they are perceived to be gender specific. In particular, in some countries the undervaluing of nursing as 'women's work' may be both a direct driver for mobile nurses to leave that country and an indirect reason why interventions to reduce outflow may be ineffective.

'Destination' countries

The policy challenges for destination countries mirror those of source countries (see Buchan and Dovlo 2004). One concern is monitoring and assessment, as the ability to monitor trends in inflow (both numbers and sources) is vital if a country is to integrate this information into its planning process. Equally important is an understanding of why shortages of health workers are occurring: is it because of poor planning, unattractive pay or career opportunities, early retirements? An initial assessment of the contributing factors for staffing shortages in any country needs to be undertaken and would include that of health worker 'wastage' to other sectors or regions within the country.

It is crucial to assess the relative contribution of international recruitment compared to other key interventions, such as home-based recruitment, improved retention and return of non-practising health professionals, in order to identify the most effective balance of interventions. This assessment has to be embedded in an overall framework of policy responses to health sector workforce issues if it is to be relevant.

A second challenge for destination countries can be characterized as the 'efficiency' challenge. If there is an inflow of health workers from elsewhere, how can this inflow be moderated and facilitated so that it contributes effectively to the health system? Policy responses have included: 'fast tracking' work permit applications; developing coordinated, multiemployer approaches to recruitment to achieve economies of scale in the recruitment process; developing multiagency approaches to coordinated placement of health workers when they have arrived; and providing initial periods of supervised practice or adaptation as well as language training, cultural orientation and social support to ensure assimilation of new workers into the country, culture and organization. A related challenge may be that of trying to channel international recruits to the geographical or specialty areas that most require additional staff.

Finally, a third challenge for destination countries concerns ethics. Is it

justifiable, on moral and ethical grounds, to recruit health workers from developing countries? The simple answer may be that it should not be justifiable to contribute to brain drain in other countries, but a detailed examination of the issue reveals a more complex and blurred picture. Active recruitment by employers or national governments in the destination country has to be contrasted with a situation in which the workers themselves have taken the initiative to move across national borders. Account must also be taken of the development of bilateral and multilateral agreements, and of the right of the individual to move.

Various types of bilateral and multilateral recruitment agreements are being developed by different recruiting countries, and some have an explicit ethical dimension or attempt to focus on encouraging a 'win–win' situation, where the source country does not lose in the process.

Policy implications

One key issue, for both country governments and international agencies, is developing a better understanding of the level and dynamics of the flows of health workers between countries, and into and out of the EU. This issue takes on greater prominence with the latest enlargement of the EU in May 2004. Often it is impossible to quantify even the most basic indicator of how many doctors or nurses have left or entered a country. While the country case studies suggest varying levels of current cross-border flows, it is apparent that active international recruitment of health professionals has become a significant element in overall human resource strategy for countries such as the United Kingdom and Ireland, while in others (e.g. Poland and Lithuania) there are suggestions that many health workers may flow westward when they have the opportunity. Within an enlarged EU further action could be supported in source and destination countries to improve the monitoring of flows; this could be undertaken in association with other agencies with an interest in this issue (OECD, WHO, ILO).

Another possibility is to move beyond monitoring flows and to develop policy interventions that manage or moderate them. One option is bilateral agreements between countries to facilitate the flow of health workers, e.g. between the United Kingdom and Norway.

The introduction of a uni- or multilateral code of practice that sets down principles for the practice of effective and ethical international recruitment could be a further option; for example, the Department of Health's Code (DoH 2001) outlined previously. This requires that NHS employers do not recruit actively from developing countries unless there is between-government agreement. So far, England is the only country to have introduced a detailed code of practice in an attempt to moderate the international recruitment of health workers.

Further, the EU as a whole could introduce some guidelines, codes or frameworks, similar to the multilateral code introduced by the Commonwealth (Commonwealth Secretariat 2002). However, this has had a limited impact because a number of Commonwealth countries, including the United Kingdom, Australia and Canada, have not signed. Some international health professional

associations have also promoted codes and principles for international recruitment (International Council of Nurses (ICN) 2001; WONCA 2002).

Whatever the source of such a framework or code, its effectiveness will rely on three factors. What is its *content*? What are the principles and practical details set out to guide international recruitment? What is its *coverage*? Does it cover all relevant employers and countries? Is *compliance* assured? Are there systems in place to monitor cross-border recruitment activity, and what are the penalties for non-compliance?

Conclusions

This chapter has examined issues related to the migration of health workers and their international recruitment. It is suggested that for some countries such migration may be of only marginal importance. However, the chapter has also highlighted that migration may currently be significant for several EU countries that are reliant on inflows of health workers to meet their staffing requirements, and for others that may experience unplanned outflows, such as some of the new Member States.

The demographics in many EU countries with an ageing population and an ageing health care workforce (see chapter on trends) may make it more likely that these countries actively encourage inflows of health workers over the next few years.

Essentially there are two viable options for policy-makers and international bodies faced with in-migration and/or out-migration of health workers. They can decide not to intervene, to moderate flows with some type of code of practice or to manage the migration process actively to enable approximation to a 'win–win', or at least not exclusively 'win–lose' situation.

Table 3.5 sets out some options for policy at local, state and international levels; some are relevant for source countries, some for destination countries, but few have been fully implemented or evaluated. The next round of policy research should focus on two aspects of migration. First, there is a clear need to improve the available data so that monitoring of trends in flows of health workers can be more effective. Second, research should focus on assessing the viability and effectiveness of the various possible policy interventions, to identify which, if any, are relevant and have the potential for mutual and beneficial impact.

The current levels of international recruitment of health workers are variable; this variation is likely to continue, based on the different impact of push and pull factors in different countries. However, at EU level, the aggregate effect of health worker migration is likely to become more prominent in the next few years, because demographic change and EU enlargement will alter the overall balance of these factors. The new Member States tend to report significantly lower levels of pay and career prospects for health workers; enlargement may thus trigger otherwise latent push factors, which may be stimulated further if western European countries exert a pull through active recruitment of doctors and nurses and other health workers. It is likely that health worker migration will be both a more prominent problem and a solution in Europe over the next

Table 3.5 Examples of potential policy interventions in international recruitment

Level	Characteristics/examples
Organizational	
Twinning	Hospitals in source and destination countries develop links, based on staff exchanges, staff support and flow of resources to source country.
Staff exchange	Structured temporary move of staff to other organization, based on career and personal development opportunities/ organizational development.
Educational support	Educators and/or educational resources and/or funding in temporary move from destination to source organization.
Bilateral agreement	Employer(s) in destination country develop agreement with employer(s) or educator(s) in source country to contribute to, or underwrite costs of, training additional staff, or to recruit staff for fixed period, linked to training and development prior to return to source country.
National	
Government-to-government bilateral agreement	Destination country develops agreement with source country to underwrite costs of training additional staff, and/or to recruit staff for fixed period, linked to training and development prior to staff returning to source country, or to recruit surplus staff in source country.
Ethical recruitment code	Destination country introduces code that places restrictions on employers – which source countries can be targeted, and/or length of stay. Coverage, content and compliance issues all need to be clear and explicit.
Compensation	Much discussed, but not much evidence in practice: destination country pays compensation (in cash or other resources) to source country. Possibly some type of sliding scale of compensation related to length of stay and/or cost of training, or cost of employment in destination country; possibly brokered via international agency?
Managed migration (can also be regional)	Country (or region) with staff-outflow initiates programme to stem unplanned out-migration, partly by attempting to reduce impact of push factors, partly by supporting other organizational or national interventions that encourage planned migration.
Train for export	(Can be a subset of managed migration) Government or private sector makes explicit decision to develop training infrastructure to train health professionals for export market to generate remittances or up-front fees.
International	
International code	As above, but covering a range of countries; its relevance will depend on content, coverage, and compliance. Commonwealth Code is an example.
Multilateral agreements	Similar to bilateral (above), but covering a number of countries (EU?). Possible brokering/monitoring role for international agency.

Source: Buchan and Dovlo (2004).

few years. As such, governments and international agencies will have to be clear about their policy standpoint.

References

Auriol, L. and Sexton, J. (2002) Human resources in science and technology: measurement issues and international mobility. *In: International mobility of the highly skilled.* Paris, Organisation for Economic Co-operation and Development.

Buchan, J. (2001) Nurses moving across borders: brain-drain or freedom of movement? *International Nursing Review,* **48**: 65–7.

Buchan, J. (2003) *Here to stay? Royal College of Nursing.* London, Royal College of Nursing (www.rcn.org.uk/publications/pdf/heretostay-irns.pdf).

Buchan, J. (2004) International rescue? The dynamics and policy implications of the international recruitment of nurses to the UK. *Journal of Health Services Research and Policy,* **9**(1): 10–16.

Buchan, J. and Dovlo, D. (2004) *International recruitment of health workers to the United Kingdom: Report for the Department for International Development.* London, DFID HSRC (www.dfidhealthrc.org/shared/publications/reports/int_rec/exec-sum.pdf).

Buchan, J., Parkin, T. and Sochalski, J. (2003) *International nurse mobility: trends and policy implications.* Geneva, Royal College of Nursing/World Health Organization/ International Council of Nurses (www.icn.ch/Int_Nurse_mobility%20final.pdf).

Buchan, J., Seccombe, I. and Thomas, S. (1997) Overseas mobility of UK based nurses. *International Journal of Nursing Studies,* **34**(1): 54–62.

Castles, S. (2000) International migration at the beginning of the twenty-first century: global trends and issues. *International Migration,* 165: 269–83.

Chanda, R. (2002) Trade in health services. *Bulletin of the World Health Organization,* **80**(2): 158–63.

Commonwealth Secretariat (2002) *Code of practice for international recruitment of health workers.* London, Commonwealth Secretariat.

Daniel, P., Chamberlain, A. and Gordon, F. (2001) Expectations and experiences of newly recruited Filipino nurses. *British Journal of Nursing,* **10**(4): 254–65.

Department of Health (2001) *Code of practice for NHS employers involved in international recruitment of health care professionals.* London, Department of Health.

Department of Health (2003) *Hospital, public health medicine and community health services medical and dental staff in England: 1992–2002. Statistical Bulletin 2003/04.* London, Department of Health.

Department of Health and Children (2002) *Nursing Policy Division, final report of the steering group.* Dublin, Department of Health and Children.

European Commission (2004a) *DGXV. Committee of Senior Officials on Public Health. Statistical tables relating to the migration of doctors in the Community from 1977 to 2000.* Brussels, European Commission.

European Commission (2004b) *DGXV. Committee of Senior Officials on Public Health. Statistical tables relating to the migration of nurses responsible for general care in the Community from 1977 to 2000.* Brussels, European Commission.

Findlay, A. and Lowell, L. (2002) *Migration of highly skilled persons from developing countries: impact and policy responses.* Geneva, International Labour Organization (International Migration Papers, No. 43).

International Council of Nurses (2001) *Position statement on ethical nurse recruitment.* Geneva, ICN (www.icn.ch/psrecruit01.htm).

International Labour Organization (2000) *Migration: a truly global phenomenon.* Geneva, ILO (www.ilo.org/public).

International Organization for Migration (2000) *World Migration Report 2000*. Geneva, IOM.

Krieger, H. (2004) *Migration trends in an enlarged Europe*. Dublin, European Foundation for the Improvement of Living and Working Conditions.

Mejia, A., Pizurki, H. and Royston, E. (1979) *Physician and nurse migration: analysis and policy implications. Report on a WHO study*. Geneva, World Health Organization.

Open Society Institute (2003) *Physician planning in Lithuania in 1990–2015*. Kaunas, Kaunas University of Medicine Press.

Organisation for Economic Co-operation and Development (2000) *Trends in international migration*. Paris, OECD.

Organisation for Economic Co-operation and Development (2002) *International mobility of the highly skilled*. Paris, OECD.

Pang, T., Lansang, M. and Haines, A. (2002) Brain drain and health professionals. *British Medical Journal*, **324**: 499–500.

Simmgen, M. (2004) Why German doctors enjoy British medicine. *Clinical Medicine*, **4**: 57–9.

Stalker, P. (1997) *Refugees and migration*. London, One World International.

Stalker, P. (2000) *Workers without frontiers: the impact of globalization on international migration*. Boulder, CO, Lynne Rienner.

Stilwell, B., Diallo, K. and Zurn, P. (2003) Developing evidence based ethical policies on the migration of health workers: conceptual and practical challenges. *Human Resources for Health*, **1**: 8.

Timur, S. (2000) Changing trends and major issues in international migration: an overview of the UNESCO programmes. *International Migration*, **165**: 255–69.

Tjadens, F. (2002) Health care shortages: where globalisation, nurses and migration meet. *Eurohealth*, **8**(3): 33–5 (www.lse.ac.uk/collections/LSEHealthAndSocialCare/pdf/eurohealth/vol8no3.pdf).

WONCA (2002) *A code of practice for the international recruitment of health professionals: the Melbourne manifesto*. World Organization of National Colleges, Academies and Academic Associations of General Practitioners/Family Physicians (www.globalfamilydoctor.com/aboutWonca/working_groups/rural_training/melbourne_manifesto.htm).

World Health Organization (2004) *International migration and health personnel: a challenge for health systems in developing countries*. Agenda item 12.11. Fifty-seventh World Health Assembly: Health Systems Including Primary Care. 22 May. Geneva, World Health Organization.

Yan, J. (2002) Caribbean nurses develop strategy for nurse shortages. *International Nursing Review*, **49**: 132–4.

Yi, M. and Jezewski, M. (2000) Korean nurses' adjustments to hospitals in the USA. *Journal of Advanced Nursing*, **32**(3): 721–9.

chapter four

Changing professional boundaries

Martin McKee, Carl-Ardy Dubois and Bonnie Sibbald

Introduction

In 2000, the World Health Report highlighted the challenges involved in achieving the appropriate mix of personnel to deliver health care (WHO 2000). What that mix might be depends on many factors. The production of health by a health care system involves not only health care personnel but also technology, information and organizational structures. The combination of these inputs will depend on their relative cost, quality and supply. In essence, health policy-makers seeking to improve the quality of care or to contain the costs of providing it should ask: who is the best person to do this job, in the particular circumstances and with the tools that are available?

In reality, the division of tasks between different health care workers reflects many considerations but evidence about who would be best is rarely one of them. There may be regulations specifying which tasks are restricted to one professional group, such as the right to prescribe, or there may be cultural norms – although unwritten these have just as great an effect. Underlying these factors is a set of issues that includes a difference in the power of different professions, often a reflection of gender relationships in society, with a predominantly male medical profession controlling a predominantly female nursing profession.

The roles adopted by different groups are not static. In part this is a reflection of the way in which health care is continually changing; advances in technology and new ways of working create new roles or make long-standing ones obsolete. Most obviously, hospitals now require a range of information technology specialists that did not exist two or three decades ago. Advances in resuscitation equipment have contributed to the emergence of a new group of emergency workers, or paramedics. Emerging evidence of the benefits of multi-professional working to tackle complex health care problems, such as treatment

and rehabilitation following stroke, is changing the dynamics of the health care team. There is a move away from the traditional medically dominated hierarchy to one in which each health care profession acts as an independent practitioner contributing to the work of the team.

The division of labour also reflects the incentives built into the health care system, often illustrated by the comparison of obstetrics and anaesthetics in the United States and the United Kingdom. In the United States, midwifery by qualified nurses has been slow to develop and many babies are delivered by medically qualified obstetricians; in the United Kingdom midwives deliver the vast majority of babies. In contrast, in the United States nurses give anaesthetics, while in the United Kingdom they are the preserve of physicians. The most obvious explanation is money. In the United States, with fee-for-service, it makes no sense for the dominant physicians to give up control of the lucrative market in deliveries. However, when operating there is no incentive to split the fee with an expensive physician. Within the United Kingdom's salaried service such incentives are absent.

This also reflects differences in supply. In the USSR, the system produced enormous numbers of physicians, often with very basic training, and paid very low wages, so there was no reason to prevent them taking on many tasks that would have been undertaken by nurses elsewhere. Indeed, the paucity of equipment and limited range of pharmaceuticals available made it difficult for them to offer anything except nursing care. In contrast, a combination of factors in western Europe, including the introduction of the European WTD and career choices (achieving a more realistic work–family balance) by an increasingly female medical workforce, is creating a serious shortage of physicians. One response is to transfer many traditionally medical roles to other health professionals, in particular nurses, and in turn transfer many basic nursing tasks to other, less extensively trained (and therefore less expensive) health care workers.

Differences also exist in the types of health professionals in each country. For example, much basic health care in the USSR was provided by feldshers, a group whose basic medical training allowed them to act independently in isolated rural facilities. Many professional groups involved in the delivery of various forms of therapy do not have equivalents in all countries. Where they do not exist their roles may be taken, to a limited extent, by nurses.

The existing division of labour in any health care system is not, therefore, sacrosanct and a range of factors is driving change. These factors have been summarized (Table 4.1). Yet change should be based on evidence. This chapter looks at some of the ways in which the skill mix is changing in different countries and examines the research evidence about what works and what does not. It assumes that the portfolio of skills possessed by those currently performing certain tasks is not necessarily the optimal one; others with narrower or more specific skills may be better. It also recognizes that health care systems are complex, dynamic and adaptive. When responsibility for a task is transferred from one professional group to another, both groups change, and so does their relative power, including the power to demand financial rewards. Thus, while a changing skill mix may lead to reductions in costs, it is naive to imagine that this outcome is inevitable. Indeed, where a task is transferred from a

Table 4.1 Factors driving changes in skill mix and possible responses

Factor	Requirement	Possible interventions
Skill shortages	Response to shortages of staff in particular occupations or professions.	Undertake skill substitution; improve use of skills.
Cost containment	Improved management of organizational costs, specifically labour costs.	Reduce unit labour costs or improve productivity by altering staff or skill mix.
Quality improvement	Improved quality of care.	Improve use and deployment of staff skills to achieve best mix.
Technological innovation	Cost-effective use of new medical technology and interventions.	Retrain staff in new skills; introduce different mix or new types of worker.
New health sector programmes or initiatives	Maximize health benefits of programme implementation, by having appropriately skilled workers in place.	Adjust staff roles; introduce new roles and new types of worker.
Health sector reform	Cost-containment, improvements in quality of care and performance, responsiveness of health sector organizations.	Adjust staff roles; introduce new skills and new types of worker.
Changes in the legislative/ regulatory environment (also a possible intervention)	Scope for changes in (or constraints on) role for different occupations, professions.	Adjust staff roles; introduce new skills and new types of worker.

Source: Buchan and Dal Poz (2002).

professional group that has had little interest in it to another that is prepared to invest greater effort in achieving health gain, it may cost more. Furthermore, changes in skill mix will often require investment in training and in structural modifications necessary for the reconfiguration of services.

Finally, a note of caution is required. Although terms such as 'doctor' and 'nurse' are used widely in international comparisons of health systems, they have obscured the tremendous diversity in roles that are associated with them. This is especially true for nursing: in some countries a nurse qualifies after very basic training in specialized high schools that gives her (and in these situations nursing is almost entirely a female occupation) very basic caring skills and negligible scope for action independent of the medical profession. In contrast, in other countries, qualification as a nurse requires a university degree and confers the right to work as an independent practitioner, initiating treatment and prescribing drugs where appropriate. These two models have little in common

and research on role transfers in one setting is of little relevance to the other, except to challenge deeply embedded beliefs about what is possible.

An analytical framework

Sibbald and colleagues (2004) have developed a taxonomy of changes in skill mix in health care (Table 4.2).

This chapter focuses on the first set of changes, related to different professional roles, drawing extensively on the review by Sibbald et al. (2004). Before this, however, it is important to reflect on one theme that appears repeatedly in this chapter: the relative lack of research. Many changes in professional roles take place incrementally, as some groups take on new roles and others give them up. Rarely are these gradual changes recognized explicitly as innovations. Indeed, frequently they are not even described in a structured way. Thus they are subject to few evaluations, especially those that would permit rigorous comparisons of different professional groups. Furthermore, even when there are evaluations, often the results can be generalized only with great caution because of the quite different contexts that exist in different systems and at different times. In addition, those interventions that are evaluated may not be typical of the systems from which they arise, or may be subject to publication bias, with successes more likely to be reported. Thus, for the interested policy-maker, the

Table 4.2 A taxonomy of changes in skill mix in health care

Changing roles	
Enhancement	Increasing the depth of a job by extending the role or skills of a particular group of workers.
Substitution	Expanding the breadth of a job, in particular by working across professional divides or exchanging one type of worker for another.
Delegation	Moving a task up or down a traditional uni-disciplinary ladder.
Innovation	Creating new jobs by introducing a new type of worker.
Changing the interface between services	
Transfer	Moving the provision of a service from one health care setting to another (e.g. substituting community for hospital care).
Relocation	Shifting the venue from which a service is provided from one health care sector to another without changing the people who provide it (e.g. running a hospital clinic in a primary care facility).
Liaison	Using specialists in one health care sector to educate and support staff working in another (e.g. hospital outreach facilitators in primary care).

Source: Sibbald et al. (2004).

greatest contribution of the published literature is to show that there is an alternative to the existing model of care and that tasks thought to be the sole preserve of one group can, in some circumstances, be undertaken by others. Whether those circumstances apply to the circumstances in which the policy-maker is working will be a matter of judgement.

Enhancement

Much enhancement of professional roles takes place without formal recognition. As professional groups adopt new technology they create ever more specialized individuals undertaking increasingly complex roles. Role enhancement, at least for physicians, is so natural that in most cases it is barely noticed. The implication is that there are no skills that physicians cannot acquire even if, in many cases, these are self-taught.

Inevitably the situation differs for other health care professionals who have traditionally inhabited an environment where enhancement of their roles is often a challenge to perceptions of what is properly the responsibility of a physician. As a consequence, such changes have more often been recognized explicitly as an enhancement of roles and thus are more likely to have been described and evaluated in academic literature.

One area where role enhancement has attracted considerable attention has been the management of patients with chronic diseases. A combination of ageing populations and more effective life-prolonging, but often complex, treatments is increasing steadily the demands on health systems. There is growing recognition that traditional models of health care are inappropriate to meet this challenge, leading health care providers to experiment with new models.

One approach involved the management of chronic diseases in nurse-led clinics in primary care settings. This represents both an enhancement of the role of nurses and a transfer from hospital to primary care. There is evidence from different countries and for several disease processes that nurse-led clinics achieve better results than traditional physician-led care (Vrijhoef et al. 2000). However, this research is difficult to generalize, given both the diversity of skills possessed by different professional groups in different countries and the range of disease processes that they may be asked to manage. For example, a Cochrane Review found improved outcome with nurse-led community-based management of chronic airways disease when the disease was moderate but not when it was severe (Smith et al. 2001). Yet in general this area has been the subject of relatively little research and several systematic reviews have concluded that what exists is often methodologically weak (De Broe et al. 2001; Smith et al. 2001; Fay et al. 2002). Specifically, while a considerable number of studies show that enhancement of nurses' roles in the management of chronic diseases can be effective, relatively few randomized studies compare this with traditional models of care.

There is more evidence looking at the expansion of the role of pharmacists: taking on the role of reviewing patient medications. A systematic review found this was generally effective in decreasing inappropriate prescribing although, in a direct comparison with a physician, the pharmacist was less effective (Beney

et al. 2000). As with other research on this topic, the authors of the review expressed caution about generalizing these studies. However, one area has considerable evidence that pharmacists are more effective than physicians in the management of anticoagulation clinics: studies from the United States and Europe report greater cost–effectiveness, in both hospital (Radley and Hall 1994; Chiquette et al. 1998) and primary care settings (MacGregor et al. 1996).

Finally, in many countries there has been considerable enhancement of the roles of emergency staff. These have moved far beyond their original roles of providing basic first aid to become skilled paramedics undertaking advanced resuscitation and initiating treatment for myocardial infarction. Again, there is less evidence than is desirable. However, one study comparing paramedics with ambulance crew who had basic life support skills found higher mortality among patients treated by the paramedics. The study authors attributed this to greater delays at the scene of the injury while resuscitation took place (Nicholl et al. 1998).

In practice, role enhancement is rarely undertaken in isolation. It often forms one element of a larger programme to change the management of chronic diseases, as in the chronic care model being implemented in many parts of the United States, which emphasizes greater self-management by patients, more structured consultations, enhanced information and decision-support systems and expanded roles for nurses, pharmacists and other health professionals (Wagner et al. 2001a). This model has been shown to improve outcomes and reduce emergency consultations for patients with several chronic disorders (Wagner et al. 2001b; Bodenheimer et al. 2002).

Substitution

Research on substituting one type of health professional for another has most frequently looked at physicians and nurses. A systematic review comparing physicians and nurses undertaking first-contact care for patients in primary care found that nurses achieved higher levels of patient satisfaction (Horrocks et al. 2002). However, they provided longer consultations and ordered more investigations, the greater resource use offsetting the cost savings from lower salaries. An added consideration is that nurses' addition to primary care teams may not necessarily reduce physician workload unless active steps are taken to prevent physicians from continuing to provide the types of care delegated to nurses (Laurant et al. 2004). Another review of nurse practitioners found that they provided as good quality of care as physicians, or better (Brown and Grimes 1995), in the routine management of chronic diseases, health promotion and the management of minor illness.

Clearly, economic analyses are especially dependent on context and Sibbald et al. note that, while the cost of training a nurse is less than for a doctor, in many countries this is balanced by nurses' reduced participation in the workforce (Sibbald et al. 2004). This may change with the increasing feminization of the medical workforce in many countries, changing gender roles in society and evolving preferences in work–leisure balance.

The higher level of patient satisfaction observed with nurses working in

primary care was also found in a review of research on nurses working in operating theatres and intensive care units in hospitals. This concluded that nurses had greater interpersonal skills, while physicians were better at resolving technical problems (Hodson 1998).

In line with the research on the enhancement of nursing roles in the management of chronic diseases, a review of nurses' partial substitution for physicians in the management of diabetes concluded that a greater role for nurses was associated with better control of blood sugar levels, the development of appropriate protocols enabling nurses to play a greater role in patient management (Renders et al. 2001).

The findings of studies of the management of conditions in primary care, where nurses have tended to undertake more interventions, contrast with the studies comparing nurse practitioners and nurse midwives with physicians in obstetric care. These have found nurses to be less likely to intervene and to achieve comparable neonatal outcomes and higher levels of patient satisfaction (Brown and Grimes 1995). Other research comparing physicians and midwives has looked at the examination of newborn babies, finding greater maternal satisfaction, technically higher quality assessments and significant cost savings associated with the use of midwives (Townsend et al. 2004).

Nurses have adopted enhanced roles in many other areas of acute care. One example is the creation of emergency nurse practitioners in emergency departments. A randomized trial found that, compared with junior physicians, nurse practitioners achieved the same outcomes but better documentation of treatment and higher levels of patient satisfaction, with nurse practitioners more likely to convey the information that patients wanted (Cooper et al. 2002). A study of nurse practitioners in British emergency departments found that they were as skilled as junior doctors at interpreting radiographs (Meek et al. 1998).

Another example is surgical nurse assistants who undertake tasks that would once have been undertaken by surgeons in training. A randomized trial of surgical nurse assistants and junior doctors working with a specialist surgeon found no difference in outcomes (Alex et al. 2004), but the authors did comment on the potential implications for surgical training, highlighting that health care facilities have roles that go beyond the immediate provision of health care to include training, research and development.

A randomized trial comparing appropriately trained nurses and junior doctors undertaking pre-operative assessment of surgical patients found no difference in the quality of assessment, although this study, performed in the United Kingdom, also found no difference in cost between the two models (Kinley et al. 2001).

Finally, some researchers have reviewed the evidence relating to replacement of physicians by other health professionals, finding little evidence in relation to a greater role by pharmacists (except for the studies of anticoagulation clinics noted previously), while dietary advice is more effective in reducing cholesterol levels when given by dietitians rather than physicians (Thompson et al. 2003). Substitution of counsellors for primary care physicians was associated with higher patient satisfaction, lower psychotropic prescribing and short-term, but not long-term, improvements in health (Bower and Sibbald 2000).

There is also a growing body of literature on the replacement of nurses by less highly qualified staff. This can take several forms (Table 4.3) (Gardner 1991; Krapohl and Larson 1996). The increasing numbers of less qualified care staff in some countries, particularly the United States, has been controversial. Commentators argue that apparent savings from lower salary costs may not be achieved because of higher rates of staff turnover and absence, as well as reduced productivity because substitute staff may have less autonomy to act independently (Orne et al. 1998). Others have criticized the low educational standard of those employed as nursing assistants (Salmond 1995). But the empirical evidence is not clear cut. Some research has found that greater use of care assistants or nurse aides does save costs (Hesterly and Robinson 1990), with no adverse effect on patient satisfaction (Bostrom and Zimmerman 1993). Other work has reported decreased quality of care and greater sickness absence (Powers et al. 1990), leading to a greater workload for the remaining qualified nurses (Garfink et al. 1991).

Finally, in laboratory-based specialties such as pathology or microbiology, as well as some other technical areas such as imaging, non-medically qualified professionals are increasingly assuming senior positions, often undergoing the same postgraduate specialist training as their medical colleagues.

Delegation

As with role enhancement, delegation in health care is widespread but seldom attracts comment and even less research. One study in the United Kingdom examined the relationship between quality of care and the different grades of nursing staff employed (reflecting their experience and training), finding that a

Table 4.3 Potential substitutes for nursing roles

Titles	*Roles*
Traditional aides/assistants/auxiliaries	Trained on the job, performing simple tasks in support of registered nurses.
Non-clinical assistants/extender clerks/aides	Undertaking non-clinical clerical and housekeeping work.
Technical assistants/operating department assistants	Assisting nurses in areas where specific technical skills are required.
Primary practice partner nursing assistants	Paired with primary nurses to maintain delivery of care.
Vocationally trained/qualified carers	Carers undergoing vocational training of several weeks or months, perhaps leading to a qualification, and taking on nursing responsibilities under the supervision of a qualified nurse or other health professional.

Source: Buchan and Dal Poz (2002), drawing on Gardner (1991) and Krapohl and Larson (1996).

greater use of higher grade staff was associated with a higher quality of care. In this case the researchers involved wrote: 'the conclusion is simple; you pay for quality care' (Carr-Hill et al. 1995). Similarly, a systematic review of care provided for patients with cancer by specialist oncologists and nonspecialist physicians, which summarized 46 studies, found that although better outcomes were achieved by specialists many of the studies contained methodological weaknesses (Grilli et al. 1998).

Comparison of medical specialists and generalists is often complicated by the fact that patients may be referred to a hospital by a generalist (but potentially very experienced) practitioner and seen by a specialist (but one who is still relatively junior). One setting in which this is especially common is in emergency rooms. One study in the United Kingdom employed GPs in an emergency department and compared their performance with that of junior hospital doctors, finding that the more experienced GPs were less likely to request investigations, prescribe or refer for a specialist opinion (Dale et al. 1995).

Innovation

The evolution of modern health care represents a continuing process of innovation, in both the skills employed and the technology to which they are applied. The process of specialization described previously in the section on role enhancement could also be considered to be a process of innovation, with similar developments taking place in other professions. For example, there are now many types of specialist nurse: managing patients with chronic diseases, providing specialized support for patients undergoing procedures such as mastectomies or colostomies, or undertaking surgical procedures. Many new roles are being created for health professionals in areas such as quality assurance.

In some countries the work of junior hospital doctors has changed greatly in the past two decades, with growing recognition that many of the tasks they performed (both administrative and clinical) do not require medical training. As a consequence new types of workers have developed, such as phlebotomists to take routine blood samples. This is becoming even more important in western Europe, with increasing restrictions on junior doctors' working hours. A study from Scotland found that nurse practitioners employed to take over some of the tasks performed by junior doctors at night could reduce the intensity of the doctors' work by almost 50% (Henderson et al. 1999).

A changing skill mix can also arise from technological innovation. For example, many once complex laboratory investigations have been superseded by simple kits. The most obvious example is pregnancy testing, which once depended on the observation of ovulation following the potential mother's urine being injected into guinea-pigs; now this is achieved with a test that can be purchased from any pharmacist. Such kits facilitate near-patient testing: former laboratory investigations can be undertaken on wards, in primary care facilities or even in patient's homes (Rink et al. 1993).

Other changes

The remaining changes identified by Sibbald et al. (2004) mostly go beyond the scope of this chapter, although in some cases innovations that are primarily changes of the location for care provision also involve changes in the type of person who provides it. One example is the development of telephone triage systems designed to divert patients from emergency departments to other, more suitable settings, such as minor injury units or the care of their general practitioner. Often this involves nurses giving telephone advice according to defined protocols. This approach's impact on demand for care remains controversial, although one study suggests that overall demand for care is redistributed but not reduced (Mark and Shepherd 2004). Such a service depends on easy access to telephones, conditions that will not apply in some parts of Europe, and research undertaken in London shows that, even in a relatively wealthy country such as the United Kingdom, there is underutilization in the most deprived areas (Burt et al. 2003).

While triage systems seek to prevent unnecessary hospital attendances and admissions, other innovations seek to reduce the time that inpatients remain in hospital. Specially trained nurses and other health professionals provide patients with the care that they would have received in hospital but in their own homes. A systematic review of such hospital-at-home schemes concluded that there was no difference in outcome for patients with a variety of medical conditions or recovering from elective surgery, with conflicting evidence for those with strokes (Shepperd and Iliffe 2001). A common finding is that patients prefer this model but their carers do not. While the duration of treatment in hospital is reduced, the overall time taken to recover is often longer and the hospital-at-home model is typically as expensive as the traditional alternative (Parkes and Shepperd 2003).

Success and failure

As the preceding review shows, it is not always more cost-effective to change who does something. Drawing on their review of evidence on changing skill mix, Sibbald et al. (2004) identified a series of issues that should be taken into account when considering whether change may be appropriate.

The first issue is whether the care being provided is effective whoever does it. In the United Kingdom the introduction of nurse-led screening clinics in primary care was ineffective in reducing morbidity and mortality because screening and lifestyle advice alone is of limited effectiveness in changing patients' lifestyles (Ebrahim and Davey Smith 2000). It only makes sense to consider who should undertake a role once it has been shown that it should be undertaken at all.

A second issue is whether there has been adequate training and support for those adopting new roles. Their needs will depend on the starting point; that is, the level of skills they already possess. For example, it will be much easier for nurses to take over the management of chronic disease clinics in countries where they have a high level of skills and are used to acting as independent

practitioners, not simply doctors' assistants. However, support goes beyond training and there is some evidence that the transfer of responsibilities from one profession to another can be facilitated by the development of evidence-based guidelines and protocols (Thomas et al. 2000).

A third issue is the existence of regulatory or legal barriers to change. Where these exist they usually specify certain activities that can be performed only by a physician, dentist, registered nurse or midwife. In some cases these are relatively non-contentious, such as the certification of death, but increasingly the status of others, in particular prescribing, is challenged. The challenges come from two sources. The first is the shift of many pharmaceuticals from prescription-only to over-the-counter status. Many active ingredients, such as simple painkillers, have always been available to anyone but these have been joined by preparations such as H_2 antagonists that, when first marketed, were prescribed only by specialists in many countries. The second is the growth in nurse prescribing, a phenomenon linked to the growth of nurse-led chronic disease management. Frequently this has required changes in legislation, which, while theoretically straightforward, may be difficult to achieve in countries where there is a politically strong physicians' lobby anxious to maintain their privileges in the face of what they consider encroachment by other professions. It may also be problematic in some countries where the legislative system is still struggling with the process of reform, especially those emerging from the political transitions of the 1990s. However, where regulatory barriers persist even though their original rationale no longer applies, the obvious solution is to remove them.

A fourth issue relates to the pattern of incentives that exist within a health care system and in particular the system by which different professionals are paid. In general, a system that rewards professionals for undertaking procedures frequently obstructs less powerful professions (generally those other than medicine) from taking them on. On the other hand, the scope to change the payment system offers a powerful mechanism to bring about change in the way things are done.

Making it happen

The review of factors predicting success or failure provides a basic list of requirements to bring about change. These include the removal of regulatory barriers, the creation of appropriate (and removal of inappropriate) financial incentives and the provision of effective training and support for those whose roles are changing. While much change is incremental and unplanned, the sum of many individual changes in response to changing circumstances, it is also true that health care systems are frequently resistant to change. There may be a case for adopting a strategic perspective, stepping aside from the day-to-day delivery of clinical care, to consider what changes are needed to respond to emerging challenges that have not yet reached the top of the agenda. For example, as Buchan showed in Chapter 3, all European countries face changes in their workforce as many confront shortages of key health professionals such as physicians and nurses. Given the long time scales between a decision to increase training and the production of trained professionals, as well as the

complexity of the changes that often are needed to support new roles, it is important that responses are developed to these looming shortages now.

Strategic planning requires an integrated programme for change, with appropriate training and mechanisms to ensure that as new ways of working are adopted, old ones are abandoned. However, innovations may also be designed to enhance quality of care, supplementing what already exists rather than replacing it. As an example, the expansion of nurse-led chronic disease clinics in general practice in the United Kingdom has not brought about a substantial reduction in the workload of GPs as it has met a previously unmet need (Campbell et al. 2003). Strategic planning should also consider the needs of those giving up responsibilities.

Developing a plan is, of course, only the first stage; it is equally important to manage the process of change, discussed further in Chapter 7. Change will be easier within a supportive or positive culture (Adams et al. 2000), with concern for 'soft' human resource issues, such as: staff satisfaction; staff development; quality of care (not simply cost-containment); strategic and systematic management of the skill mix change, coordinated by senior management; development of a methodology for change that is shaped by employee participation; support for training and staff development; and commitment to redeployment of existing staff.

Other factors recognized as important include support for middle managers, consultation with key stakeholders, good teamworking (with effective leadership and a reflexive way of working) and continuity of leadership, something that is often elusive (Harris et al. 2000).

Seeing the whole picture

Health systems are not mechanical machines but complex adaptive systems where a change in one area often leads to unanticipated changes in another. Major changes, such as the closure and transfer of hospital facilities, can impact adversely on both remaining staff and those transferred to other facilities (Armstrong-Stassen et al. 2001). These effects are exacerbated by poor communication and the increased workload arising from poorly planned change. Yet change can be successful, leading to improved job satisfaction and decreased burnout (Burke 2002).

Ideally change produces win–win situations but in practice there will be both winners and losers. Protocol-driven care pathways were viewed positively by nurses, as they enhanced their autonomy, yet negatively by physicians, who saw them as restrictions (Degeling et al. 2001). Even where the role of a professional group is not changed explicitly, it may lead to negative perceptions when role changes lead to reorganization of existing hierarchies (Leverment et al. 1998). Thus, nurses' adoption of new roles has created legitimate expectations of greater professional autonomy. It should not reinforce the perception of subservience to medicine.

Changes in roles are frequently part of a larger process involving the creation of extended teams of health care workers, each with distinct packages of skills. This may bring about improvements in the quality of care but it also produces

risks as larger, more diverse teams are more difficult to coordinate. Such changes require the development of explicit mechanisms to foster this coordination, including protected time for meetings, with consequent reductions in the time available for direct patient care. Those seeking to bring about change need to take account of this and to balance the potential benefits of larger teams with the greater transaction costs generated. The challenges become even greater when care that has been provided in a single location is divided among several. The greater use of modern information systems, in particular electronic patient records, is seen as a solution to this problem, although often, in practice, the results are disappointing.

Conclusions

The reason why some tasks are the responsibility of one profession and not another is frequently an accident of history. As health needs change, with new patterns of disease and new opportunities to prevent and treat them, so too human resources must adapt to respond to these changing circumstances. It is important that health policy-makers anticipate these changes and take action that will support appropriate change.

There is rarely a simple answer to the question of who should undertake a particular activity. While words such as 'doctor' or 'nurse' may be the same, their meanings differ. Roles that can be assumed easily by one group in one country may seem unimaginable in another without major investment in change management. Despite the growing volume of research on changing skill mix in the health care sector, contextual differences make it difficult to extrapolate from one setting to another. This is especially true for comparisons of cost–effectiveness, given the differing prices of inputs.

Instead, what this research can do is challenge preconceived notions and suggest that things can be done differently. Whether it is appropriate to introduce change will depend on the specific circumstances. Here the aphorism 'if it isn't broken, don't fix it' seems especially appropriate, as change inevitably has a cost; where there is a problem, either existing or anticipated, then action will be needed.

This chapter has identified a series of issues that should be taken into account when introducing change. The first is to be sure that what is to be done is worth doing, regardless of who should do it. If it is worth doing and it seems likely that it would be better with a different mix of staff, then attention should be directed to training, creating appropriate financial and other incentives to change and removing regulatory barriers. It is important that the change should be seen within its broader context so that defunct activities are discarded and released capacity is redeployed, and that any adverse impact on those most affected, the health care staff, is minimized by effective human resource policies.

References

Adams, A. et al. (2000) Skill-mix changes and work intensification in nursing. *Work, Employment and Society*, **14**: 541–55.

Alex, J. et al. (2004) Surgical nurse assistants in cardiac surgery: a UK trainee's perspective. *European Journal of Cardiothoracic Surgery*, **25**: 111–15.

Armstrong-Stassen, M., Cameron, S.J. and Horsburgh, M.E. (2001) Downsizing-initiated job transfer of hospital nurses: how do the job transferees fare? *Journal of Health and Human Services Administration*, **23**(4): 470–89.

Beney, J., Bero, L.A. and Bond, C. (2000) Expanding the roles of outpatient pharmacists: effects on health services utilisation, costs, and patient outcomes. *Cochrane Database of Systematic Reviews*, **3**: CD000336.

Bodenheimer, T., Wagner, E.H. and Grumbach, K. (2002) Improving primary care for patients with chronic illness: the chronic care model. Part 2. *Journal of the American Medical Association*, **288**: 1909–14.

Bostrom, J. and Zimmerman, J. (1993) Restructuring nursing for a competitive health care environment. *Nursing Economics*, **11**(1): 35–41.

Bower, P. and Sibbald, B. (2000) On-site mental health workers in primary care: effects on professional practice. *Cochrane Database of Systematic Reviews*, **3**: CD000532.

Brown, S.A. and Grimes, D.E. (1995) A meta-analysis of nurse practitioners and nurse midwives in primary care. *Nursing Research*, **44**: 332–9.

Buchan, J. and Dal Poz, M.R. (2002) Skill mix in the health care workforce: reviewing the evidence. *Bulletin of World Health Organization*, **80**: 575–80.

Burke, R.J. (2002) Work experiences and psychological well-being of former hospital-based nurses now employed elsewhere. *Psychological Reports*, **91**(3/2): 1059–64.

Burt, J., Hooper, R. and Jessopp, L. (2003) The relationship between use of NHS Direct and deprivation in southeast London: an ecological analysis. *Journal of Public Health Medicine*, **25**: 174–6.

Campbell, S. et al. (2003) Is the quality of care in general medical practice improving? Results of a longitudinal observational study. *British Journal of General Practice*, **53**: 298–304.

Carr-Hill, R.A. et al. (1995) The impact of nursing grade on the quality and outcome of nursing care. *Health Economics*, **4**: 57–72.

Chiquette, E., Amato, M.G. and Bussey, H.I. (1998) Comparison of an anticoagulation clinic with usual medical care: anticoagulation control, patient outcomes, and health care costs. *Archives of Internal Medicine*, **158**: 1641–7.

Cooper, M.A. et al. (2002) Evaluating emergency nurse practitioner services: a randomized controlled trial. *Journal of Advanced Nursing*, **40**: 721–30.

Dale, J. et al. (1995) Primary care in the accident and emergency department: II. Comparison of general practitioners and hospital doctors. *British Medical Journal*, **311**: 427–30.

De Broe, S., Christopher, F. and Waugh, N. (2001) The role of specialist nurses in multiple sclerosis: a rapid and systematic review. *Health Technology Assessment*, **5**: 1–47.

Degeling, P., Kennedy, J. and Hill, M. (2001) Mediating the cultural boundaries between medicine, nursing and management – the central challenge in hospital reform. *Health Services Management Research*, **14**: 36–48.

Ebrahim, S. and Davey Smith, G. (2000) Multiple risk factor interventions for primary prevention of coronary heart disease. *Cochrane Database of Systematic Reviews*, **2**: CD001561.

Fay, J., Jones, A. and Ram, F.S. (2002) Primary care based clinics for asthma. *Cochrane Database of Systematic Reviews*, **1**: CD003533.

Gardner, D.L. (1991) Issues related to the use of nurse extenders. *Journal of Nursing Administration*, **21**(10): 40–5.

Garfink, C.M., Kirby, K.K. and Bachman, S.S. (1991) The university hospital nurse extender program. Part IV, what have we learned? *Journal of Nursing Administration*, **21**: 26–31.

Grilli, R. et al. (1998) Do specialists do it better? The impact of specialization on the processes and outcomes of care for cancer patients. *Annals of Oncology*, **9**: 365–74.

Harris, C., McBride, A. and Marchington, M. (2000) *Developing the concept of the 'good' employer in the NHS*. Manchester, Health Organisations Research Centre, UMIST.

Henderson, N.C. et al. (1999) The influence of a nurse practitioner on out of hours work intensity for surgical house officers. *Scottish Medical Journal*, **4**: 2–3.

Hesterly, S.C. and Robinson, M. (1990) Alternative caregivers: cost-effective utilization of RNs. *Nursing Administration Quarterly*, **14**: 18–23.

Hodson, D.M. (1998) The evolving role of advanced practice nurses in surgery. *AORN Journal*, **7**: 998–1009.

Horrocks, S., Anderson, E. and Salisbury, C. (2002) Systematic review of whether nurse practitioners working in primary care can provide equivalent care to doctors. *British Medical Journal*, **324**: 819–23.

Kinley, H. et al. (2001) Extended scope of nursing practice: a multicentre randomised controlled trial of appropriately trained nurses and pre-registration house officers in pre-operative assessment in elective general surgery. *Health Technology Assessment*, **5**: 1–87.

Krapohl, G.L. and Larson, E. (1996) The impact of unlicensed assistive personnel on nursing care delivery. *Nursing Economics*, **14**(122): 99–110.

Laurant, M.G.H. et al. (2004) Impact of nurse practitioners on workload of general practitioners: randomised controlled trial. *British Medical Journal*, **328**: 927–30.

Leverment, Y., Ackers, P. and Preston, D. (1998) Professionals in the NHS – a case-study of business process re-engineering. *New Technology Work Employment*, **13**: 129–39.

MacGregor, S.H. et al. (1996) Evaluation of a primary care anticoagulant clinic managed by a pharmacist. *British Medical Journal*, **312**: 560.

Mark, A.L. and Shepherd, I.D. (2004) NHS direct: managing demand for primary care? *International Journal of Health Planning and Management*, **19**(1): 79–91.

Meek, S. et al. (1998) Can accident and emergency nurse practitioners interpret radiographs? A multicentre study. *Emergency Medical Journal*, **15**: 105–7.

Nicholl, J. et al. (1998) The costs and benefits of paramedic skills in pre-hospital trauma care. *Health Technology Assessment*, **2**: 17.

Orne, R.M. et al. (1998) Caught in the cross fire of change: nurses' experience with unlicensed assistive personnel. *Applied Nursing Research*, **11**: 101–10.

Parkes, J. and Shepperd, S. (2003) Discharge planning from hospital to home (Cochrane Review). In: *The Cochrane Library*, Issue 1. Oxford: Update Software.

Powers, P.H., Dickey, C.A. and Ford, A. (1990) Evaluating an RN/co-worker model. *Journal of Nursing Administration*, **20**: 11–15.

Radley, A.S. and Hall, J. (1994) The establishment and evaluation of a pharmacist-developed anticoagulant clinic. *Pharmaceutical Journal*, **252**: 91–2.

Renders, C.M. et al. (2001) Interventions to improve the management of diabetes in primary care, outpatient, and community settings: a systematic review. *Diabetes Care*, **24**: 1821–33.

Rink, E. et al. (1993) Impact of introducing near patient testing for standard investigations in general practice. *British Medical Journal*, **307**: 775–8.

Salmond, S.W. (1995) Models of care using unlicensed assistive personnel. Part II: Perceived effectiveness. *Orthopaedic Nursing*, **14**: 47–58.

Shepperd, S. and Iliffe, S. (2001) Hospital at home versus in-patient hospital care. *Cochrane Database of Systematic Reviews*, **3**: CD000356.

Sibbald, B., Shen, J. and McBride, A. (2004) Changing the skill-mix of the health care workforce. *Journal of Health Services Research and Policy*, **9**(1): 28–38.

Smith, B. et al. (2001) Home care by outreach nursing for chronic obstructive pulmonary disease. *Cochrane Database of Systematic Reviews*, **3**: CD000994.

Thomas, L. et al. (2000) Guidelines in professions allied to medicine. *Cochrane Database of Systematic Reviews*, **2**: CD000349.

Thompson, R.L. et al. (2003) Dietary advice given by a dietitian versus other health professional or self-help resources to reduce blood cholesterol. *Cochrane Database of Systematic Reviews*,**3**: CD001366.

Townsend, J. et al. (2004) Routine examination of the newborn: the EMREN study. Evaluation of an extension of the midwife role including a randomised controlled trial of appropriately trained midwives and paediatric senior house officers. *Health Technology Assessment*, **8**(14): 1–112.

Vrijhoef, H.J., Diederiks, J.P. and Spreeuwenberg, C. (2000) Effects on quality of care for patients with NIDDM or COPD when the specialised nurse has a central role: a literature review. *Patient Education and Counselling*, **41**: 243–50.

Wagner, E.H. et al. (2001a) Improving chronic illness care: translating evidence into action. *Health Affairs (Millwood)*, **20**: 64–78.

Wagner, E.H. et al. (2001b) Chronic care clinics for diabetes in primary care: a system-wide randomized trial. *Diabetes Care*, **24**(4): 695–700.

WHO (2000) *The World Health Report 2000. Health systems: improving performance*. Geneva, World Health Organization.

chapter five

Structures and trends in health profession education in Europe

Elizabeth K. Kachur and Karl Krajic

Introduction

What is happening in the education of health professionals in Europe? Is health professions' education (HPE) adapting to the new challenges laid out in the introductory chapters of this book? Has HPE become an agent of reform, a motor of innovation to help to create a workforce that can manage the challenges imposed by social and economic changes, new knowledge and new technologies?

While these questions may seem straightforward, describing European developments in HPE is not. Despite major efforts towards homogenization one must take account of the deep-rooted political, economic, sociocultural and historical diversity that has existed for centuries. This chapter attempts to clarify the situation by describing some aspects of the current status of HPE; comparing Europe with global developments further helps to sketch out a picture. To manage complexity we have decided to focus on medicine, since its situation is more transparent, but we also look at nursing wherever possible. The chapter starts with a cognitive framework to clarify some basic features of HPE systems as they interact with relevant environments. It concludes with recommendations for researchers and policy-makers, providing encouragement to advance the field through further studies and careful planning.

HPE: an autonomous system in a turbulent environment

The prime function of HPE is to select, train and socialize people who are willing and able to fulfil occupational roles in health care. In a static society this could

be a comparatively simple task, even though the work of health professionals deals with human life and well-being and thus is often risky and complex. The classic solution was to train for core competences in master–apprentice relationships, secondary to everyday practice. A theoretical and ideological basis was provided well in advance of clinical training, in more or less separate institutions. While such strategies have worked, recent developments make this educational model less appropriate for HPE.

To a large extent HPE's transformation is owing to external pressures, not internal developments. The systems in the social environment of HPE have become more complex and are undergoing dynamic change processes, as laid out in other chapters of this book. Changing demography and epidemiology (e.g. the ageing population) and changes in the knowledge base and available technology affect the content of health care work. The globalization of the economy (with increased competition and investment opportunities), changes in health welfare state policies and political integration processes in Europe are among the factors that affect the organizational framework of health care. Although these pressures may be contradictory, HPE is expected to adapt to these changes, and actively to contribute to national and EU-wide problem solutions and reform.

In order to be effective, HPE has to become a well-organized enterprise that is grounded in universal knowledge/scientific evidence and not just based on local traditions. Educating health care workers has to move beyond being just a secondary role of experienced practitioners and scientists (although these professionals will continue to be important). Teaching or, more precisely, facilitating learning requires specific professional roles, dedicated departments and institutions and communications in a much wider-ranging scientific and professional discourse. The latter takes place in specialized journals (e.g. *Medical Education, Medical Teacher, Nurse Education Today*), annual conferences (e.g. Association for Medical Education in Europe (AMEE), European Federation of Nurse Educators (FINE)) and listserves (e.g. MEDIMED). Many of these networks extend far beyond national or even continental borders. The backgrounds of those who become deeply involved in HPE range from health care providers to educators to scientists to biostatisticians. Such variety has helped to make this an innovative field.

Basic medical training occurs primarily in universities, which maintain a closer link to science and research than to health care systems (Stichweh 1994). This can result in an academic indifference to current daily practice that may render significant portions of training irrelevant. Early clinical exposure and learning methodologies that focus on clinical cases (e.g. problem-based learning) are part of the response to such criticism. Interestingly, as basic medical education is becoming more clinical, HPE for other professions (e.g. nursing) has become more academic by making bachelor degrees an entry requirement for the profession. However, regardless of whether the movement is to or from clinical practice, to or from universities, HPE is striving towards more autonomy.

How to influence HPE: a model from the quality movement

We have selected a quality improvement model as a framework for our exploration of the topic. Human resources (professional health care workers) are the output of HPE but a central input to the health care system. Health policy-makers may want to intervene in HPE to influence health care by changing one central input.

Based on the framework devised by Donabedian (1982), HPE can be understood as a system that produces *outcomes* (professional health care workers in specific numbers, with a specific level of knowledge and skills and particular attitudes that may affect actions such as resource consumption) through *processes* (selection, teaching, learning, assessment, socialization and professionalization) that are to a wide extent determined by specific *structures* (institutions, teaching staff, access rules, curricula) (Figure 5.1).

Health policy-makers want the right numbers of staff with the right knowledge, skills and attitudes to fit the needs of health care organizations and consumers, avoiding under- and oversupply, under- and overqualification. If they are responsible for organizing or financing education, they might also be concerned about the resources that are being consumed. Even if HPE takes place

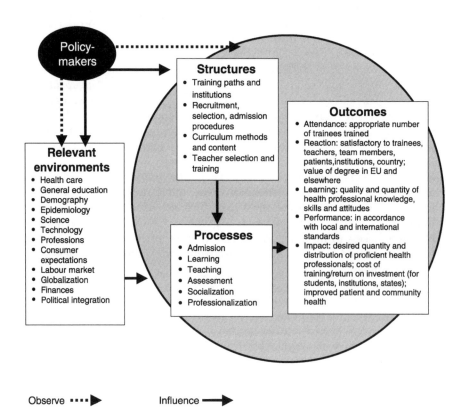

Figure 5.1 Influencing outcomes of HPE: the challenge for health policy-makers.

in organizations formally under their authority, policy-makers have to accept that they can exert their influence upon structures alone. Outcomes are the result of processes, and processes are what is happening in the teaching and learning settings during daily interactions. It is likely that there will also be time lags before new outcomes materialize. In planning and designing interventions, policy-makers have to take into account the following concurrent forces.

- *Developments in the general system of education push for more sophisticated training programmes.* New theories, e.g. adult learning (Knowles 1990), and new technologies are being disseminated widely. Trainees' expectations have increased sharply and society as a whole expects HPE to use the best available educational technologies for selecting, instructing and socializing professionals. HPE has to keep up with general education developments so that it does not become hopelessly outdated.
- *International political developments aim at standardizing HPE to facilitate globalization and integration.* Professionals' international mobility has been an important force in reshaping HPE in Europe. Qualifications must be acceptable beyond national borders. However, the Bologna Process, which seeks to facilitate collaboration in higher education, is creating mixed effects as it is focusing on neither quality improvement in HPE nor health care. Instead, it tries to solve problems of legal harmonization, clarification of equivalence and other managerial concerns. In contrast, the WHO-sponsored World Federation for Medical Education (WFME) is attempting to influence medical training institutions by establishing specific quality standards, setting out guidelines for basic, postgraduate and continuing education in 2003.
- *Scientific progress and health care technology development require that practitioners stay up to date.* Basic HPE must be concerned about future professional practices and prepare trainees for careers that may span up to 50 years. This forces basic and graduate (specialized) training programmes frequently to update what is being taught and ultimately will move HPE towards 'maintenance of licensure' requirements.
- *Economic opportunities and constraints require the inclusion of managerial and financial perspectives.* Since education necessitates resources at individual, local, national and/or global levels, the prospect of financial rewards and limitations can have a major impact. Loans and scholarships have widened or narrowed access to training, and legislative appropriations and grant initiatives have helped to open and close academic programmes, as evidenced by the case studies.
- *Occupational groups can exert political pressures.* Professional organizations and labour unions often have input to numerus clausus (an annual ceiling on the number of students allowed to enter professional training) determinations and are party to licensing and accreditation decisions. Since these are member organizations they represent the interests of individuals who are already established in an occupation. Consequently, they are not always at the forefront of innovation.
- *Societal expectations of, and attitudes to, individual health professions change.* A profession's image in society can have a great impact on the candidate pool (e.g. female workforce participation). The emancipation of patients,

facilitated by changes in access to information, has driven HPE towards imparting more patient-centred interaction styles.

In summary, health policy-makers interested in influencing HPE outcomes through rules, regulations and organizational and financial provisions must make sure that they monitor systematically the HPE structures and processes, as well as pressures from relevant environments. In their role as agents for quality assurance and development they can play a proactive role by evaluating whether these influences create a balanced response in the HPE system; in other words, whether HPE reacts to population demands for better communication skills as strongly as it does to new products marketed by health care industries.

Monitoring outcomes and processes

HPE outcomes can be understood with the help of the Kirkpatrick pyramid model for evaluating educational programmes, which was modified by Harden et al. (1999).

- *Participation* is often measured as attendance at a training event or enrolment on a programme. It is the most basic level of assessing whether the goals of an educational programme have been achieved.
- Collecting *reactions* is a very commonly utilized second level of evaluation. Typically this is done via questionnaires asking participants to indicate their level of satisfaction with the programme. An increase in popularity of qualitative research has led to a more extensive use of in-depth interviews and focus groups.
- The next level is the *assessment of knowledge, skills and attitudes* gained through the programme. Assessments include strategies such as multiple-choice tests or performance-based tests (e.g. objective structured clinical exams, OSCEs; Harden et al. 1975). Frequently evaluators also look into self-reported learning gains either via scaled surveys or by asking participants to identify their 'take-home points'.
- Still more relevant for health policy is the assessment of *performance in practice* (e.g. ascertained from chart reviews). Unfortunately, such evaluations often present logistical challenges; furthermore, it may be difficult to attribute behaviour changes solely to specific educational programmes.
- To monitor *impact* – that is, the changes in actual patient care outcomes – epidemiological data, patient compliance or satisfaction are used often. Needless to say, a vast range of intervening factors co-determine the final outcomes, 'contaminate' the results and thus may make definite attributions impossible.

Monitoring *process* in HPE is keeping track of the selection, learning, teaching, assessment, socialization and professionalization that take place in a programme. Typically this is undertaken by the educational institutions themselves, as part of their management strategies. However, given the complex interplay of psychological and social phenomena, the training process is often treated as a 'black box', leaving the focus on input and output. To map out

accurately the multitude of processes and their determining factors requires the application of scientific methods and usually this is attempted only in research projects. While it will still take much effort to unlock all the mechanisms of education, educational research methods have become more sophisticated. Initiatives such as best evidence medical education (BEME) are searching actively for a better understanding of how lay people are transformed into professionals.

Influencing structures

In order to assure and develop the quality and quantity of HPE, the 'producer' of HRH, policy-makers can influence the following structures through policies, laws, audits, licensures and accreditations:

- training paths (basic, specialized and continuing education) and their associated institutions;
- recruitment, selection and admission procedures;
- curriculum content, instructional and assessment methods;
- teacher selection and training.

A description of these key structures of HPE in Europe (particularly medicine and, to a lesser extent, nursing) makes up much of the rest of this chapter. We try to determine to what extent HPE has become a system in its own right and how it is changing in the face of harmonization and other developments in the different parts of Europe.

Key elements of HPE: the current situation

Training paths and institutions: what are the stages of training and where does training occur?

Across Europe there have been significant variations in the educational paths trainees have to travel in order to achieve and maintain professional status. These differences range from the type of training institution (e.g. university or non-university) to the number of years and academic hurdles passed in order to advance to the next level. Gradually discrepancies are being reduced as part of the EU harmonization process, but so much variety remains that mobile health care professionals benefit greatly from guide books that navigate the maze (e.g. Eysenbach 1998; Darling 2000). Table 5.1 outlines the current typical training paths for medicine and nursing.

Basic medical training occurs primarily at public universities as, unlike in the United States, there are only a few private institutions in Europe. For mid-level professionals, private institutions are more numerous but that training is moving gradually to universities and thus to the public sector. New degree programmes are being created. Rappold (2003) showed in a review of the 15 Member States of the EU before 2004 that nursing training occurs at a post-secondary level in 11, in two it occurs on a secondary level and in another two both options are available. Ancillary staff, such as laboratory technicians or

Table 5.1 Educational paths for medicine and nursing in Europe

	Basic (undergraduate) education	(Post) graduate education (specialization)	Continuing professional development
Medicine	Medical school 5–6 years	Residency 2–6 years	Continuing medical education (CME), lifelong
	Initial years pre-clinical/basic science, later years clinical rotations (university-based)	Depending on specialty (hospital- and community-based)	Recommended or required for continuing certification and career development; up-skilling and cross-training (public or private)
Nursing	Nursing school 3–4 years	Graduate school 1–6 years	Continuing nursing education, lifelong
	Initial years foundation courses, later years clinical rotations (university and non-university based)	Specialization, masters and doctoral degrees (university-based)	Recommended or required for continuing certification and career development; up-skilling and cross-training (public or private)

nurses' aides, are often trained at special high schools or through some specialized courses not associated with a university. New licensing requirements resulted in the emergence of new institutions that have taken on responsibility for national testing.

Regardless of the profession or training level, in order to offer certificates or degrees that are acknowledged and usable elsewhere, institutions typically require accreditation by central and regional governments or professional bodies. This is part of their quality assurance profile and serves legal, contractual and professional purposes. Efforts are under way to develop accreditation programmes not just within particular states but also at EU level, and even worldwide through agencies such as the WFME. Regulating bodies may require a certain number of training hours, specific types of courses or rotations to be provided by an institution or completed by a candidate. Increasingly, such agencies are less likely to provide a stamp of approval based on minimum requirements. They are becoming aware of their unique opportunities to enhance HPE.

HPE in Europe is tightly regulated by law rather than left under the purview of individual institutions as in other parts of the world. This has promoted more consistency within countries but has also hampered progress because laws are slow to change. EU membership requirements have added a new layer of standards that give rise to new local laws and regulations.

Basic and postgraduate training (specialization)

EU Directive 93/16/EEC (*Official Journal* L165, 07/07/1993, pp. 1–24) requires basic medical training (medical school) to consist of six years (5500 hours) of university-based theoretical and practical training. Most countries are aiming towards this standard. A notable exception is the United Kingdom or countries that have based their training on that model (e.g. Malta, Ireland), where medical school lasts for five years. The United Kingdom is also starting four-year programmes that, as in the United States, students enter after obtaining a university degree (e.g. a bachelor degree). Not all countries have uniform lengths of study. Most countries now require even those medical school graduates who do not want to specialize to complete a period of closely supervised work (an internship) before granting them a licence to practise medicine independently.

The training of medical specialists is also regulated by EU Directive 93/16/EEC. Countries vary in the definition and availability of specialties and subspecialties but there is a tendency towards harmonization. For example, in Lithuania the number of medical specialties was reduced from 96 to 19. Typically, residency training lasts for two to five years, with surgical specialties maintaining the upper end of the spectrum. General practice has become a specialty in its own right and is no longer a default selection for those who do not have the academic credentials or endurance to enter a hospital-based specialty. General practice requires at least two years of full-time vocational training that includes at least six months of hospital work and at least six months in a primary care practice for any physician working in a public setting. Since primary care specialties are relatively new, they are not as bogged down in traditions and are more likely to employ advanced and innovative educational techniques. Using a specialist degree typically requires completion of a final exam, which frequently includes multiple-choice tests and practical evaluations. More recent developments include the assessment of taped encounters with actual patients to determine patient-centredness (Campion et al. 2002). Europe is becoming similar to the United States, where no one is truly employable without postgraduate training, and insurance companies and health care providers neither contract with nor employ undertrained providers.

Postgraduate training has a rich tradition of migration, with medical school graduates going to countries such as the United Kingdom or the United States for the duration of their residency and/or for additional fellowships. To facilitate such movements agencies have been set up in the receiving countries to identify standards and verify credentials. In the United Kingdom the relevant agency is the General Medical Council (GMC), in the United States it is the Educational Commission of Foreign Medical Graduates (ECFMG). Agencies such as the EU-initiated ERASMUS programme facilitate exchange between academic programmes in the basic training years.

Based on EU Directive 89/595/EEC (*Official Journal* L341, 23/11/1989, pp. 30–32), basic nursing training must last at least three years (4600 hours) and is to be university-based, culminating in a bachelor degree. This is a major change from the high school or trade school type of education that is still in place in many countries. Figure 5.2 illustrates the many consequences of the necessary upgrading throughout Europe. There is a need to develop new curricula, find

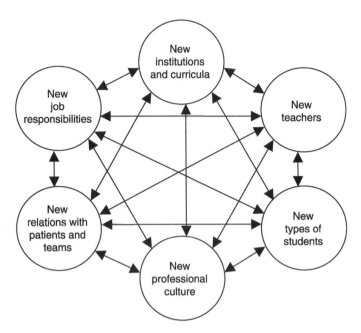

Figure 5.2 The ripple effects of upgrading a health profession.

new teachers and close, start and possibly move some programmes to new institutions. Applicant pools and student bodies will change in educational level, maturity and career aspirations. New training opens up more job responsibilities and work restructuring also affects the other professions on a team, whose roles and responsibilities may undergo some scrutiny and redefinition. Major adjustments in the professional culture can be expected. Bridging courses have been developed to update the existing workforce who trained under the old system.

Nursing specialization is being introduced in many countries for the first time; the European Network of Nurses' Organizations (ENNO) has developed a framework for such training. It may be necessary to import instructors or prepare abroad to develop fully the new fields in each country. Doctorate programmes and degrees are rare but planned for the near future. Among the many hurdles is the development of the necessary research capacity (Cooke and Green 2000).

Continuing professional development (CPD)

The training that occurs after basic and postgraduate education, and possibly specialist certification, has changed greatly in the past decade. First, there was a name change from continuing medical or nursing education to CPD. This brought an underlying philosophical change that moved from simple upgrades in knowledge to a more comprehensive view of working in a profession that includes communication and leadership skills (Peck et al. 2000).

The changing demands of the health care system have resulted in a variety of CPD training efforts. Upgrading can range from lectures and brief courses to more extensive efforts that may lead to advanced degrees (e.g. short-tracks, bridging courses). Clearly, if advanced academic studies suddenly become a job requirement this can be problematic for those who entered the profession originally because they prefer more practical work. In cross-training, a professional's skills set is stretched horizontally, without demanding new diplomas. But the expansion of one person's professional role can cut into those of others. Depending on the rigidity of assigned responsibilities, other health care providers or administrators may oppose the use of the newly acquired knowledge and skills in everyday practice. Typically this is a severe disincentive to competency expansion. Retraining aims at changing specialty (e.g. from subspecialty to primary care) and is even more challenging because people choose their professions for many complex reasons. Past attempts to change specialists into primary care providers have shown that while trainees were able to learn new information and skills, attitudinal changes, such as adopting a new professional identity, are more difficult to achieve (Lember 1996).

The fast turnover of knowledge, the rapid deployment of new technologies and new data on skills decay have pushed for recertification or revalidation. Often the latter is linked to CPD by a requirement for completion of a certain number of CPD hours/credits. Nevertheless, even in a country with a strong professional tradition like France, CPD remains uncoordinated and fragmented. Continuing education is recommended but usually not required and even when it is required there are few, if any, sanctions in place for unmet standards. While government-employed health care professionals are likely to undergo more scrutiny, only rarely is the ability to work privately suspended. However, before long, it can be expected that professionals in all settings will be held personally accountable for keeping their competencies up-to-date.

While the first step towards lifelong learning is to require a certain number of continuing education credits (primarily based on attendance and the amount of time spent on activity), newer developments push for periodic assessments that may range from multiple-choice tests to practice audits (e.g. chart reviews or electronic monitoring systems). Practice audits are considered of particular value since they target performance in daily life, not just competence, and tie into a movement of continuous quality improvement (CQI). Medical errors are common but a significant portion are preventable. However, they are in large part caused by systems failures and thus the potential impact of CPD is often overestimated.

No longer is HPE viewed as a one-time, finite event that ends with graduation or licensure. Instead, training is seen as a lifelong process that requires updating, prevention of deskilling and continuous reinforcement of professional values. Step-by-step CPD is becoming a strong component of HPE. Increasingly organized by academic institutions and professional organizations, training events are assessed for their educational value as part of an accreditation process. Although it is gradually losing its association with pharmaceutical sales pitches and entertainment, a large portion of CPD in some countries is still sponsored by the pharmaceutical industry.

In many places it is not clear who should pay for CPD. Some governments are

reluctant to take on this responsibility and, with the prospect of recertification, often the cost shifts to the health care professionals themselves. Thus continuing education credits are becoming a valuable commodity and efforts are under way to make them exchangeable between countries. An agreement between Europe and the United States permits mutual recognition; clearly Europeanization and even globalization is encouraged.

Recruitment, selection, admission procedures: who gets to be trained?

Most countries have a numerus clausus to control the number of students admitted to educational institutions and ultimately to the health professions. Such entry level limits are typically arrived at by collaboration between education and health ministries, with input from professional organizations. However, in many countries these policies have led to shortages. A prime example is nursing, where the concern is to produce sufficiently high numbers of graduates to sustain professional skills, and to impart identities that will keep them in the active workforce for longer (Hasselhorn et al. 2003). There are also legitimate concerns about an oversupply of certain health care providers in some countries, which can lead to waste at both individual and societal levels. But even the ubiquitous reports of physician oversupplies in the 1980s and 1990s have increasingly been challenged by descriptions of specific shortages. Thus the talk is more about imbalances than about simple trends in one direction or the other (WHO 2002).

Unfortunately, it is not easy to forecast health profession needs. It requires: extensive, comprehensive databases on present and past staffing resources and health care needs; equal involvement of all stakeholders and not just the voice of more vocal interest groups; and the ability to think outside the box and to contemplate the unthinkable (e.g. EU-wide institution of the WTD, significant levels of health professional migration). Such basic requirements for good decision-making are not always in place when committees determine the numerus clausus for a specific profession in a certain country. Large fluctuations in the number of new trainees can have an immediate impact on educational institutions, which may suddenly require significantly more or fewer facilities and teachers. Certain types of curricula may become unmanageable for large class sizes and require the establishment of new training institutions. It takes years (and many financial and administrative hurdles) for a school to go from the drawing board to inauguration. Given the long training cycles, especially those of physicians, often the impact of these decisions is not felt until decades later.

Usually a numerus clausus is introduced in basic training but, with limited numbers of training positions, there are also restrictions on advancement to postgraduate levels. In some countries this has caused significant waiting times and unemployment among physicians. In other countries medical specialty training positions and locations are distributed according to exam results. Those at the bottom of the list may only have the choice to enter primary care. Here the effort to control national supply needs may not be compatible with the talents of an individual. As noted previously, specialty preferences align with

features of personality and arbitrary assignment of specialties does not result in the best workforce.

Since selection decisions are often based on exam results and academic achievement during high school, there is little guarantee that high-performing candidates also have the personalities and humanitarian qualities needed for success in the caring professions. Multiple-choice tests may predict little more than the ability to perform well in future multiple-choice tests, single tests may not reliably predict consistent performance levels and academic achievement during turbulent teenage years may not provide a clear picture about future capabilities. None the less, few people argue that current admission strategies are worse than chance. Even in the Netherlands, the only country that applies a lottery, those with the best high school performances can enter the medical school of their choice.

In anticipation of harmonization and an increase in student exchange the ERASMUS Project, in collaboration with the Association of Medical Schools of Europe (AMSE), reviewed the admission procedures and selection instruments in Europe. AMSE seeks to provide a forum for deans and the administrative personnel of medical schools both in and outside the EU. In this respect they resemble the United States-based Association of American Medical Colleges (AAMC) (Ebach and Trost 1997). The key models are summarized in Table 5.2 and the advantages and disadvantages of each are highlighted.

In the United Kingdom over recent years there has been a trend to encourage students with prior university degrees to enter medicine. This follows the model well established in the United States and initiated in the past decade in Australia. The aim is to obtain a more diverse and more mature applicant pool. In nursing the entry age is 17 years and 12 years of prior schooling are required in most EU Member States (Rappold 2003).

Feminization is a trend observed in the candidate pool of most health professions. The number of women entering the caring professions is increasing worldwide, leading some commentators to consider the positive (e.g. potentially better communication between providers and patients) and negative (e.g. loss of prestige) impact of this phenomenon. The majority of nurses have always been women and this creates major socialization problems for the slowly increasing numbers of male nursing students (Stott 2004).

There is little information about the racial and ethnic distributions among trainee health professionals. This has been less of an issue in Europe than in the United States, where the admission of underrepresented minorities in the health professions has been a special concern for decades. There the aim is to make the health care workforce resemble the ethnic distribution of the patient populations. With increased mobility between EU Member States and worldwide, this is likely to become an important topic in Europe too. Raising the numerus clausus offers the potential to introduce more diversity in the candidate pool. However, it will only result in a more diverse workforce if all trainee groups complete their studies at the same rate.

In addition to the necessary academic credentials there can also be a financial barrier to entering a health profession. Given that much training occurs in government institutions that may provide stipends, the financial obstacles to studying in Europe are fewer than in some other parts of the world. But even in

Table 5.2 Trainee selection strategies

	Before studies		During studies
	Random/lottery	Based on prior academic achievement and aptitudes exhibited in interviews, essays or psychological tests	Based on academic achievement and exhibition of aptitudes during basic training
Rationale	Everyone who is eligible should have an equal chance to study	Only those who best fulfil the entry criteria should be admitted	Everyone who is eligible should have an equal chance to start training; academic hurdles determine promotion
Advantages	Cost-effective	Institutional resources are preserved Country-wide admission tests limit costs School-based admission tests increase control	Institution has maximum control
Disadvantages	Does not utilize any knowledge available about candidates' suitability	Knowledge base is easier to measure than personality and humanistic commitment	Large class sizes in beginning Significant levels of attrition lead to wasted resources

Source: adapted from Ebach and Trost (1997).

Europe there are the dual problems of high living expenses and limited earning potential. A recent review of medical student debt by the British Medical Association (BMA) estimated that British medical students owed about €18 000 by the end of their basic training (Carvel 2002). Such a financial burden may be unacceptable for some cultural groups, thus putting medical education out of their reach.

Curriculum methods and content: what is being taught and how?

Currently there are many shifts in curricula and instructional and assessment strategies, as summarized in Figure 5.3. Although they are more evident in some countries, with variability among the professions, at least traces of these new

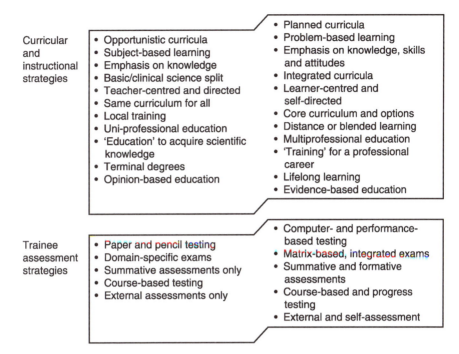

Curricular and instructional strategies

- Opportunistic curricula
- Subject-based learning
- Emphasis on knowledge
- Basic/clinical science split
- Teacher-centred and directed
- Same curriculum for all
- Local training
- Uni-professional education
- 'Education' to acquire scientific knowledge
- Terminal degrees
- Opinion-based education

- Planned curricula
- Problem-based learning
- Emphasis on knowledge, skills and attitudes
- Integrated curricula
- Learner-centred and self-directed
- Core curriculum and options
- Distance or blended learning
- Multiprofessional education
- 'Training' for a professional career
- Lifelong learning
- Evidence-based education

Trainee assessment strategies

- Paper and pencil testing
- Domain-specific exams
- Summative assessments only
- Course-based testing
- External assessments only

- Computer- and performance-based testing
- Matrix-based, integrated exams
- Summative and formative assessments
- Course-based and progress testing
- External and self-assessment

Figure 5.3 Methodological shifts in HPE.

educational methodologies can be found everywhere. Underlying many of these changes is HPE's reorientation towards 'adult learning' (Knowles 1990). The basic principles of this theory postulate that adults (and health profession trainees are considered as such) are voluntary participants in educational processes. In order to foster learning education has to be purposeful, have meaning, relevance, clear goals and objectives, necessitate active involvement and include feedback and reflection. Typically such requirements cannot be met by the traditional HPE methods (e.g. attending lectures where trainees remain passive).

There is a trend towards planning and organizing learning opportunities, rather than leaving them to chance. Educators are also becoming aware of the 'hidden curriculum', which includes all the subliminal messages given to trainees by the way that courses and institutions emphasize specific subjects (e.g. selection of the content of exams) (Hafferty 1998).

There is a movement towards customizing education. Instead of a blind requirement for the completion of all programmes by everyone, there is now a tendency to assess particular training needs (based on prior knowledge or future career interests) and then to design a course of study that can use the training time (always too short) more efficiently. Clearly there is a need for a group of core educational events, but the curriculum can be rounded out through electives and selectives that offer choices.

Another manifestation of independence and individualization is distance

learning. Learning-by-mail has been in place for some time, especially in CPD. With the advent of computers and the Internet new possibilities are emerging. The Open University in the United Kingdom has been a leader in establishing such training programmes for nursing and social work and attempted (unsuccessfully) to create a medical school in this fashion. More recently a worldwide collaboration of medical institutions developed The International Virtual Medical School (IVIMEDS). In a barter-type system, schools share web-based resources or 'learning objects'. By combining these into a curriculum and adding face-to-face instructions the initiative hopes to establish a cost-effective, easy-access alternative for the pre-clinical years of medical school. Such a programme would be built on blended learning (i.e. a mixture of distance and in-person educational offerings), viewed as the most effective approach.

HPE's reorientation towards professional careers (rather than just a scientific discipline) makes the basic/clinical science split that has permeated HPE less viable. Gradually curricula are becoming more integrated, as illustrated in Figure 5.4. 'Early clinical exposure' is a buzz phrase that is making its way into European medical education. Some schools pride themselves on providing patient contact in week one. Such encounters are likely to occur in ambulatory care settings, clinics and private offices since there is a simultaneous movement towards community-based training (Boaden and Bligh 1999). To make early clinical exposure effective, educational programmes need to provide adequate preparation, structure and debriefing (Kachur 2003).

In addition to a greater integration of basic and clinical sciences, *vertical integration*, there is also *horizontal integration*: a merging of subjects that used to be taught simultaneously. Initially this manifested itself in systems-based curricula where students focus on one aspect of the body at a time. There is now a trend towards case- or problem-based learning (PBL) (David et al. 1999) where all learning objectives from basic, social, clinical or population science domains are embedded in a patient case scenario. Typically students work in small groups with an emphasis on independent learning. In some places this is linked with initiatives to train different professions together.

The focus on the application of knowledge, rather than knowledge alone, and the importance of practical skills has also encouraged the development of performance-based assessments such as OSCEs (Harden et al. 1975). Trainees rotate through a series of 'stations', in each of which they perform a specific clinical task that is evaluated with the help of rating forms containing predetermined performance criteria. This method allows sampling of competencies under standardized conditions and has led to the development of clinical skills

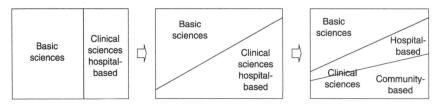

Figure 5.4 Shifts in the basic/clinical science distribution in medical education.

labs. Whether for initial practice or assessment, simulations that range from standardized patients to computer-based machines are becoming a standard in HPE at all levels (Tekian et al. 1999).

Assessment has become more sophisticated, satisfying psychometric characteristics such as reliability and validity (Newble and Cannon 2001). In addition to final exams to make promotion decisions (i.e. summative assessments), programmes also introduce tests that focus on feedback and act as another instructional tool (formative assessments). Tests given to all trainees at regular intervals (e.g. quarterly) are referred to as progress tests (Van der Vleuten et al. 1996).

In recent years, some topics have emerged that seem critical for current and future practice. While the degree of intensity may vary according to location and professional field, the topics listed in Table 5.3 are at the forefront of curriculum change in many institutions.

In the past the focus of education has been on biomedical knowledge and skills acquisition. However, it has become increasingly evident that curricula need to be broadened to address attitudes or values too. These range from professionalism and lifelong learning to an orientation towards prevention and resource preservation. Typically they are difficult to impart, yet much of the success of HPE will depend on the accomplishment of such attitudinal objectives.

Conclusion: an agenda for the future

Developments in HPE have implications for both researchers and policy-makers. Researchers need to focus on the following issues.

- *Raising the level of programme evaluation from mere attendance and satisfaction data*. Researchers need to go beyond satisfaction data and include learning, performance and patient care outcomes in their programme evaluation designs. They must move up the Kirkpatrick/Harden pyramid (Harden et al. 1999) in order to provide more in-depth analysis of the impact of HPE's new structures and processes on all of its stakeholders.
- *Using more sophisticated methods to explore more complex research questions*. As research in medicine has become more systematic and stringent in its scientific discourse, HPE must adopt more rigour. Although randomized controlled trials may not always be possible, HPE can expand descriptive investigations to become more comparative, clearly identify local context in order to illuminate the applicability of findings and orient itself on the most advanced theoretical models related to learning, teaching and socialization.
- *Disseminating research results across institutions, nations, languages and professions*. Increased communication through consultations, conferences and publications will be vital to move the field forward. English has emerged as a primary language, which inevitably disadvantages many. Yet there is a need for a common language and strategies will need to be found to share more promptly the good work that is being done and the insights that are being gained across Europe.

Policy-makers also have a role and must keep in mind the following issues.

Table 5.3 Curriculum topics that cross discipline and national lines

Curriculum topic	Selected reasons for current and future importance
Professionalism/ethics	Public and media look at health care professions more critically than before (e.g. reports on corruption in public health care).
	If professions do not regulate themselves better, external agencies will take over (some have).
Health care economics	Health care systems are changing (evidenced by the case studies), professionals need to learn how to work within them and advocate for their patients.
	Providers have more responsibility for cost-containment and resource allocation.
Error reduction and continuous quality improvement	Medical errors have come to the forefront of public attention.
	Health care professionals are made responsible for identifying best practices and adhering to standards and guidelines; they are held accountable for their actions (e.g. lawsuits).
Medical informatics	Computers help to manage the dramatically increasing knowledge base and facilitate evidence-based practice.
	Electronic record-keeping is becoming more widespread.
	Computer-based instructions can disseminate training programmes across geographical barriers and scheduling limitations.
Prevention	Prevention is cost-effective.
	Population-based thinking is becoming more prevalent.
	Behaviour change (e.g. smoking cessation, traffic safety/accident avoidance) are important factors in reducing morbidity and mortality.
Cultural competence	There is a global migration of patients and health care professionals.
	Language barriers and a lack of cultural competence can interfere with health care.
	Complementary/alternative medicine is used widely.
Geriatric care	Populations are ageing rapidly.
Genetics	The Genome project may revolutionize future care.
	Concerns about ethical complications.
Primary care	A strong primary care system may lead to more efficient and cost-effective health care delivery.
	Primary care is seen as enhancing prevention.
Teamwork	Most clinical work is performed in teams.
	'Disruptive innovations' and automation permit certain tasks to be passed down to lower-level practitioners and technicians (Christensen et al. 2000).
	Most errors are systems-based.

Continued overleaf

Table 5.3 *Continued*

Curriculum topic	Selected reasons for current and future importance
Community-based care	Expensive, unnecessary and potentially dangerous hospital care is becoming less popular.
	Ambulatory and home care are used increasingly.
	Rural health care is understaffed and often neglected.
Telemedicine	Networks and new delivery mechanisms of care are being created.
	Opportunity to provide care to underserved rural and remote sites.

- *Basing decisions on evidence.* While HPE research, arguably, remains limited in scope and depth, it is a growing resource for making more effective decisions. Initiatives such as BEME will eventually provide clear information about what does and does not work. Policy-makers can have a significant impact on the quality and quantity of data collection by allocating appropriate resources and demanding an outcome-based orientation.
- *Acknowledging the need for a long-term perspective.* There is a significant lag time in HPE so there cannot be an immediate translation into a better workforce, better care or a better functioning health care system. Yet societies cannot afford to postpone improvements, even if they necessitate more up-front resources. Administrative sophistication requires a long-term perspective that takes account of diverse factors. As systems become more interrelated within Europe and globally, policy-makers need to keep a close watch on the international scene to realize fully future opportunities and challenges.
- *Involving all stakeholders.* In the past health care workforce decisions were influenced mainly by political forces and powerful professional groups. Little consideration was given to trainees and patients, although they are in essence the end-users of HPE. If no attention is paid to their short- and long-term needs, education-based human resource initiatives are more at risk of producing undesirable side-effects or even failing.

Acknowledgement

The authors would like to thank Ms Elisabeth Rappold, sociologist and nursing scientist from Vienna University, for her very helpful advice.

References

Boaden, N. and Bligh, J. (1999) *Community-based medical education. Towards a shared agenda for learning.* London, Arnold.

Campion, P. et al. (2002) Patient centredness in the MRCGP video examination: analysis of large cohort. Membership of the Royal College of General Practitioners. *British Medical Journal*, **28**(325, 7366): 691–2.

Carvel, J. (2002) BMA warns on debt of medical students. *Guardian*, 3 December.

Christensen, C.M., Bohmer, R. and Kenagy, J. (2000) Will disruptive innovations cure health care? *Harvard Business Review*, Sept/Oct: 102–11 (www.indymedia.org.uk/media/2003/10/279486.pdf).

Cooke, A. and Green, B. (2000) Developing the research capacity of departments of nursing and midwifery based in higher education: a review of the literature. *Journal of Advanced Nursing*, **32**(1): 57–65.

Darling, K.E.A. (2000) *Guide to working in Europe for doctors*. Edinburgh, Churchill Livingstone.

David, T. et al. (1999) *Problem-based learning in medicine: a practical guide for students and teachers*. London, Royal Society of Medicine.

Donabedian, A. (1982) *Explorations in quality assessment monitoring. Vol II: The criteria and standards of quality*. Ann Arbor, MI, Health Administration Press.

Ebach, J. and Trost, G. (1997) *Admission to medical schools in Europe*. Lengerich, Pabst Science Publishers.

Eysenbach, G. (1998) *Medicine and medical education in Europe: the Eurodoctor*. Stuttgart, Georg Thieme Verlag.

Hafferty, F.W. (1998) Beyond curriculum reform: confronting medicine's hidden curriculum. *Academic Medicine*, **73**(4): 403–7.

Harden, R.M. et al. (1975) Assessment of clinical competence using objective structured examination. *British Medical Journal*, **1**(5955): 447–51.

Harden, R.M. et al. (1999) BEME Guide No. 1: best evidence medical education. *Medical Teacher*, **21**(6): 553–62.

Hasselhorn, H.-M., Tackenberg, P. and Müller, B.H. (2003) *Working conditions and intent to leave the profession among nursing staff in Europe*. Report No. 7, SALTSA and NEXT (www.next.uni-wuppertal.de/index.html).

Kachur, E.K. (2003) Observation during early clinical exposure – an effective instructional tool or a bore? *Medical Education*, **37**(2): 119–25.

Knowles, M.S. (1990) *The adult learner. A neglected species*. Houston, Gulf.

Lember, M. (1996) Family practice training in Estonia. *Family Medicine*, **28**(4): 282–6.

Newble, D.I. and Cannon, R.A. (2001) *A handbook for medical teachers*, 4th edn. Dordrecht, Kluwer Academic.

Peck, C. et al. (2000) Continuing medical education and continuing professional development: international comparisons. *British Medical Journal*, **320**: 432–5.

Rappold, E. (2003) Ein überblick über europäische plegeausbildungen. *Österreichische Pflegezeitschrift*, **12**: 34–5.

Stichweh, R. (1994) *Wissenschaft, universität, professionen*. Frankfurt am Main, Suhrkamp.

Stott, A. (2004) Issues in the socialisation process of the male student nurse: implications for retention in undergraduate nursing courses. *Nurse Education Today*, **24**(2): 91–7.

Tekian, A. et al. (1999) *Innovative simulations for assessing professional competence*. Chicago, University of Illinois at Chicago, Department of Medical Education.

Van der Vleuten, C.P.M., Verwijnen, E.M. and Wijnen, W. (1996) Fifteen years of experience with progress testing in a problem-based learning curriculum. *Medical Teacher*, **18**: 103–9.

World Health Organization (2002) *Imbalances in the health workforce. Report of a technical consultation*. Geneva: WHO (www.who.int/hrh/documents/en/consultation-_imbalances.pdf).

chapter six

Managing the performance of health professionals

Charles Shaw

Introduction

One of the most important developments in health care systems in recent decades has been the emergence of a growing body of literature on the subject of health care quality. Early work highlighting unexplained variations in the delivery of health care led to a realization that some long-established health care interventions lacked evidence of effectiveness and some were being administered in circumstances where they were ineffective. Subsequent work has included a much greater understanding of what works (drawing on growing numbers of formal evaluations of interventions) and in what circumstances (drawing on research that identifies the opportunities and constraints acting at a health system level in relation to the delivery of high-quality care). Further, it identifies the ways to bring about change in order to ensure the provision of optimal care within a given system. This chapter focuses on the latter, looking specifically at the contribution to high-quality care of individual health professionals and the teams in which they operate.

While maintaining this focus, it is essential to note the importance of the other elements of this process (Healy and McKee 2002). No matter how motivated health professionals are, their ability to provide optimal quality care is determined by their access to the necessary resources, particularly the physical resources such as well-designed facilities, appropriate technology and effective pharmaceuticals, as well as knowledge resources, such as the growing body of evidence of the effectiveness of interventions and the means of delivering them.

Much of the published literature revolves around defining the roles of clinicians – especially doctors but increasingly nurses and other health professionals – in relation to consumers, managers and purchasers. Professional interactions traditionally have operated on the basis of trust, but this is coming under increasing scrutiny, with growing recognition of the damage that can be caused

by those who fall below the threshold of acceptable practice (Maynard and Bloor 2003). Thus, many stakeholders, including those in the clinical professions, agree that the delivery of health care should be more transparent, patients should be better informed and the 'contract' between doctors and clients should become implicit rather than explicit.

This chapter describes some of the mechanisms that are used to ensure health professionals' high-quality performance. Many of the examples are drawn from a recent review of national policies on quality improvement in Europe (Shaw and Kalo 2002).

However, before these practical mechanisms can be explored, the objectives and underlying values that determine them must be identified. The first section, on policy issues, deals with definitions, aims and the context of clinical performance management. The second, on organizational issues, deals with structures and pathways of communication and accountability. The third looks at specific mechanisms that are either external or internal to the clinical team and the host organization. Finally, the practical requirements for effective performance management are identified, including time, information, managerial support and funds.

Policy issues

What is clinical performance management?

Martínez and Martineau (2001) define performance management as 'essentially about measuring, monitoring and enhancing the performance of staff to the extent that they contribute to overall organizational performance'. Reporting on a major study of performance in 15 countries (including Portugal, Spain and the United Kingdom), they note: 'Few health care organizations, particularly those in the public sector, use performance management approaches. There was not a common understanding . . . of what was meant by performance, or how performance could be measured in practice' (Martínez and Martineau 2001). Only two of the systems they examined used performance management as an 'interrelated set of policies and practices that, put together, enable the monitoring and enhancement of staff performance'.

This is changing in many countries (Table 6.1) but such approaches can have several goals. Thus, while a strategy developed in Ireland refers to performance management in the context of workforce development, others associate it with safety: protecting the public against dangerous practices or incompetent individuals; increased productivity, such as reduced waiting time; or enhanced quality of clinical practice, as illustrated by the development of many clinical guidelines. Thus, the aims of performance management must first be made explicit, not least because, as Martínez and Martineau note:

> . . . not all health care organizations are primarily performance oriented or value performance in the same manner. For example, achieving high levels of employment or job security may be pursued by some national health systems as a primary objective, over and above staff performance . . . Focus

Table 6.1 Explicit national policies on performance

State	Year	Requirements
Czech Republic	2000	Decree 458/2000 requires performance measurement, case-mix management, practice guidelines, accreditation of facilities
Estonia	1998	Quality policy working group: clinical guidelines, (re)licensing of professionals and institutions, certification of specialists, accreditation of hospitals and polyclinics, patient and public satisfaction studies
Ireland	2001	National health strategy (Department of Health and Children's Services 2001) sets explicit goals for high performance
Lithuania	1998	Regulations on clinical audit in hospitals and external inspection (Ministry of Health of Republic of Lithuania 1998a, b)
Norway	1996	National strategy for quality improvement in health care. Defines legal accountability through local government and professional self-regulation
United Kingdom	1998	'A first class service: quality in the new NHS' proposes clinical governance, lifelong learning and professional self-regulation – and a statutory duty of quality (Department of Health n.d.)

on enhancement immediately changes the nature of performance management from the often quoted 'to verify that staff are doing their jobs properly' to the far more positive 'to ensure that staff get the necessary help to do their jobs well'. While the first approach favours control and measurement, the latter emphasizes positive supervision and staff development.

Who manages performance?

The design and operation of a performance management system should be based not only on the explicit values that define 'performance' but also on the relationship between those whose performance is being assessed and their managers. The independent surgeon in a private clinic, the public employee in a state hospital and the family physician contracted to a health authority all have relationships with management but these are very different and often non-explicit.

One of the central issues to emerge from public enquiries, studies of medical error and charters of patients' rights is clinicians' accountability (particularly doctors'). To whom are they accountable and by what mechanisms? This is exemplified by the conclusions of a public inquiry undertaken in England following revelations of poor outcomes among children requiring complex cardiac surgery in Bristol (Bristol Royal Infirmary 2001). It recommended a number of important changes to the regulation of doctors and other health care professionals in the United Kingdom, including continuing professional

development, annual appraisal and regular revalidation of the licence to practice.

This is a major change from the previous emphasis on professional self-regulation. As the then editor of the *British Medical Journal* stated in 1999, 'The old system – based on an expectation that professionals would keep up-to-date and do something about poorly performing colleagues combined with some half hearted systems of self-regulation – is dead' (Smith 1999).

While the pace of change in the United Kingdom has been especially rapid, similar trends can be detected elsewhere. In France, several initiatives begun in the late 1990s sought to boost regulatory mechanisms within the health care system with the aim of enhancing quality and cost-containment (Or 2002). These included new information systems to facilitate the collection of data on the quality and costs of care, systematic accreditation for hospitals and ambulatory care, strengthening of continuing medical training and adoption of mandatory clinical practice guidelines or 'references'.

As in the United Kingdom, these moves can be seen as departures from a profession's traditional characteristic of a capacity for self-regulation. In western European countries, this has given clinicians (particularly doctors) relative immunity from management until recently. Now many countries are struggling to find the ideal balance between statutory, central, external control and voluntary, local, internal self-regulation. In practice many methods of performance management lie between these two extremes.

In western Europe, to variable degrees and with variable success, doctors have espoused self-regulation as an antidote to command and control. In many parts of CEE the control of health care traditionally has been more hierarchical, focused on inputs (rather than outcomes), and professional initiative has been discouraged. This has produced a generally negative view of performance management among clinicians.

A main finding from international research is the importance of context. The situation in each country is influenced by its history and the relative power of the health (and especially medical) professions compared to other key stakeholders. Thus each country needs to examine the strengths and weaknesses of existing structures and processes rather than trying to impose an off-the-peg solution from elsewhere. They also need to examine the definitions, values and priorities of the various stakeholders including the public, the professions and the organizations delivering and funding health care as they seek to develop appropriate mechanisms.

Making policy explicit

The main message of this section is the importance of making the policies on performance management explicit. In particular it is important to be clear about the goals of the system and who is responsible for achieving them. In addition, effective management of performance requires explicit systems that enable objective measurement of achievement and practical mechanisms for changing behaviour. The expectations of regulators, professions and institutions must be realistic, understandable, measurable and clearly stated.

Organizational issues

National structures

Many countries have established national resource centres, either within the Ministry of Health or as independent agencies, to define, measure and even manage various elements of performance. Increasingly, in western Europe these centres are governed by stakeholders' independent representatives and are dominated neither by civil servants nor by clinical professions. Even in countries where the health system is organized within a federal framework, at regional, cantonal or provincial level, such resource centres often operate at national level to achieve economies of scale. In addition, there is very active sharing of experience among these organizations within Europe and with their counterparts elsewhere, particularly those in Canada and Australia.

A wide range of roles can be undertaken by such organizations. The exact mix within any single organization often reflects its historical development, in particular the institutional framework within which these roles have developed in that country. Thus, all European countries have some system for maintaining a register of certain health care professionals, often combined with a mechanism for taking action against those who fail to meet the standards expected. Some countries, especially those where many health care facilities are owned by non-governmental organizations, the private sector or local government, may have accreditation agencies to ensure that these facilities meet certain standards. Others, especially those where the facilities are owned by central government, may have inspection agencies that fulfil a similar role.

All countries have systems to ensure the quality of pharmaceuticals that are in use. Within the EU this function is complemented by the European Medicines Agency (EMEA). Most countries also have systems for ensuring the safety of technology. In some countries these roles, traditionally limited to ensuring that products are safe, have been complemented by institutional responses concerned with the relative effectiveness and cost–effectiveness of different pharmaceuticals and technology, and in some cases of integrated packages of care. An example is the National Institute for Clinical Excellence (NICE) in the United Kingdom. The complexity of these roles and the very varied institutional configurations within which they exist in different countries defies simple description. For example, The National Centre for Quality Assessment in Health Care (Centrum Monitorowania Jakości w Ochronie Zdrowia (CMJ)), created in Krakow in 1994 by the Ministry of Health, is responsible for: providing health professionals with training in quality and performance; setting organizational standards and undertaking accreditation of health care institutions; monitoring patient satisfaction and clinical performance; developing national guidelines and standards for medical procedures; and evaluating medical technology (Strózik 2005).

Local structures

Each institution or network also needs clear accountability for the clinical performance of senior and junior staff and trainees. The shape of this accountability structure will reflect the role, attitudes and competence of clinicians in general management. For example, the Health Supervision Act S3 in Norway states that 'The county medical officer shall ensure that anyone providing health care has established an internal control system and is supervising their own activities in such a manner as to prevent short-comings in the health services' (Ministry of Health and Social Affairs Norway 1999).

Within an institution, the performance of clinicians can be managed either at individual or at team/departmental level. Integration of these two approaches (e.g. participation in peer review as a criterion of individual appraisal) requires data to be shared not only between departments but also between neighbouring institutions (e.g. to aggregate clinical experience) and national agencies (e.g. to verify licensing with medical chamber).

Performance management and the individual clinician

This section sets out the elements that would form a comprehensive local performance management system. These involve a documented continuum of personal development from initial appointment to resignation or retirement. Most health care organizations apply some of the elements listed below; despite good intentions, few apply all.

Job description

Recruitment should be based on a specific statement of the content of the job (job description), as well as a list of the essential and desirable criteria that will be used to select the most appropriate candidate (person specification). These should encompass the knowledge, attitudes and skills that relate to the particular post.

Work programmes

While there is a need to maintain a degree of flexibility, where this is possible there may be benefits in establishing a weekly or monthly description of scheduled work undertaken by an individual clinician, such as attending clinics, theatre sessions, ward rounds and meetings, as well as more flexible sessions such as teaching, research and management.

(Hospital) 'by-laws'

These consist of a general statement of operational rules by which the facility operates, agreed by the governing board. These should include the work of clinical staff, such as organizational policies, systems for maintaining accurate clinical records, mechanisms for introducing new drugs and technologies,

punctuality, supervision arrangements, responsibility for teaching and disciplinary procedures. Although these are common in North America and Australasia, those in many parts of Europe are less likely to make specific reference to the work of clinicians.

Selection and appointment procedures

Appointments should be consistent with existing labour law: new posts should be advertised, candidates should submit written applications and opinions should be sought from referees who can comment on the work of the individual. In particular it is important to ensure transparency and compliance with equal opportunity laws, not only because this is both fair and a legal requirement but also because it makes it easier to appoint the best candidate. It is good practice for appointment panels to include an external assessor. Appointments should be conditional upon acceptance of local 'by-laws' and national conditions, and current licensing and insurance status should be validated by reference to the relevant official body.

Contract

A written contract is essential and should define mutual expectations (e.g. a work plan for employees, the scope and limitation of clinical privileges – termed 'credentialing' in North America and Australia), the duration of initial appointment and criteria for appraisal, review or reappointment. The explicit definition of the scope and limits of clinical practice rights should apply to work undertaken privately as well as publicly; dual practice creates many incentives for abuse, although this does not happen often in practice.

Internal appraisal

Individual performance should be reviewed regularly by the individual's supervisor or by a peer group, using agreed documented measures. Some countries have also adopted systems for revalidation (Shaw and Kalo 2002) or mechanisms to confirm or modify the range of clinical procedures that can be undertaken.

Appraisal may be summative, as part of performance management, or formative, contributing to professional education and self-directed learning (Taylor et al. 2002). Conlon (2003) has expanded this taxonomy, summarizing methods of performance review.

- *Appraisal* (appraisee-centred), involving reflection: formative; developmental; confidential.
- *Assessment* (personal), involving measurement: targets/audits/standards; complaints; significant events.
- *Performance management* (organization), involving comparison with others: assessment against organizational agenda.
- *Revalidation* (external/public), involving licensing: summative; declaration of fitness to practise.

Systems of appraisal are being implemented increasingly in industrialized countries, although, as Martínez and Martineau (2001) have noted, much of what takes place under this label relates to behavioural issues rather than actual performance. Furthermore, they found that it was rarely undertaken as part of service planning and management processes. In particular they found that the rating of staff often took priority over efforts to help them work better, so that performance enhancement was an afterthought, with staff appraisal being turned against those concerned. They noted that staff appraisal was often used as a means to blame staff for managerial incompetence and they argued that the potential to transform existing appraisal systems into more sophisticated performance management systems should not be taken for granted, as moving from a civil service culture to a performance-oriented culture would be complex and take time.

Continuing professional development

Participation in a funded programme of education based on periodic individual review is a common expectation of clinicians employed in western Europe. Managers see this as an investment in the future and regulators consider it a basic requirement for continued licence to practise (see external recertification, below).

External peer review

Reciprocal visiting is driven by professional and often unidisciplinary organizations and has a long tradition as a form of peer review, especially in relation to the recognition of training posts. It has also been applied to service development, such as in the hospital specialties programme in the Netherlands (CBO Visitatie) (Klazinga et al. 1998).

Peer review generally is supported and endorsed by the clinical professions as a means of self-regulation and clinical improvement, and integrates well with requirements for undergraduate, specialty and continuing professional development. But it is typically specialty-based, not covering whole hospitals. The results are often confidential and not publicly available.

External recertification

In recent years, professional regulatory authorities in many countries have engaged in the difficult process of ensuring that medical practitioners engage in continual updating of their skills (Southgate and Dauphinée 1998). To this end, they have developed performance assessments with the dual aim of protecting patients and of enhancing doctors' clinical performance. Often these assessments are linked to the recertification or revalidation of practitioners (Bashook and Parboosingh 1998).

In reality, many states (especially some of the NIS of the former USSR) have no coherent system for licensing nurses or allied staff. They also have relatively weak mechanisms to review the continuing competence of doctors and dentists,

in terms of either national licensing (e.g. revalidation) or local hospital appointments (e.g. recredentialing).

Box 6.1 Systems of external review in selected countries

Attestation in the Russian Federation

Continuous learning and attestation (individual accreditation that either confirms or upgrades the status of the physician) are promoted by the Ministry of Health of the Russian Federation. Physicians undergo further training every five years, lasting one month and culminating in an exam. On successful completion of this training, physicans are promoted to the *second* category, followed by the *first* category after another five years and finally the *highest* category – which needs to be reconfirmed every five years. Physicians who have had no further medical training for at least five years have no category. In 2000 only 19% of physicians had the highest grade, 22% were in the first category and 7% were in the second category; 50% of physicians had no category (Danishevski 2005).

Revalidation in the United Kingdom

Revalidation (also known as recertification) is 'the regular demonstration by all practising doctors that they remain up to date and fit to practice medicine' (Catto 2003). It is one method of attempting to assess performance, leading to the provision of a licence to practise. In 1995, the first edition of the General Medical Council standards document *Good Medical Practice* (GMC 2001) was published. Each doctor is required to provide information under the seven major headings in that document in order to maintain a licence to practise: good professional practice; relationship with patients; working with colleagues; maintaining good practice (keeping up to date); teaching and training; health; probity.

Certification and recertification in ambulatory care in Germany

'Licensed specialists have also to be certified on the basis of additional training, experience, participation in audit and volume of special procedures (about 30% of the catalogue of ambulatory services) in order to enter into service contracts. Requirements for re-certification are fixed in the contracts and vary depending on the service in question. The different approaches include minimum volumes of procedures done within a year (e.g. 200 colposcopies within one year), or case-verification and evaluation of skills of the physician (with thresholds for sensitivity for example)' (Weinbrenner and Busse 2005).

The clinical team

One of the consistent messages to emerge when there are problems in the delivery of health care is that errors and failures are rarely caused by ignorant or deviant individuals, but more often by incompetent systems that conspire to allow mistakes to happen. As Farmer et al. (2002) have noted:

> Increasing attention is being directed towards finding ways of assessing how well doctors perform in clinical practice. Current approaches rely on strategies directed at individuals only, but, in real life, doctors' work is characterized by multiple complex professional interactions. These interactions involve different kinds of teams and are embedded within the overall context and systems of care.

For years accreditation standards have focused on relationships between departments. Performance management now should also focus on teamworking, communication and continuity of care. Approaches for managing the performance of clinical teams range from internal peer review to external inspection.

Internal peer review

This comprises the regular, multidisciplinary review of current practice, measured against evidence-based standards as incorporated into guidelines, care pathways and local protocols. Many countries have abandoned planning systems based on resource norms, such as the number of doctors per 1000 population, in favour of objectives focused on results. However, in many cases it is difficult to measure outcome reliably, or it takes too long to assess; for example, cancer survival is typically assessed as survival to five years. In such cases, performance may be measured better in terms of process (e.g. what preventive, diagnostic or therapeutic interventions are delivered). Of course, this requires a demonstrable association between the provision of the intervention in question and the probability of a successful outcome. Thus, 'best practice' should be based on good evidence from research rather than history, political dogma or personal preference. Such clinical standards (service frameworks, pathways, practice guidelines, protocols) range from the general to the specific, from formative to summative tools. However, the quality of guidelines has improved greatly in recent decades, in part because of the international diffusion of good practice through initiatives such as the Cochrane Collaboration and the AGREE Collaboration of 2003 (Burgers et al. 2003).

The effectiveness of internal review processes depends on the quality of not only the standards used (many guidelines are insufficiently evidence-based or are out of date) but also the assessment process (much clinical audit is unsystematic) and the data that are used (data collection systems often are driven by administrative requirements rather than relevance to clinical practice).

External assessment

Many countries have systems of inspection or accreditation, some of which relate to institutions such as hospitals, some to specific activities such as laboratories. Voluntary external assessment programmes (e.g. peer review and accreditation) may focus on clinical teams, departments or whole institutions (Shaw 2003). Traditionally, these focused on hospitals, but programmes for primary care teams are developing in several European countries, including the Netherlands, Poland (Walonczyk 2002), Portugal (MoniQuOr 1998) and the United Kingdom.

Incentives and resources for changing performance

Change management

It has long been apparent that the publication of guidelines for clinical practice does not ensure that they will be adopted. There is now a considerable body of research on changing clinical practice, much of it from the Cochrane Collaboration (Grimshaw and Russell 1993; Oxman et al. 1995; Grol 1997; Moulding et al. 1999). This research reveals that the problems and solutions of change management relate to the behaviour of people and organizations rather than the technical issues involved. Drawing on this evidence, it is possible to identify four sets of strategies that, together, increase the probability that change will be achieved (Woodward 2000).

- *Predisposing strategies*: educational materials, conferences, outreach visits, local opinion leaders, self-assessment.
- *Enabling strategies*: practice rehearsal, clinical guidelines, care maps, reminders, patient-mediated interventions, computer-based clinical decision support.
- *Strategies for reinforcing changes in behaviour*: audit and feedback, peer review.
- *Multifaceted strategies*: combinations of the above.

The final point is crucial as now there is considerable evidence that a combination of interventions has a greater effect on clinician behaviour than a single one used in isolation (McKee and Healy 2002).

The mechanisms that facilitate change can be divided into four categories: information, support, incentives and system change.

Information

Feedback reinforces and sustains improvement against predefined standards or peer-group benchmarks. Benchmarking can encourage debate between clinicians and managers and collaboration between participating hospitals and practices. The process of using information often identifies its weaknesses, thereby leading to improvements in data quality. While it is unusual for routinely collected information alone to be used to identify with certainty the nature of a problem or what should be done about it, it is often useful for determining potential problems that are susceptible to more detailed study. Thus, for

example, a study of variations in clinical practice undertaken in England showed widespread variation in activity levels in general surgery, urology, trauma and orthopaedics, ear, nose and throat and ophthalmic surgery. This led to discussions about the possible explanations (Bloor and Maynard 2002).

Information is required not only on the pattern of care being provided but also on the evidence needed to inform how it should be provided. Hence, it is essential that health care professionals have access to sources of information in libraries and, increasingly, via the Internet.

Support

Change can be sustained by peer group pressure, such as participation in audit meetings, assisted by feedback on comparative performance, where relevant. This was notably effective in implementing guidelines for preventive care in general practice in the Netherlands (Hulscher et al. 1998).

In some countries, especially those with no tradition of using evidence in the development of health policy, problems can arise through the lack of peer support. This has been reported in the Russian Federation, where international consultants were able to provide support for those pioneering new ways of working (Tillinghast 1998).

Support is especially important for trainees (Atherton et al. 1999). Educational programmes should ensure that they include a means to resolve identified weaknesses, recognizing that many instances when individuals fail to take appropriate action are owing to wider system factors rather than a lack of knowledge.

Responsive training should extend beyond improving clinical skills and knowledge to develop clinicians' capacity to improve the performance of the institution. Measurement of clinical performance still does not feature in the traditional undergraduate curriculum of clinicians in many countries. Most staff need a systematic introduction to peer review and management in their own workplace, as well as the continuing development of clinical skills and knowledge.

Incentives

The Institute of Medicine report *Crossing the Quality Chasm* emphasizes the need to align payment policies with performance improvement (Institute of Medicine 2001). Financial barriers created by inappropriate payment methods can create significant disincentives to the provision of high-quality care. Most incentive systems focus on organizations rather than individuals, but ultimately they too are affected by the indirect incentives that are created.

Non-financial rewards

Grindle and Hildebrand (1995) argue that a pay packet is not the only motivator, even in low-income countries. People want to feel that the organization has an important and clear mission and that they are part of this endeavour. Job satisfaction is important, in that they should enjoy the work they do and feel it to be

worthwhile. People should regard themselves as part of a well-regarded profession or occupation that has social status in society. They want recognition and respect from peers and managers for the tasks that they do well (Martínez and Martineau 2001).

While most health staff derive satisfaction from doing their jobs better, more tangible incentives have been used, such as high-profile quality awards, certificates of approval and money. A French review of the association between physician payment and the costs, process or outcomes of care (Chaix-Couturier et al. 2000) found that:

- fund-holding or capitation decreased the volume of prescribing by up to 24%, and hospital days by up to 80% compared with fee-for-service;
- financial incentives may reduce access and continuity of care and create conflicts of interest between doctor and patient;
- an annual cap on doctors' income resulted in referrals to colleagues when the target income was reached.

The authors concluded that financial incentives can reduce the use of resources, improve compliance with practice guidelines and facilitate the achievement of targets. This approach has been used explicitly in the GPs' contracting system in the United Kingdom. Practices are assessed on the basis of their performance in four domains: clinical standards; organizational standards; patient experience; additional services (NHS Confederation n.d.).

Elsewhere, less ambitious methods have been used to change specific aspects of clinicians' behaviour. For example, in Norway, some general practitioners received a fixed block grant from the local municipality in addition to fee-for-service remuneration and patient co-payments. A new system based on capitation was introduced with the objective of creating incentives to increase the number of patients on the list and to reduce the workload for each patient by increasing referrals to specialist care (Iversen and Luras 1998).

System change

Business process re-engineering is a concept borrowed from industrial management. It involves an examination of the different elements involved in delivering a specific service. An example is the approach taken to reduce the delay between arriving at a hospital with a myocardial infarction and receiving thrombolytic treatment (door-to-needle time). Studies of the process of care have revealed many possible delays, such as problems with ambulances, inefficient admission procedures, waits for the admitting doctor and onward referral to cardiology units, waits for porters, diversion via radiology departments before reaching the coronary care unit (CCU) and poorly located refrigerators used to store the drug. These studies have informed the development of new clinical pathways, frequently involving emergency department staff being authorized to institute therapy prior to admission to the CCU, with completion of patient registration following treatment and admission.

Studies of clinical pathways often suggest ways of reconfiguring referral patterns and clinical specialties. These may be informed by evidence that some technical procedures produce better results in the hands of frequent users

(the volume–outcome link), though this needs to take account of the risk that moving specialty services to distant centres can merely make them less accessible (Phillips and Luft 1997). However, it is important to consider each case individually, as a review published in 1997 concluded that:

> The literature on links between volume of clinical activity and clinical outcomes suggests that for some procedures or specialties there may be some quality gains as hospital or physician volume increases. In other areas the research suggests an absence of significant volume gains. Generalisation is clearly not possible on the basis of these results. (Sowden et al. 1997)

Public disclosure of clinical performance

Many examples of comparative measures of health service performance have been published, with the goals of improving transparency, assisting patients to make informed choices and encouraging poor performers to improve. However, as one commentator noted:

> Little is known about the kind of performance information the public wants to see, thinks is useful, or actually uses. There are concerns that publicly available performance measures will encourage health care providers to focus on producing information which looks good rather than patient care that is good. (Buchan 1998)

The available experience highlights major problems with data. In many cases, data have not been sufficiently complete, accurate or detailed to enable adjustment for severity, except in those situations (in the United States) where massive investment in information systems has gone far beyond what is available outside certain specialist registers in Europe. In addition, in many cases the small numbers involved make it impossible to eliminate the play of chance. However, one of the greatest problems is the scope that it presents for opportunistic behaviour as clinicians either avoid treating patients at greatest risk (whose severity is apparent but not captured by information systems) or use their discretion to increase the recorded frequency of complications, thus making their case load appear more complex than it is (Entwhistle et al. 1996; Marshall et al. 2000). An American review of disclosure concluded that there is limited empirical evidence of either its influence on the clinical and managerial practices of professionals and organizations or its impact on the quality of care for health service users (Leatherman and McCarthy 1999). This conclusion was shared by a series of commentaries reviewing the experience of public disclosure as a change management tool in Australia (Collopy 1999), Sweden (Mebius 1999) and the United Kingdom (Coles 1999). These concluded that the benefits of public disclosure of performance information were not yet proven but that it may improve health care through changes in consumer, professional, managerial and organizational behaviour.

Resources for performance improvement

When asked what would most improve quality in health care, many clinicians and managers reply, 'more staff, more equipment, more money'. This review has found little empirical evidence to support this but some basic needs are evident.

Time

Systematic clinical performance review, by whatever method, must displace patient contact time. Work plans and contracts must recognize this as a legitimate activity both for individuals and for clinical teams. The implementation of medical audit in the United Kingdom estimated that 5% of a full-time clinician's time is spent on regular systematic review. This replaced some of the time spent on more traditional and anecdotal clinical meetings but also generated more work for clerical staff in retrieving and refiling large numbers of case records for analysis.

Data

Much use has been made of individual and aggregated patient and service data for performance improvement. Computer-based clinical support systems have been shown to improve diagnosis and treatment (Hunt et al. 1998) and to reduce errors, particularly in prescribing. Clinicians need to receive regular feedback of performance against agreed standards using complete, accurate and timely data; comparisons over time and with other similar clinical units should be available and reliable.

Many facilities, particularly hospitals, have numerous fragmented manual and computer records, often using incompatible systems of coding and operation, which could be catalogued and developed for quality improvement. Even the poorest facilities usually keep registers of outpatients, emergencies, admissions, prescriptions, diagnostic tests, operations and nursing and medical care, which can yield valuable data. Technical support with statistical analysis, documentation and logistics reduces the loss of clinical time.

Conclusions

From this review of experience, particularly in Europe, four key elements emerge as principles for managing the performance of clinicians. The first is the need to clarify the values, objectives, accountability and stakeholders involved in performance improvement. The second is the need to define explicit standards of performance based, as far as possible, on research-based evidence. Third, it is necessary to establish valid measures of compliance with agreed standards. Finally, there must be effective systems to induce appropriate change in both organizations and individuals.

References

Atherton, F., Mbekem, G. and Nyalusi, I. (1999) Improving service quality: experience from the Tanzanian Family Health Project. *International Journal for Quality in Health Care*, **11**: 353–6.

Bashook, P.G. and Parboosingh, J. (1998) Recertification and the maintenance of competence. *British Medical Journal*, **316**: 545–8.

Bloor, K. and Maynard, A. (2002) Consultants: managing them means measuring them. *Health Service Journal*, **112**: 10–11.

Bristol Royal Infirmary (2001) *Learning from Bristol: the report of the public inquiry into children's heart surgery at the Bristol Royal Infirmary 1984–1995*. CM 5207. London, Bristol Royal Infirmary.

Buchan, H. (1998) Different countries, different cultures: convergent or divergent evolution for health care quality? *Quality in Health Care*, **7**(suppl.): S62–7.

Burgers, J.S. et al. (2003) Towards evidence-based clinical practice: an international survey of 18 clinical guideline programs. *International Journal for Quality in Health Care*, **15**(1): 31–45.

Catto, G. (2003) Improving professional competence – the way ahead? *International Journal of Quality Health Care*, **15**: 375–6.

CBO Visitatie (www.cbo.nl/algemeen/english/folder20030512164118/default_view).

Chaix-Couturier, C. et al. (2000) Effects of financial incentives on medical practice: results from a systematic review of the literature and methodological issues. *International Journal for Quality in Health Care*, **12**: 133–42.

Coles, J. (1999) Public disclosure of health care performance reports: a response from the UK. *International Journal for Quality in Health Care*, **11**: 104–5.

Collopy, B.T. (1999) Public disclosure of health care performance reports: what do we lose in giving information? *International Journal for Quality in Health Care*, **11**: 98–101.

Conlon, M. (2003) Appraisal: the catalyst of personal development. *British Medical Journal*, **327**: 389–91.

Danishevski, K. (2005) Case-study: Russia. *In*: Dubois C.-A., McKee, M. and Nolte, E., eds, *Human resources for health in Europe*. Copenhagen, European Observatory on Health Systems and Policies.

Department of Health (n.d.) *A first class service: quality in the new NHS* (www.dh.gov.uk/assetRoot/04/04/48/91/04044891.pdf).

Department of Health and Children's Services (2001) *New health strategy. November 2001*. Dublin, Department of Health and Children's Services (www.doh.ie/hstrat).

Entwhistle, V.A. et al. (1996) Supporting consumer involvement in decision-making: what constitutes quality in consumer health information? *International Journal for Quality in Health Care*, **8**: 425–37.

Farmer, E.A. et al. (2002) Assessing the performance of doctors in teams and systems. *Medical Education*, **36**(10): 942–8.

General Medical Council (2001) *Good medical practice*. London, GMC.

Grimshaw, J.M. and Russell, I.T. (1993) Effect of clinical guidelines on medical practice: a systematic review of rigorous evaluations. *Lancet*, **342**: 1317–22.

Grindle, M. and Hildebrand, M. (1995) Building sustainable capacity in the public sector: what can be done? *Public Administration and Development*, **15**: 441–63.

Grol, R. (1997) Beliefs and evidence in changing clinical practice. *British Medical Journal*, **315**: 418–21.

Healy, J. and McKee, M. (2002) Improving performance within the hospital. *In*: McKee M. and Healy J., eds, *Hospitals in a changing Europe*. Buckingham, Open University Press.

Hulscher, M.E.J. et al. (1998) Tailored outreach visits as a method for implementing guidelines and improving preventive care. *International Journal for Quality in Health Care*, **10**: 105–12.

Hunt, D.L., Haynes, R.B. and Hanna, S.E. (1998) Effects of computer based clinical decision support systems on physician performance and patient outcomes: a systematic review. *Journal of the American Medical Association*, **280**: 1339–46.

Institute of Medicine (2001) *Crossing the quality chasm: a new health system for the 21st century*. Washington, DC, NAP (www.nap.edu/pdf/0309072808/pdf_image/193.pdf).

Iversen, T. and Luras, H. (1998) *The effect of capitation on GPs' referral decisions*. Oslo, University of Oslo, Health Economic Research Programme.

Klazinga, N.K., Lombarts, K. and van Everdingen, J. (1998) Quality management in the medical specialties: the use of channels and dikes in improving health care in the Netherlands. *International Quality Review (Quality Review Bulletin)*, May: 240–50.

Leatherman, S. and McCarthy, D. (1999) Public disclosure of health care performance reports: experience evidence and issues for policy. *International Journal for Quality in Health Care*, **11**: 93–8.

McKee, M. and Healy, J. (2002) Improving performance in the hospital. *In*: McKee, M. and Healy, J., eds, *Hospitals in a changing Europe*. Buckingham, Open University Press.

Marshall, M.N. et al. (2000) Public disclosure of performance data: learning from the US experience. *Quality in Health Care*, **9**: 53–7.

Martínez, J. and Martineau, T. (2001) Introducing performance management in national health systems: issues on policy and implementation. London, Institute for Health Sector Development (www.hlspinstitute.org/files/project/15034/IN8-Martinez.pdf).

Maynard, A. and Bloor, K. (2003) Trust and performance management in the medical market place. *Journal of the Royal Society of Medicine*, **96**: 532–9.

Mebius, C. (1999) Public disclosure of health care performance reports: comments and reflection from Sweden. *International Journal for Quality in Health Care*, **11**: 102–3.

Ministry of Health and Social Affairs Norway (1999) *The national strategy for quality improvement in health care*. Oslo, Board of Health.

Ministry of Health of Republic of Lithuania (1998a) *On regulations of internal audit* [in Lithuanian]. Valstybes zinios, 89: document no. 2469.

Ministry of Health of Republic of Lithuania (1998b) *On regulations of State Medical Audit Inspection at the Ministry of Health* [in Lithuanian]. Valstybes zinios, 34: document no. 914.

MoniQuOr (1998) *Assessment and monitoring of organisational quality in health centres*. Lisbon, Lisbon Instituto de Qualidade em Saude (IQS) (www.iqs.pt).

Moulding, N.T., Silagy, C.A. and Weller, D.P. (1999) A framework for effective management of change in clinical practice: dissemination and implementation of clinical practice guidelines, *Quality in Health Care*, **8**: 177–83.

NHS Confederation GMS contract negotiations (www.nhsconfed.org/gmscontract/).

Or, Z. (2002) *Improving the performance of health care systems: from measures to action (a review of experiences in four OECD countries)*. Paris, OECD (Labour market and social policy occasional papers no. 57).

Oxman, A.D., Thomson, M.A. and Davis, D.A. (1995) No magic bullets: a systematic review of 102 trials of interventions to improve professional practice. *Canadian Medical Association Journal*, **153**: 1423–31.

Phillips, K.A. and Luft, H.S. (1997) The policy implications of using hospital and physician volumes as 'indicators' of quality of care in a changing health environment. *International Journal for Quality in Health Care*, **9**: 341–8.

Shaw, C. (2003) Measuring against clinical standards, *Clinica Chimica Acta*, **333**: 115–24.

Shaw, C. and Kalo, I. (2002) *A background for national quality policy in health systems.* Copenhagen, World Health Organization (www.euro.who.int/document/ e77983.pdf).

Smith, R. (1999) Managing the clinical performance of doctors. *British Medical Journal,* **319**: 1314–15.

Southgate, L. and Dauphinée, D. (1998) Maintaining standards in British and Canadian medicine: the developing role of the regulatory body. *British Medical Journal,* **316**: 697–700.

Sowden, A., Aletras, V. and Place, M. (1997) Volume of clinical activity in hospitals and health care outcomes, costs and patient access. *Quality in Health Care,* **6**: 109–14.

Strózik, M. (2005) Case-study: Poland. *In*: Dubois, C.-A., McKee, M. and Nolte, E., eds, *Human resources for health in Europe.* Copenhagen, European Observatory on Health Systems and Policies.

Taylor, C.M., Wall, D.W. and Taylor, C.L. (2002) Appraisal of doctors: problems with terminology and a philosophical tension. *Medical Education,* **36**(7): 667–71.

Tillinghast, S.J. (1998) Can Western quality improvement methods transform the Russian health care system? Joint Commission. *Journal on Quality Improvement,* **24**(5): 280–98.

Walonczyk, J. (2002) *Program akredytacji praktyk lekarzy rodzinnych* (*Program of accreditation of Family Physicians*). Seventh Polish Conference on Health Protection, Krakow, 22–24 April.

Weinbrenner, S. and Busse, R. (2005) Case-study: Germany. *In*: Dubois, C.-A., McKee, M. and Nolte, E., eds, *Human resources for health in Europe.* Copenhagen, European Observatory on Health Systems and Policies.

Woodward, C.A. (2000) *Strategies for assisting health workers to modify and improve skills. Developing quality health care – a process of change.* Copenhagen, World Health Organization (WHO/EIP/OSD/00.1) (www.who.int/health-services-delivery/disc_papers/ Process_Chabge.pdf).

chapter seven

Health care managers as a critical component of the health care workforce

Ann Mahon and Ruth Young

Introduction

Health care organizations have always been among the most difficult of entities to manage, but the ever-increasing complexity of the health care industry means that today's managers are being faced with greater challenges, and greater opportunities, than ever before (Barner 1996; Adams and Hirschfeld 1998; Martínez and Martineau 1998; Baker 2002; OECD 2002, 2003). This is especially so in Europe, where managers are working in the context of governments' different attempts to respond to the wide-ranging political, sociological and economic transformations that are driving radical, fast-moving changes in health care systems across the continent (Flynn and Strehl 1996; Lane and Ersson 1996; Kanavos and McKee 1998; Figueras et al. 2004).

For the purposes of this chapter these drivers can be viewed at two levels, reflecting the fact that especially (but not only) within the EU, individual countries retain primary responsibility for health care delivery that is also affected by wider legislative developments. It follows that managers are faced with both country-specific policy reforms and the collateral effects of ostensibly non-health-related European and global policies as they impact upon and become embedded within individual countries. For instance, the European Union Treaties (as interpreted by the European Court of Justice (ECJ)) are opening up opportunities for patients to act as cross-border consumers and for health care workers to become internationally mobile on the basis of mutual recognition of training and qualifications (Busse 2000). As another example, the WTD has reduced weekly hours of work, with important implications for the delivery of a system of care that has long depended on some groups working very long hours (Pickersgill 2001). It is against this complex background that this chapter

focuses on the following questions about health care managers as a group within the broader health care workforce in Europe.

- What do we know about the health care management workforce in Europe?
- Can a common framework be developed to derive a common understanding of health care managers and their role?
- What are the key management challenges arising from current reforms: why are managers important?
- What are the implications of these changes for Europe's health care managers in the future?

The main purpose of this chapter is thus to develop a dynamic and unified framework for describing and analysing the role of the health care manager in a changing Europe. The chapter also attempts to combine the construction of this theoretical model with its application, drawing on empirical work in different European countries to illustrate the challenges and opportunities arising from the various elements of health care reform.

What do we know about the health care management workforce in Europe?

A key observation in relation to health care mangers in Europe is that the literature rarely, if ever, recognizes them as a critical component of the health workforce in their own right. Instead, they are discussed primarily in terms of the roles they play in relation to doctors, nurses, therapists and other professional and non-professional workers who deliver health care. A second important issue is the lack of empirical data about the European health care management workforce. This translates into a distinct lack of clarity about how many health care managers are needed, where and with what skills, in order to deliver services efficiently and effectively. And what are acceptable levels of management costs? Such questions are equally relevant in countries like Belgium, France, Norway, Sweden and the United Kingdom, where there is a tradition of modelling need and attempting to match supply to demand for health care professionals (e.g. doctors and nurses); and Austria, Germany, Spain, the NIS of the former USSR and others, where it is simply left to the market to achieve workforce adjustments (Bloor and Maynard 2003; Young et al. 2003).

These gaps are explained partly by the difficulties of definition that exist in relation to management and public management generally and health care management specifically. Despite the lack of data, however, there is a generally growing recognition of gaps between workforce supply and demand – at both senior and middle management levels – across Europe (Davies 2001).

Of course, the most fundamental question is whether it is at all possible to think of Europe's health care managers as a workforce group in their own right. It is this key topic that the remainder of this chapter attempts to address.

Can a unified framework be developed to derive a common understanding of health care managers and their role?

In this part of the chapter we outline three frameworks for analysing the health care management workforce, focusing on:

- managers as people socialized differently into their roles;
- the detailed content of an individual manager's everyday role;
- managers within the broad context of their health care system.

Although presented initially as three separate and distinct frameworks, together these form a dynamic and unified model for describing and explaining the roles and experiences of health managers within different European health care systems. Each framework is introduced in turn, with specific examples drawn from different European countries, before the frameworks are incorporated into a unifying conceptual model.

Framework 1: Managers as people socialized differently into their roles

Seen through this lens, it is possible to identify three types of health care manager that have evolved differently in health care systems across Europe.

Type A: the professional manager, more typical of western Europe. This is a view that sees health care management as a distinct professional role, i.e. managers have recognized status and sets of skills stemming from the acquisition (in the public or private sectors) of accepted, specialist management training and qualifications. This professional health care manager is most developed in countries such as the United Kingdom (Buchan and Maynard 2005), but is also evolving elsewhere (e.g. Spain and Germany: Lopez-Valcarcel et al. 2005; Weinbrenner and Busse 2005).

For our purposes, it is important to note that reform is a key driver of the expansion of health care management as a profession in many countries. For example, with continuing devolution and decentralization, posts that were purely administrative (i.e. clerical or secretarial) increasingly require management skills and qualifications. The same is true of certain clinical positions (Leat 1994; Forbes and Prime 1999). Another emerging trend is the move into professional management from other fields, such as medicine and nursing (Harrison and Smith 2003; Lopez-Valcarcel et al. 2005). In this instance, moving tends to constitute a complete departure from clinical practice and status. The key feature of type A is that managers are a group in their own right, pushing for equal status with other health care professions.

Type B: administrator/manager, less-formalized role, more typical of Member States who joined after 2004. In many eastern European countries, by contrast, it is the medical profession that tends to dominate health care management (together with accountants, often termed economists, in finance). This applies in both the traditionally predominant hospital sector and newer entities like the social/ health insurance organizations established in the 1990s (Karski et al. 1999; Busse and Wisbaum 2000; Hlavacka et al. 2000). Past differences in status between

doctors, nurses and other staff were simply reproduced as the vacuum was filled by a discipline unheard of before the fall of communism.

The same medical dominance is also true in other new Member States such as Malta (Azzopardi Muscat and Grech 2005). For all these countries, the issue is how to broaden the appeal of health care management to a wider pool of skilled labour, inside and outside the health sector. The relatively new concept of the health care manager who has a set of distinct roles and responsibilities is still developing, in terms of who is suitable to carry out the role and also in its transition from what traditionally has been a public sector *administration* paradigm.

Type C: clinician-managers, a growing trend, particularly in western Europe. This brings together the previously distinct domains of management and administration with clinical practice in a process that some see as producing a 'new breed' or 'hybrid' type of public/health care manager (Leat 1994; Forbes and Prime 1999; Llewellyn 2001). The impetus comes from a range of policy initiatives in virtually all health care systems, which attempt to tie the activities of clinicians, particularly physicians, closer to the goals of health care organizations (Llewellyn 2001). These initiatives include the development of tighter systems of financial management and of moves that frame medical and other clinical activity within a managerial approach. Senior doctors, typically departmental heads, have developed roles that transcend the clinical–managerial interface (Hasselbladh and Kallinikos 2000). In addition, new clinical roles (such as specialist nurses and nurse practitioners in the United Kingdom) are being developed with a specific management agenda to respond to evolving service needs (Walshe et al. 1999). The development of this type of manager has profound implications for: (a) broadening the definition and associated roles/activities of the health care manager; (b) considering the organizational support needed for incumbents; (c) the transformation of both clinical and managerial professions.

Overall, framework 1's approach indicates that the concept of health care management is potentially quite different in countries across Europe. So too are the ways in which individual health care managers are socialized into their roles. The predominance of different types of manager is reflected in countries' contrasting levels of investment in, and approaches to, preparing individuals for the management role. Essentially, more professionalized managers have achieved greater status as a consequence of their enhanced exposure to education and development. It follows that in most western European countries there are specialist health care management programmes, initially developed solely for professional managers but that now recruit clinicians. In addition, health care managers are represented increasingly on nonspecialist programmes (such as masters of business administration and masters of public administration), which, while targeted traditionally at senior managers, increasingly recognize the needs of middle managers too (Livian and Burgoyne 1997). Managers can also access distance-learning and in-house management and leadership programmes designed to meet emerging needs.

By contrast, in much of eastern Europe, health care management training developed later, often with technical and financial assistance from the EU and the wider international community (Cerniauskas et al. 2000; Jesse et al. 2000; Albrecht et al. 2002; Azzopardi Muscat and Grech 2005). A key question here is

whether existing courses are providing what the system will need. In Poland and Hungary, for example, there has been an emphasis on hospital management (a sector being downsized) rather than areas that are recognized future priorities, such as public health and collaborative working between hospitals and other sectors (Gaal et al. 1999; Bobak et al. 2002). Moreover, many countries have yet to give formal recognition to management qualifications obtained at home or abroad (Hlavacka et al. 2000).

Such factors (professionalization/status, types of education and training, differences in background between clinicians and managers) are highly relevant to our exploration of health care management across Europe. They impact on understanding and attitudes and, as a result, how the job of management is carried out on a day-to-day basis. As a specific example, note the contrasting stances that different types of health care professional take to key elements of health service modernization in the United Kingdom (Table 7.1). According to this model, nurse managers are the most supportive of modernization and are seen as significant change agents and role models. By contrast, physicians' attitudes often pose a considerable challenge to managers wishing to implement change.

As another example, implementation of the WTD (in particular its application to junior doctors who in the past delivered a significant proportion of hospital care) in English hospitals reveals differences in managerial approaches. For some, particularly doctors, the directive is an unwelcome intrusion from a bureaucratic state and has little legitimacy. This has led to resistance, which is slowing or blocking initiatives to deal with its impact in some places (Mahon et al. 2003). Importantly, such findings also raise questions about the position of clinician-managers, made even more relevant by the fact that they are a growing group within the health care management workforce overall. As Degeling et al. (2003) observed, 'conflicts of priority . . . exist even among holders of common objectives'; but clinician-managers are being asked to combine professional

Table 7.1 Attitudes of different United Kingdom professionals to health service modernization

Modernization aspect	Doctor clinicians	Nurse clinicians	Doctor managers	General managers	Nurse managers
Recognize connections between clinical decisions and resources	Oppose	Oppose	Support	Equivocal	Support
Transparent accountability	Oppose	Oppose	Support	Support	Support
Systematization	Oppose	Equivocal	Oppose	Support	Support
Multidisciplinary teams	Oppose	Support	Oppose	Equivocal	Support

Source: adapted from Degeling et al. (2003).

cultures, and to work within a context in which 'the various professions [may differently] interpret policy initiatives'. This may lead to problems around both professional and role identity.

To sum up, although European health care managers are a heterogeneous group in terms of the social and cultural characteristics brought to the job, it is possible to develop a broad categorization. A key question is the extent to which the three different types of managers are identifiable across the different health systems within Europe. If, as it appears, it is a question of emphasis rather than the categories being mutually exclusive, then greater interchangeability between, and comparative analysis across, different countries and the continent as a whole is possible.

Framework 2: Detailed content of an individual manager's everyday role

A second way of analysing the health care management workforce is in terms of the roles they perform at the level of the organization, i.e. the context in which they work on a day-to-day basis.

As Appleby (2001), citing the United Kingdom NHS Executive, states, 'the general definition of a manager . . . [in the context of health care is] "someone with a supervisory responsibility – or [someone who] performs a support function, e.g. planning rather than a clinical or operational function".' Within that, at an organizational level, it is possible (Maliqi et al. 2003) to distinguish between the following types of management.

- *Strategic management* involves, inter alia, defining the role and purpose of the organization and its relationship with the external environment. This, in turn, involves setting the organization's high-level vision and goals, i.e. its overall direction, and formulating strategies and objectives to achieve them.
- *Service (or operational) management* covers the basic tasks that an organization must perform in order to achieve its objectives. It includes, inter alia, the allocation of resources and the management and development of internal structures, systems and processes. As just one example, managers need to anticipate the impact of new medical, pharmaceutical and information technologies, selecting those likely to provide the greatest cost–benefit to patients and their organization. They also have to negotiate their way through complex budgets and contracting/service agreement arrangements, priority setting and accessing and utilizing resources without risking long-term financial viability (Ham and Honigsbaum 1998; Savas et al. 1998).
- *Managing (through) people*; for example, managers must liaise with, and mediate between, different groups of professional and non-professional workers, dealing with individual staff and their representative bodies and trade unions. Traditionally this is the area of human resources management (HRM), but it is important to note that management roles increasingly are incorporating many aspects traditionally associated with HRM.

At another level, it is possible to distinguish variation in the scale and scope of activities undertaken by managers in different organizations and in different

departments within the same organization (Institute of Healthcare Management 1999). The scale of activity of a typical manager ranges from a relatively small primary care practice to a large hospital with hundreds of staff and a budget of millions of euros. The scope of responsibilities includes general administration and management, together with more specialist roles that require additional training. The latter might include: scientific, therapeutic or technical support; human resources/personnel; finance; medical records; quality; facilities; or even, in some countries, property management. Thus managers operate at different organizational levels (senior and middle management) and in different functional areas, making complex decisions that are likely to have both short- and long-term impacts on their organizations and their outcomes.

Finally, it is possible to describe what health care managers do in terms of the skills required to perform the different management tasks (strategic, service or HRM) just described. Mintzberg's classic model provides a useful means of understanding what (health care) managers do (Mintzberg 1990). From this viewpoint, health care managers are seen to undertake interpersonal, information and decisional roles (Figure 7.1). Again, the combination of these roles may vary according to a given manager's formal/informal status, level within the organization and the context in which he or she operates. All of these are considered in more detail later.

In all of the above roles, a key aspect of managers' tasks is to balance the potentially competing demands of the numerous interest groups to which they, and their organization, are accountable. This not only includes other senior and middle managers and clinical staff in the context of HRM, but also (going back to strategic and service management) covers patients, local communities and the general public (Calnan et al. 1998). Perhaps even more importantly, managers must deal with the impacts of government and the other (e.g. professional) bodies that regulate, fund and influence health care reform (Kokko et al. 1998). Indeed, responsibility for implementing and managing the various reform initiatives instigated by government is the part of health care management that cuts across managers' roles, whatever the detailed content of their job.

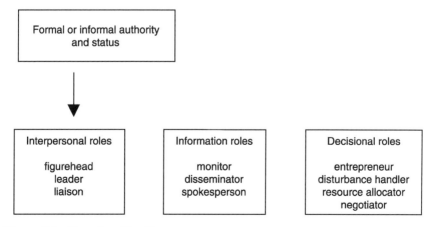

Figure 7.1   The roles of health care managers.

Framework 3: Managers in the broad context of their health care system

Finally, for the purposes of our European-level discussion of the health care management workforce, it is important to consider the significance of different health and social welfare systems from a political economy perspective. In our third framework, therefore, we outline some of the broader historical, economic, political, cultural and environmental factors that have impacted on who managers are (framework 1) and what they do (framework 2). We focus on the features underlying continuing differences across Europe (often based on specific national histories) and on possible areas of convergence (for instance, emerging as a result of the need for all countries to respond to wider European and global forces, often through similar types of health care reform).

Several 'difference factors' impact on frameworks 1 and 2. For example, there are significant variations in the funding models of different countries with essentially tax-based or social insurance systems (respectively known as the Beveridge and Bismarck models) (Ham 1997). There are also (country and intra-country) variations in and renegotiation of the boundaries of service delivery models. This includes the balance of: hospital, primary and community-based health and social services; generalist gatekeepers (GPs/family doctors) versus a greater emphasis on specialist primary care providers; and public versus independent sector provision. Within the private sector there are also differences of emphasis between private for-profit, voluntary and not-for-profit providers. These range from individual practitioners to churches, charities and national or international companies (Forder et al. 1996; Kendall and Anheier 1999; Bartlett and Blackman 2001). In turn, such developments are influenced or constrained by a country's broader economic, social and political context and its history in terms of, for example, the influence of unionized labour, public attitudes to government, constitutional arrangements, vested interests and national culture (OECD 2003).

It is possible to develop these arguments here only as far as it suits our purpose in identifying frameworks for analysis. From this perspective, it must be emphasized that by altering the political and institutional contexts that provide the platform for health care activity, particular system configurations and evolutionary trajectories will have impacted on all of the factors we have described so far. This includes managers' status and the overall nature and perception of their role (framework 1) and the organizational context within which managers are required to operate or the tasks they carry out day-to-day (framework 2) (Pettigrew et al. 1992; Andrews et al. 2003). In particular, questions of ethos – social democratic public service, liberal market, state hierarchy and so on – have a strong bearing on the managerial (including the health care reform) task and how it is carried out (Flynn and Strehl 1996; Osterle 2001; Le Grand 2003).

So, for example, some managers in systems that face capacity constraints (e.g. the United Kingdom's) may be preoccupied with managing waiting lists. By contrast, others may be focused on aspects of the contracting process. For example, post-Soviet systems in eastern Europe have inherited a large hospital sector, so managing the shift to a more community-based health (e.g. home nursing, mental health services) and social care (e.g. day centres, residential

care) model is a key management task (Gaal et al. 1999; Karski et al. 1999; Cerni-auskas et al. 2000; Hlavacka et al. 2000; Jesse et al. 2000; Albrecht et al. 2002). Finally, in the context of health care (and wider public sector) reform, it is important to note that countries will have different priorities and different areas where, for historical and cultural reasons, it is not possible for assertive action to be taken (OECD 2003). Put simply, management interventions that work well in one country may not be transferable to another.

Overall, despite the variation in system trajectories, it should be emphasized that all European countries are facing common pressures. On the one hand, they need to control expenditures; on the other, they are struggling to meet rapidly accelerating health care demand (e.g. owing to demographic change). Growing pressures for more decentralized governance simply add another common driver so that managers in the public sphere are forced to plan for an increasingly turbulent future. Of course, this is just one component of a much wider process that stems from a globalized and increasingly competitive world economy, which forces revision of the European economic and social model that has underpinned the EU since its inception. Another example of wider forces' impact on the context for health care management relates to the increasing mobility of professionals, requiring regulatory frameworks that reach beyond those of individual states (Evetts 2002).

The increasing tendency to address health issues at European level is also relevant when considering international trends. This includes: the expansion of European law into the health arena (European Commission 2002, 2004); the spread of ideas facilitated by cross-national research (Saracci et al. 1998); and attempts to harmonize professional education (Brearley 1995).

While it is important to recognize the diverse contexts in which managers are embedded, the ways in which the 'increasingly convergent set of pressures for change, shaped in part and reflected in part by European integration' (Martin 1997) are acting are equally critical. For example, are we witnessing the emergence of some new managerial structures that owe more to the commonality of contemporary pressures than the differentiation of past models? If so, then there may be an argument that something that could justifiably be labelled a 'European health care manager' is emerging. At the very least, health care managers need to be aware of the increasing European dimension to their work and its implications for themselves and their organizations (Kanavos et al. 1999).

In addition, it could be argued that the fact that most European countries, regardless of political, economic and cultural histories, have been actively reforming or modernizing their health care systems in response to wider forces is a unifying feature in its own right. In western Europe there have been reforms at least since the 1970s; in CEE most significant changes have emerged since the late 1980s and the fall of communism (Ham 1997; Figueras et al. 2004).

Health system reform as a key unifying feature?

Every European country will respond differently to the varied external and internal factors that are driving change in their health care systems. A common unifying feature is that recent reforms have tended to be inspired by market-based

approaches that, in the post-war period, were not associated with health care. In other words, management theories, concepts and practice developed in business and the private sector have extended into health care, moving away from more traditional models based on public administration. The global term for this trend is new public management (NPM), the key features of which are summarized in Box 7.1 (Hood 1995; Ferlie et al. 1997).

NPM has its critics. One argument is that it directly imports notions of financial efficiency from profit-making organizations and takes no account of the distinctive features of public sector organizations in general and health care organizations in particular (e.g. Flynn and Strehl 1996; Stewart 1998). Another is that as a global concept NPM may create an artificial sense of convergence in health policy and reform implementation, when in reality there are significant inter- and intra-country differences in the scale, scope or even existence of different forms of change (Lynn 1998). Nevertheless, NPM does provide a useful framework: first, to describe the general scope of reform in different European countries; second, to develop a greater understanding of the common features of the health care manager role, and why managers are important, across Europe.

More specifically, it would appear that countries undertaking health care reform (initially at least) have focused on only one model of NPM: efficiency measures (NPM1). For example, demand management has been used in an effort to contain costs, increasing co-payments for drugs and certain procedures. Other systems, such as those of the United Kingdom and Spain, have attempted to address perceived inefficiencies through the use of contracts with public and independent sector health and social care providers, and with organizations and individual practitioners. Each of the above methods is also being used, to differing degrees, in CEE. However, while efficiency clearly remains a prominent feature of reform agendas – because of the common need to address basic financial challenges in health and social welfare systems across Europe – there have also been many changes associated with other models of NPM. These include:

- regulation and governance (NPM4), often involving the creation of new national institutions, as in France and the United Kingdom, and entirely new accreditation and regulatory systems developed and planned for both individual and organizational providers in the Czech Republic, Poland etc.;
- decentralization (NPM2), a feature of recent reforms in most east European countries;
- organizational culture (NPM3), recognized as key in the United Kingdom NHS Plan, for example;
- increased recognition of user voices (NPM4), evidenced, for instance, by the establishment of patient representative groups and their input into debates about health priorities in Estonia, Hungary, Lithuania and Slovenia.

Overall, application of these different NPM models highlights the diversity of themes and issues emerging from different national reform agendas. It also illustrates the challenges that are common to health care managers, despite the fact that Europeans work in a range of health systems with differences in economic and political environments, organizational structures and cultures.

Box 7.1 Key features of new public management

New public management model 1 (NPM 1): the efficiency drive

This model of NPM attempts to make 'bureaucratic' public sector organizations more business-like, efficient and rational. Eight core themes are associated with this model of NPM.

- Increased attention to financial control; a strong concern with value for money; strengthening of the finance function of organizations; growth of more elaborate cost and information systems.
- Stronger general management system; clear target-setting and performance monitoring; shift of power to senior management.
- Extension of audit, both financial and professional; insistence on more transparent views of performance; protocols; standards.
- Increased stress on provider responsiveness to consumers; greater role for non-public sector providers; more market-mindedness.
- Deregulation of the labour market; erosion of national pay agreements; short-term contracts.
- Reduction in the self-regulating power of the professions; shift in power from professionals to management; drawing professionals into management; more transparent forms of professional regulation.
- Some empowerment of less bureaucratic and more entrepreneurial management but with tight retrospective accountability.
- New forms of corporate governance; marginalization of elected representatives and trade unionists.

New public management model 2 (NPM 2): downsizing and decentralization

Public sector organizations are perceived as large, bureaucratic, hierarchical, overcentralized, inflexible, insensitive and unmanageable. Seven core themes are associated with this model.

- Extension of the early stress on market-mindedness to more elaborate and developed quasi-markets; shift from planning to quasi-market mechanisms for allocating resources.
- Move from management by hierarchy to management by contract. Creation of more loosely coupled public sector organizations at a local level.
- Split between a small strategic core and a large operational periphery.
- Delayering and downsizing; move to flatter organizational structures; staff reductions at higher and lower tiers.
- Split between public funding and independent sector provision.

- Move from command and control associated with NPM model 1 to new styles of management such as management by influence; an increased role for network forms of organization; stress on strategic alliances between organizations as a new form of coordination.
- Attempt to move away from standardized forms of service to a service system characterized by more flexibility and variety.

New public management model 3 (NPM 3): in search of excellence

Within this model there is strong emphasis on organizational culture (Deal and Kennedy 1981; Peters and Waterman 1982; Senge 1990). Highly rationalistic approaches are challenged and there is attention to values, culture and roles. Hence, it is concerned less with structures and more with the place and role of people in their organizational context. This model can be subdivided into bottom-up and top-down approaches. Two core themes are associated with this model.

- Bottom-up form: emphasis on organizational development and learning. Top-down backing for bottom-up product champions; radical decentralization with performance judged by results.
- Top-down form: explicit attempts to secure culture changes; projection of a top-down vision; managed culture change programmes; stress on charismatic forms of top-down leadership.

New public management model 4 (NPM 4): public service orientation

The fourth model of NPM presents a fusion of private and public sector management ideas, taking ideas from the private sector and applying them in a public sector context. It includes a strong focus on securing the services' accountability to consumers/customers and citizens (Osbourne and Gaebler 1992). Five core themes are associated with this model.

- Major concern with service quality.
- Management process reflects service user concerns and values.
- Desire to shift power from appointed to elected bodies.
- Stress on the development of societal learning over and above the delivery of routine services.
- A continuing set of distinctive public service tasks and values; stress on securing participation and accountability as legitimate concerns of management in the pubic sector.

Towards a dynamic and unifying framework for understanding the role of the European health care manager

We referred earlier to the difficulty of defining health care management, and our subsequent discussion has shown the diversity of managers within the European health care workforce: their professional and clinical backgrounds; the roles they are performing; the settings they are working in; and the key management challenges they are facing. Despite this diversity we have been able, at the broadest level and by the use of some key analytical frameworks, to identify a general understanding of health care management across Europe, essentially:

• activities directed towards developing and achieving the aims and objectives of health care organizations;
• taking responsibility for implementing and managing reform initiatives;
• undertaking these within a formal health care system.

Three frameworks for understanding the role of health care managers have been introduced. The first focuses on the process of socialization and the associated norms and values; the second adopts the approach developed by Mintzberg and is concerned with what managers do, i.e. the dimensions or content of their job; the third is concerned with the broader policy context that ultimately determines the role of the manager. These three frameworks can be constructed into an overarching conceptual model that emphasizes the changing (i.e. ever reforming) nature of health care managers' roles (Figure 7.2) and potentially is

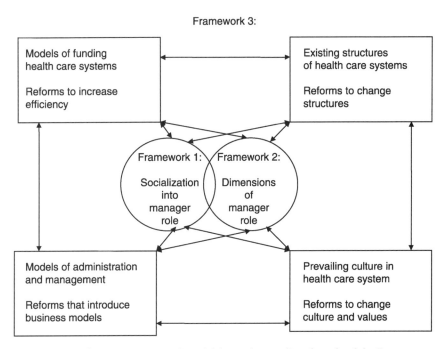

Figure 7.2 A dynamic conceptual model for understanding the role of the European health manager.

applicable to all health care systems. In this model we wish to emphasize the dynamic nature of relationships between our three approaches to analysing the health care management workforce: the ever-changing policy context (framework 3), which includes existing and proposed features of health care systems, *both influences and is influenced by* socialization processes and experiences (framework 1) and the content of the manager's job (framework 2).

It is outside the scope of this chapter to provide a detailed and full account of the interaction between reform and the role of health care managers across Europe. Instead, in the next section, we employ specific illustrative examples of the challenges faced by Europe's managers generally in the context of reform, and how similar policy reforms are received and present different challenges (and opportunities) within different health care systems. Overall, in considering managers as a critical component of the European workforce, it seems particularly important to note, with other commentators (Adams and Hirschfeld 1998; Martínez and Martineau 1998), that policy-makers have *underestimated* their role in reform implementation. Indeed, changes 'are often implemented without consulting managers or taking into account the need for management to lead and be an active part of the change' (Maliqi et al. 2003). In the remainder of this chapter, our aim is to show just why it is that managers are so important and should not be overlooked in the reform process. It is possible also to gauge the interactions between the different dimensions by using the model set out in Figure 7.2.

What are the key management challenges arising from reforms: why are managers important?

Reforms have enormous implications for health care managers. They are critical if change is to produce the intended improvements in organizational performance and the responses to wider societal pressures that are vital to sustain health system performance across Europe. This section is necessarily selective, focusing on key areas to illustrate managers' critical role, including:

- the role of the manager as change agent per se;
- dealing with changing stakeholder and organizational relationships;
- managing knowledge in the context of reform;
- building organizational capacity for change and improvement through HRM.

The role of the manager as change agent

Health care management is a highly complex field. As we have shown, a vast range of environmental factors, both internal and external to an organization, will impact on its performance. This ranges from levels of investment in staff development, working environments, cultures and information systems to changes in budgetary processes, the civil service and health care systems and whether changes are instigated on a system-wide or piecemeal basis (OECD 2003).

Although it is difficult for research to separate the effects of different factors and establish which, if any, are key to success, a growing body of knowledge recognizes the specific role of managers in this context (Pettigrew et al. 1992; Andrews et al. 2003; Gould-Williams 2003). Even though managers have little control over many factors that impact on their organizations, they are well placed to anticipate them and negotiate adequate organizational responses. Specifically, this kind of leadership is a vital component in the context of reform in its own right – vital for harnessing those same environmental factors as they interact to facilitate change and bring about service improvement (Figure 7.3).

Clearly, there is no single best solution to any management challenge. But there is a need to balance the competing and potentially conflicting interests of different stakeholders and come to the most appropriate option, given all of the resources available (WHO 2000). Indeed, the context in which a health care organization achieves its aims and objectives (reforming or otherwise) is so complex that without firm, clear leadership and strong, effective management practices it is almost inevitable that it will lose direction.

Importantly, from an NPM viewpoint, many of the recent reforms in European

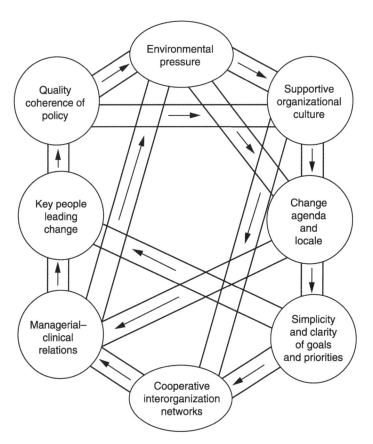

Figure 7.3   Factors facilitating change in organizations (from Pettigrew et al. 1992).

health care offer particularly strong opportunities for managerial leadership (as opposed to traditional public administration) precisely because they emphasize the need for outcomes, outputs and results rather than improved processes alone. It is also apparent that the multiple policy objectives seen in most countries will produce inevitable tension between objectives.

Under these circumstances, managers are vital if organizations are to prioritize reform objectives effectively. They are also important as a resource that can be freed up to focus specifically on the work necessary to overcome implementation difficulties (other groups, such as clinicians with responsibilities for service provision, may find this more difficult). This emphasizes how improved processes are necessary for achieving results; managers' roles in this context are illustrated below. Overall, it is clear that the concept of the manager as a change agent in reform is one that cuts across all the emerging roles associated with health care management, across Europe.

Dealing with changing stakeholder and organizational relationships

One major result of reform is the continuing renegotiation of relationships between key health care stakeholders, in particular: the relationships between the state and the clinical professions (especially medicine); different types of organization within the health care sector; clinical and managerial professions; and the health sector, i.e. the professions and patients/users (McKinlay and Arches 1985; Coburn et al. 1997; Evetts 2002). For the purposes of exploring the critical nature of managerial roles in this context, these changes can be viewed at three levels (Harrison and Ahmad 2000).

- *The micro-level*: at which doctors, for example, are perceived as losing control over the content of their job, including treatment and work patterns. In this context, managers are seen to gain influence because change is brought about by measures such as the introduction of clinical guidelines (Dowswell et al. 2001) and the implementation of the WTD (Mahon et al. 2003).
- *The meso-level*: focuses on the changing corporatist relationships between organizations, the professions and the state, essentially via increased demand for externalized control mechanisms. Using doctors as our example, we can show how professionals are being asked to become more involved in audit, evidence-based practice, peer review etc. – referred to as 'moral persuasion initiatives' (Degeling et al. 2003). Where there is a history of antagonism and tensions between the state and medicine (as in France, Germany, Sweden and the United Kingdom) such developments can meet challenges to their implementation. This is especially the case in countries where heavy-handed methods have been used, leading to a 'regulatory approach' to managing clinical performance.
- *The macro-level*: the key theme is how different parts of the health care system relate and integrate. A specific example is the increased recognition of the limitations of curative care versus the importance of preventive approaches. Also relevant is the increasing emphasis on patient/user and public

empowerment and involvement in organizational decision-making, rather than all key decisions being made by doctors, managers or other professionals (Glendinning et al. 2002). Finally, changes in macro-level relationships are being brought about by developments such as the rise of new models of (e.g. networked) organization, the greater use of partnerships between existing organizations and new types of (contracted) relationships across both the public and private sectors (Forder et al. 1996; Goodwin et al. 2003).

At all three levels, these changing relationships require careful handling if organizations are, at the very least, to remain effective or, more importantly, to improve performance. In the context of micro- and meso-level renegotiations with medicine, for example, it is clear that radical organizational, cultural and attitudinal changes are necessary if the balance of power is to shift demonstrably (Pickin et al. 2001). This creates an obvious leadership role for high-level managers.

In the context of the macro-level changes described above, the implications are also so broad that they require dedicated work to bring them about. It is also important to emphasize that networks tend to be characterized by flat organizational structures and are underpinned by soft values such as trustworthiness and egalitarianism. The same is true of patient and public involvement. Hence, management approaches that emphasize interpersonal skills and negotiation are key. Such developments in collaboration and coordination are required not least to address the agendas being introduced by a focus on the wider public health. When combined with concepts of an increasingly globalized world, it becomes clear that 'if the health care needs of this new millennium are to be met, more radical approaches to collaborative work will need to be explored' (O'Brien-Pallas et al. 2001). Of course it is important to remember that such new ways of working may present serious challenges in terms of management practice. Past health care management viewed the hospital as its focal point and employed 'command and control' rather than collaborative styles (Goodwin et al. 2003).

Managing knowledge in the context of reform

Another persistent theme in the literature (and indeed the case studies commissioned for this study) is the increasing emphasis on evidence and evidence-based clinical practice. However, this is not matched by information for making sound *management* decisions and forecasts, especially in relation to the professional workforce. Importantly, the reform agenda itself also needs informed choices based on adequate information and research evidence. Given that initiatives often suffer from a lack of continuity, underfunding or withdrawal of resources, it is even more important that organizations document learning so as not to lose it. By contrast, studies of health care reforms frequently show that organizations pay insufficient attention to monitoring, evaluating and transferring good practice systematically (Glendinning et al. 2002; Hyde et al. 2003).

At the same time, in other respects there is an increasing amount of information available within health care organizations, and between them and other

stakeholders. Many aspects of health care reforms involve the introduction of new information systems: those reflecting financial flows, activity and productivity data, quality indicators and so on. Yet even where these new systems are implemented successfully their reliability, validity and usefulness to the organization may vary.

Managers are key in determining whether and how data are converted into usable information and in developing an organizational culture receptive to its implications. In this context, a recent survey of 132 central government organizations in 20 OECD countries (including ministries of health and social care) provides timely insights into knowledge management's development as a strategic-level activity in the European public sector. One important finding is that strategic management roles, in particular, are evolving. Managers increasingly oversee the work of 'more knowledgeable' (in some areas) staff such as clinicians, understand the importance of capturing currently 'undocumented knowledge' from employees and attempt to overcome resistance (e.g. among middle managers) to the new systems and processes put in place to do this. A recent British inquiry commented: 'Bristol was awash with data. There was enough information from the late 1980s onwards to cause questions about mortality rates to be raised both in Bristol and elsewhere had the mindset to do so existed' (BRI Inquiry Secretariat 1999). In the context of knowledge management, therefore, relationships with staff – and hence HRM – are vital (OECD 2003).

Building organizational capacity for change and improvement through HRM

A key feature of many health care reforms in most European countries is the demand that the traditional emphasis on production and distribution of existing types of staff is matched by efforts to tailor staff to deliver more responsive, user-oriented health services. In other words, improving current skills (of teams and individuals), changing staff behaviour and developing new (combinations of) professional and non-professional skills are seen as important means of improving the quality of services delivered. It seems obvious, therefore, that if reform objectives are to be achieved, health care organizations need, almost as a prerequisite, to develop their staff appropriately.

Even more obvious, perhaps, is the need for effective communication to ensure staff commitment to change. Clearly, no organization can make changes, improve performance and maintain these high levels without good HRM. At a central level, managers need to oversee any changes in organizational structures and staffing levels to ensure that essential parts of the system continue to function effectively throughout the process of reform. They also need to establish processes of negotiation and good relationships with trade unions and professional bodies. This will ensure that service redesign projects that are likely to affect staff roles, or their terms and conditions, can be implemented as smoothly as possible. Finally, these managers need to put in place practical systems, such as staff appraisal based on results or outputs, career management, HR planning and local pay bargaining arrangements, where appropriate, based on a clear view of how they will help the organization achieve its strategic aims and objectives.

Managers at all levels of an organization need to make the most effective, timely use of this information in the day-to-day management of their own staff (Martínez and Martineau 1998). At the very least there is a need for effective management so that clinical staff, in particular, do not feel threatened by poor knowledge of what change will involve. It has become even more important to address the quality of the working environment and the needs of employees in this way given the significant problems with the recruitment and retention of high-quality workers, especially clinical professionals, in the public sector in many European countries (OECD 2002).

Overall, what becomes clear in the context of HRM is that once again health care managers are key to making full use of the talent within their organizations. At a broader (regional, national and perhaps European) level, however, HR management and development both need to be better integrated within health care policy and planning processes. This calls for many countries to make a focused effort to improve HR practices as part of the reform process. Here, too, managers can make a critical contribution to the debate with professional bodies, trade unions, education and training providers and government.

Conclusions: what are the implications for Europe's health care managers?

This chapter began with the question: 'is it appropriate to talk about the European health care manager?' What we have attempted to demonstrate is that, while we are unable to provide a tight definition of some internally coherent groups, simply asking the question is sufficient to provide the entry point to a rewarding debate. First, we were able to set out some frameworks that reveal the prime dimensions shaping European diversity as it affects health care management. Second, we proposed a dynamic and unified conceptual model for describing and analysing the relationships between those frameworks, i.e. between health care systems with their different reforming agendas (framework 3) and socialization into (framework 1), and domains of, the managerial role (framework 2). We were able to speculate about features (particularly regarding reform) that might be emerging in common across roles and systems, indicating some of the factors that might be pulling health care managers in the same direction. However, we are also sure that variety across Europe will continue to be the norm, since these common forces will be played out against the contingent circumstances of history, position and culture.

Within this diversity, it is evident that everywhere the shape of the health care manager's role is evolving in response to dynamic processes of change. Where this role has not existed, circumstances are leading to its creation; where it has a long history, the pressures we have described are moulding its configuration and importance. One clear feature of this reconfiguration is that the boundaries between clinical and managerial professions and practice are becoming more blurred. It follows that while health care managers may not explicitly be considered a critical workforce component, at least as indicated by national statistics, the roles that increasingly they are called upon to perform are crucial and have clear elements in common.

Given the unprecedented pressures from the external environment (especially demographic change affecting demand for care and the 'workforce deficit'), one of health care managers' most vital roles is as shock absorbers, mediating change to preserve vital day-to-day continuity of quality service provision. Inevitably this draws them into reactive and crisis management activities. We have emphasized managers' importance as medium- and long-term strategists for the health care sector. Importantly, this requires that managers across Europe are trained properly for the wider role of confronting change in this way.

In addition, we have emphasized that fundamental shifts in health systems are transforming health care organizations and their workforces. This too creates a demand for changes in the role and competencies of managers working within organizations. Since the process of implementation is one that requires active leadership and management, it also gives managers another important role – that of change agents in the process of reform. In this context we have emphasized that managing and, in particular, leading change requires a range of personal abilities including interpersonal, political, negotiation and networking skills. Overall, it is clear that at national and European levels managers themselves (individually, via their health care organizations and through representative groups) are important in promoting the need for professional managers and ensuring that they have the necessary tools.

Inevitably there are debates about how far harmonization of management education and development is desirable or feasible (Brearley 1995). Our proposition is that this may be less important than making sure that Europe's health care managerial workforce is prepared for the future – in the full acknowledgement of the complexity of its role as set out here. As has been argued elsewhere (Warden and Griffith 2001), there is a clear need for longer-term planning of both recruitment numbers and the education and training needed to produce managers with the appropriate skills (leadership and technical) to meet emerging needs. It is also a priority to retain the current workforce and to attune their roles and tasks more effectively to meet a new range of demands on their expertise. Succession planning and career development is the natural adjunct to defining the scope of the health care manager's role.

Finally, from the European perspective taken by this book, there is clearly scope for greater coordination across Member States in order to identify the components of best practice and to facilitate the benefits that arise from the movement and interaction of professionals. At the same time (as with the other components of the health care workforce, such as doctors, nurses and therapists) there is a need for Europe to ensure that it avoids any tendency to engage in a zero-sum game of competitive bidding for the best. This may benefit few but disadvantage many.

References

Adams, O.B. and Hirschfeld, B. (1998) Human resources for health – challenges for the 21st century. *World Health Statistics Quarterly*, **51**: 28–32.

Albrecht, T. et al. (2002) *Health care systems in transition – Slovenia*. Copenhagen, European Observatory on Healthcare Systems.

Andrews, R., Boyne, G.A. and Walker, R.M. (2003) Strategy content and organizational performance: an empirical analysis. National Public Management Research Conference. Washington, 8–11 October.

Appleby, J. (2001) Management costs – cut and run. *Health Service Journal*, 5 July: 33–4.

Azzopardi Muscat, N. and Grech, N. (2005) Case-study: Malta. *In*: Dubois, C.-A., McKee, M. and Nolte, E., eds, *Human resources for health in Europe*. Copenhagen, European Observatory on Health Systems and Policies.

Baker, G.R. (2002) Healthcare managers in the complex world of healthcare. *Frontiers of Health Services Management*, **18**(2): 23–32.

Barner, R. (1996) The new millennium workplace: seven changes that will challenge managers – and workers. Quoted in: Ninemeier, J., The changing role of managers in the health workplace. *The Futurist*, **30**(2): 14–18 (ww.iahcsmm.com/basic_man_0998.htm).

Bartlett, H. and Blackman, T. (2001) Models of care. *In*: Blackman, T., Brodhurst, S. and Convery, J., eds, *Social care and social exclusion: a comparative study of older people's care in Europe*. Basingstoke, Palgrave.

Bloor, K. and Maynard, A. (2003) Planning human resources in health care: towards an economic approach – an international comparative review. York/Ottawa, Canadian Health Services Research Foundation (www.chsf.ca).

Bobak, M. et al. (2002) Advancing public health: 10 years of transition in central and eastern Europe and the newly independent states of the former Soviet Union. Background paper for USAID Conference, Washington, 29–31 July.

Brearley, S. (1995) Harmonisation of specialist training in Europe: is it a mirage? *British Medical Journal*, **311**: 297–9.

BRI Inquiry Secretariat (1999) *BRI inquiry paper on commissioning, purchasing, contracting and quality of care in the NHS internal market*. London, BRI Inquiry Secretariat.

Buchan, J. and Maynard, A. (2005) Case-study: United Kingdom. *In*: Dubois, C.-A., McKee, M. and Nolte, E., eds, *Human resources for health in Europe*. Copenhagen, European Observatory on Health Systems and Policies.

Busse, R. (2000) *Health care systems in transition – Germany*. Copenhagen, European Observatory on Health Care Systems.

Busse, R. and Wisbaum, W. (2000) *Health care systems in transition – Czech Republic*. Copenhagen, European Observatory on Health Care Systems.

Calnan, M., Halik, J. and Sabbat, J. (1998) Citizen participation and patient choice in health reform. *In*: Saltman, R.B., Figueras, J. and Sakellarides, C., eds, *Critical challenges for health care reform in Europe*. Buckingham, Open University Press.

Cerniauskas, G., Murauskiene, L. and Tragakes, E. (2000) *Health care systems in transition – Lithuania*. Copenhagen, European Observatory on Health Care Systems.

Coburn, D., Rappolt, S. and Borugeault, I. (1997) Decline versus retention of medical power through restratification: an examination of the Ontario case. *Sociology of Health and Illness*, **19**(1): 1–22.

Davies, J. (2001) What does it all add up to? *Health Service Journal*, 5 July: 28–31.

Deal, T.E. and Kennedy, A.A. (1981) *Corporate cultures; the rites and rituals of corporate life*. Reading, MA, Addison-Wesley.

Degeling P. et al. (2003) Medicine, management and modernisation: a 'danse macabre'? *British Medical Journal*, **326**: 649–52.

Dowswell, G., Harrison, S. and Wright, J. (2001) Clinical guidelines: attitudes, information processes and culture in English primary care. *International Journal of Health Planning and Management*, **16**: 107–24.

European Commission (2002) Decision No. 1786/2002/EC of the European Parliament and of the Council of 23 September 2002 adopting a programme of Community

action in the field of public health (2003–2008) – Commission Statements. *Official Journal of the European Communities*, L 271, 09/10/2002: 1–12.

European Commission (2004) New EU centre for disease prevention and control adopted. Press release: IP/04/427 (http://europa.eu.int/rapid/start/cgi/guesten.ksh?p_action.-gettxt=gtanddoc=IP/04/427\0\RAPIDandlg=ENanddisplay=).

Evetts, J. (2002) New directions in state and international professional occupations: discretionary decision-making and acquired regulation. SASE 13th Annual Meeting on Socio-economics Knowledge: The Wealth of Nations. University of Amsterdam, 28 June to 1 July.

Ferlie E. et al. (1997) *The new public management in action*. Oxford, Oxford University Press.

Figueras, J., McKee, M. and Lessof, S. (2004) An overview. *In:* Figueras, J. et al., eds, *Health systems in transition: learning from experience*. Copenhagen, European Observatory on Health Systems and Policies.

Flynn, N. and Strehl, F. (1996) *Public sector management in Europe*. London, Prentice Hall.

Forbes, T. and Prime, N. (1999) Changing domains in the management process: radiographers as managers in the NHS. *Journal of Management in Medicine*, **13**(2): 105–13.

Forder, J., Knapp, M. and Wistow, G. (1996) Competition in the mixed economy of care. *Journal of Social Policy*, **25**(2): 201–21.

Gaal, P., Rekassy, B. and Healy, J. (1999) *Health care systems in transition – Hungary*. Copenhagen, European Observatory on Health Care Systems.

Glendinning, C. et al. (2002) *National evaluation of notifications for use of the Section 31 partnership flexibilities of the Health Act 1999: final report*. Department of Health, NPCRDC, University of Manchester and Nuffield Institute, University of Leeds.

Goodwin, N. et al. (2003) *Managing across diverse networks of care; lessons from other sectors*. Policy Report, NHS Service Delivery and Organisation Programme.

Gould-Williams, J. (2003) The importance of HR practices and workforce trust in achieving superior performance: a study of public-sector organisations. *International Journal of Human Resource Management*, **14**(1): 28–54.

Ham, C. (1997) *Health care reform: learning from international experience*. Buckingham, Open University Press.

Ham, C. and Honigsbaum, F. (1998) Priority setting and rationing health services. *In:* Saltman, R.B., Figueras, J. and Sakellarides, C., eds, *Critical challenges for health care reform in Europe*. Buckingham, Open University Press.

Harrison, S. and Ahmad, W.I. (2000) Medical autonomy and the UK state 1975 to 2025. *Sociology of Health and Illness*, **34**(1): 129–46.

Harrison, S. and Smith, C. (2003) Neo-bureaucracy and public management: the case of medicine in the National Health Service. *Competition and Change*, **7**(4): 243–54.

Hasselbladh, H. and Kallinikos, J. (2000) The project of rationalization: a critique and reappraisal of neo-institutionalism in organisation studies. *Organisation Studies*, **21**(4): 697–720.

Hlavacka, S. et al. (2000) *Health care systems in transition – Slovakia*. Copenhagen, European Observatory on Health Care Systems.

Hood, C. (1995) Contemporary public management: a new global paradigm? *Public Policy and Administration*, **10**(2): 104–17.

Hyde, P. et al. (2003) *A catalyst for change? A national evaluation of the Changing Workforce Programme*. Final report to the Department of Health. Manchester, MCHM and MSM, University of Manchester.

Institute of Healthcare Management (1999) *Healthcare management careers information*. London: IHM (www.ihm.org.uk/content.asp?pageID=185).

Jesse, M. et al. (2000) *Health care systems in transition – Estonia*. Copenhagen, European Observatory on Health Care Systems.

Kanavos, P. and McKee, M. (1998) Macro-economic constraints and health challenges

facing European health systems. *In*: Saltman, R.B., Figueras, J. and Sakellarides, C., eds, *Critical challenges for health care reform in Europe*. Buckingham, Open University Press.

Kanavos, P., McKee, M. and Richards, T. (1999) Cross-border health care in Europe. *British Medical Journal*, **318**: 1157–8.

Karski, J.B., Koronkiewicz, A. and Healy, J. (1999) *Health care systems in transition – Poland*. Copenhagen, European Observatory on Health Care Systems.

Kendall, J. and Anheier, H.K. (1999) The third sector and the European Union policy process: an initial evaluation. *Journal of European Public Policy*, **6**(2): 283–307.

Kokko, S. et al. (1998) The role of the state in health reform. *In*: Saltman, R.B., Figueras, J. and Sakellarides, C., eds, *Critical challenges for health care reform in Europe*. Buckingham, Open University Press.

Lane, J.E. and Ersson, S.O. (1996) *European politics: an introduction*. London, Sage.

Leat, P. (1994) Physicians in health care management: 1. Physicians as managers: roles and future challenges. *Canadian Medical Association Journal*, **150**(2): 171–6.

Le Grand, J. (2003) *Motivation, agency and public policy: of knights and knaves, pawns and queens*. Oxford, Oxford University Press.

Livian, Y.F. and Burgoyne, J.G. (1997) *Middle managers in Europe*. London, Routledge and Kegan Paul.

Llewellyn, S. (2001) 'Two-way windows': clinicians as medical managers. *Organisation Studies*, **22**(4): 593–623.

Lopez-Valcarcel, B.T., Quintana, C.D.D. and Cocorro, E.R. (2005) Case-study: Spain. *In*: Dubois, C.-A., McKee, M. and Nolte, E., eds, *Human resources for health in Europe*. Copenhagen, European Observatory on Health Systems and Policies.

Lynn, L.E. (1998) The new public management: how to transform a theme into a legacy. *Public Administration Review*, **58**: 231–7.

McKinlay, J.B. and Arches, J. (1985) Towards the proletarianisation of physicians. *International Journal of Health Services*, **15**(2): 161–5.

Mahon, A. et al. (2003) *European working time directive pilots: an early evaluation*. Manchester, Manchester Centre for Healthcare Management.

Maliqi, B., Dorros, G.L. and Adams, O. (2003) *Management matters: coping with the crises of management and managers in the health system. Evidence and information for policy*. Geneva, World Health Organization.

Martin, B. (1997) Reform of public sector management. A relevant question for unions in the public sector? Background paper prepared for EPSU/ETUI Conference, Brussels, 23–24 October.

Martínez, J. and Martineau, T. (1998) Rethinking human resources: an agenda for the millennium. *Health Policy and Planning*, **13**(4): 345–58.

Mintzberg, H. (1990) The manager's job: folklore and fact. *Harvard Business Review*, **68**(2): 163–76.

O'Brien-Pallas, L. et al. (2001) Integrating workforce planning, human resources, and service planning. *Human Resources for Health Development Journal*, **5** (Dec/Jan): 1–3.

OECD (2002) *Public service as an employer of choice. OECD Policy Brief*. Paris, Organisation for Economic Co-operation and Development.

OECD (2003) *Public sector modernisation. OECD Policy Brief*. Paris, Organisation for Economic Co-operation and Development.

Osbourne, D. and Gaebler, T. (1992) *Reinventing government: how the entrepreneurial spirit is transforming the public sector*. Reading, MA, Addison-Wesley.

Osterle, A. (2001) *Equity choices and long-term care policies in Europe*. Aldershot, Ashgate.

Peters, T.J. and Waterman, R. (1982) *In search of excellence: lessons from America's best run companies*. New York, Harper and Row.

Pettigrew, A., Ferlie, E. and McKee, L. (1992) *Shaping strategic change*. London, Sage.

Pickersgill, T. (2001) Editorial: the European Working Time Directive for doctors in training. *British Medical Journal*, **323**(1): 1266.

Pickin, C. et al. (2001) Promoting organisational capacity to engage with active lay communities; developing a model to support organisational change for health. *Journal of
Health Services Research and Policy*, **7**(1): 34–42.

Saracci, R., Olsen, J. and McMichael, A. (1998) Europe's health research: getting the right
balance. *British Medical Journal*, **316**: 795.

Savas, S., Sheiman, I. and Maarse, H. (1998) Contracting models and provider competition. *In*: Saltman, R.B., Figueras, J. and Sakellarides, C., eds, *Critical challenges for health
care reform in Europe*. Buckingham, Open University Press.

Senge, P. (1990) *The fifth discipline: the art and practice of the learning organization*. New York,
Doubleday.

Stewart, J. (1998) Advance or retreat: from the traditions of public administration to the
new public management and beyond. *Public Policy and Administration*, **13**(4): 12–27.

Walshe, A., Crumbie, A. and Reverley, S. (1999) *Nurse practitioners: clinical skills and professional issues*. London, Elsevier.

Warden, G.L. and Griffith, J.R. (2001) Ensuring management excellence in the healthcare
system. *Journal of Healthcare Management*, **46**(4): 228–37.

Weinbrenner, S. and Busse, R. (2005) Case-study: Germany. *In*: Dubois, C.-A., McKee, M.
and Nolte, E., eds, *Human resources for health in Europe*. Copenhagen, European Observatory on Health Systems and Policies.

WHO (2000) *Public service reforms and their impact on health sector personnel. Critical questions: a tool for action* (WHO/EIP/OSD/01.2).

Young, R. et al. (2003) *The international market for medical doctors: perspectives on the position-
ing of the UK*. Report to Department of Health. Manchester, MCHM and NPCRDC,
University of Manchester.

chapter eight

Incentives in health care: the shift in emphasis from the implicit to the explicit

Alan Maynard

Introduction

All organizational structures in health care contain incentives, i.e. incitements to action or inaction. In health care systems, the purpose of action is to deliver evidence-based health care efficiently, equitably and within budget constraints. This requires health care professionals to have the clinical capacity to diagnose the patient's condition and an ability to deliver, from a range of possible interventions (including doing nothing), what is cost-effective for the patient and within the capacity of the institution to fund.

The tradition in medicine is for clinical practice to be individual and isolated, with muted peer review. Where review exists it is often based on opinion rather than systematic collection and management of comparative data about clinical activity and patient outcomes at the level of the individual practitioner. This tradition has been sustained by implicit incentives such as trust, duty and professional self-regulation. However, there is concern that these implicit mechanisms may be insufficient and explicit incentives, financial and non-financial, increasingly are being used to ensure quality of care.

Such incentives can be used to achieve intermediate and final outcomes. For instance, they can be used to improve the national and local recruitment of health care professionals, as well as the retention of professionals in a health care system or local organization, such as a clinic or hospital. They can also be used to manipulate the behaviour of health care professions; for example, to induce high levels of activity and improved quality of patient care. However, in some of the NIS of the former USSR, some new Member States and the remaining candidate countries, sometimes there is inadequate funding to pay staff. Even when they are paid, often the provision of care is altered by systems of

informal payment (e.g. Bulgaria, Hungary, Poland and Romania). Here, the priority may be to ensure funding and then slowly and cautiously to reform the structure of incentives at the margin (e.g. the Hungarian primary care 'experiments'). As in many low- and middle-income countries, the challenge in such systems is to provide basic packages of care in an efficient and equitable manner.

This is also a challenge in the high-income countries of western Europe. Although these have fewer problems of inequalities of access and utilization of health care they are significant (Jones and van Doorlaer 2004). Unlike the NIS of the former USSR and sub-Saharan Africa, where the average length of life is declining, the countries of western Europe continue to show evidence of enhanced length and quality of life (Nolte and McKee 2004). However, while this is due in part to their health care systems, their use of funding remains inefficient and in need of improvement by the careful use and evaluation of incentive reform.

This chapter examines the use and impact of incentives in European health systems. It begins with a brief discussion of the nature of the health care market and the nature of implicit and explicit incentives, followed by a review of the deficiencies of the health care industry, i.e. the problems that reformed incentive structures may reduce.

Background

The health care market is permeated with uncertainty. When a patient presents to a practitioner in the health care system there is uncertainty about diagnosis, treatment and rehabilitation. This led Arrow (1963) to conclude:

> when there is uncertainty, information and knowledge becomes a commodity . . . The buyer does frequently not know the value of information in any meaningful sense; if indeed, he knew enough to measure the value of information, he would know the information himself. But information, in the form of skilled care, is precisely what is being bought from most physicians.

Doctors have a comparative advantage in their knowledge of diagnosis and treatment options in medicine. As a consequence of this information asymmetry the patient delegates part or all of the decision-making to the doctor, who becomes an agent of the patient. If this agency relationship were perfect, the doctor would make choices that are only in the best interests of the patient. However, usually this relationship is imperfect and doctors consequently pursue not only their patients' interests but also their own preferences for income, leisure and professional satisfaction (Evans 1984). Doctors' power to induce demand for patient care has led to the development of professionalism and self-regulation and, more recently, performance management to protect patients from exploitation.

Most transactions in the health care market involve not only doctors and patients, but also the purchasers and providers of health care, both public and private. Consequently doctors can be regarded as 'double agents' (Blomquist 1991). They owe a duty not only to their patients but also to their health care

systems. As crucial decision-makers in the allocation of care and funding for themselves and their clinical teams, doctors are agents of the hospitals and clinics in which they work, and their funders – both government and private insurers.

Deficiencies in health care delivery

There is increasing international concern about value for money in the delivery of health care, largely as a consequence of growing evidence about the effectiveness of care. Early work looked at variations in medical practice in the United States and Europe, epitomized by the work of Wennberg and others at the Dartmouth Medical School in the United States. They compared the activities and outcomes of care processes for Medicare patients (the elderly) in New Haven and Boston and showed that, despite similar demographic characteristics, there were variations in the adjusted rates of discharge (47%), readmission (29%), length of stay (15%) and reimbursement (79%) between the two cities. Mortality rates were identical, while expenditure in Boston was nearly double that of New Haven (Wennberg et al. 1987, 1989, 2004).

More recently the Dartmouth group showed that US Medicare per capita spending in 2000 in Manhattan was more than twice that in Portland, Oregon, at $10 550 per enrolee compared with $4823. This was due to differences in the volume of services rather than illness, socioeconomic status or the price of services. 'Residents in high spending regions received 60% more care but did not have lower mortality rates, better functional status or higher satisfaction' (Fisher and Wennberg 2003).

In one study, potential savings of 30% were estimated if high spenders were to reduce expenditure to the level of regions offering lower treatment rates (Fisher 2003). This literature also illustrates that the value of additional specialist care may be zero or negative: the higher level of such providers in the east of the United States does not improve health as measured in this study. This should alert health workforce planners to the need to consider the benefits (in terms of improved length and quality of life) of increased staffing and increased staff activity. More specifically, these variations in clinical practice oblige managers to focus on the outcomes achieved by specialists, general practitioners and nurses. In terms of improving patient outcome, where would the greatest gain be achieved at least cost from additional investment in these competing skill groups?

Wennberg has argued consistently, for 30 years, that these variations are significant signals of waste and that they are related to physician choice of both activity level and case mix. 'The amount and cost of hospital treatment in a community have more to do with the number of physicians there, their medical specialties and the procedures they prefer than the health of residents' (Wennberg and Gittelsohn 1973). Similar literature, chronicling long-evident variations in practice, has been documented in the United Kingdom and other European countries (McPherson et al. 1982; Yates 1987, 1995; Bloor and Maynard 2002).

A related issue is the renewed interest in medical errors, following the

(American) Institute of Medicine report that estimated that medical errors killed between 44 000 and 98 000 Americans each year (Kohn et al. 1999). One retrospective analysis of errors in the United Kingdom detected an error rate of over 10% (Vincent et al. 2001). In Australia similar work showed an error rate of over 16%, although use of the American methodology reduced this to 10% (Wilson et al. 1995).

Such errors can occur in surgery (e.g. a Welsh case in which the surgeon removed the healthy, rather than diseased, kidney), the use of pharmaceuticals (use of the wrong drug or the right drug in the wrong dosage) and inadequate control of hospital infections (in particular, because of poor hand hygiene) (Pittet and Boyce 2001). Some errors are inevitable. However, the challenge is to learn from mistakes and invest in efficient risk management strategies. Yet often such strategies are neither evidence-based nor evaluated. They must be realistic, recognizing that the efficient rate of error may not be zero and that striving to extend the life of very ill patients by a few days may produce minor health benefits at great cost.

At the same time there seems to be remarkable reluctance to measure success, i.e. patient outcome. The past decade has seen an emerging literature on the measurement of failure, such as inpatient mortality or mortality 30 days after intervention. It has demonstrated the complexities of risk adjustment and also the unsurprising effects on clinical behaviour when publishing such data; in particular, the adoption of opportunistic behaviour that changes the diagnostic labels applied to patients or the way that they are treated, not to help them achieve a benefit but to reduce the risk of reported failure (Dranove et al. 2002).

However, most patients leave hospital alive and it seems surprising that the systematic measurement of relative success in improving the functional quality of life of patients is practically absent. One of the few exceptions in Europe is the British United Provident Association (BUPA), a private insurer in the United Kingdom. In response to a particular case of bad surgical practice, since 1998 BUPA has used a quality of life measure (the Short Form 36) on entry to hospital and three months after intervention to monitor changes in health status after adult elective surgery as a means of monitoring performance (Vallance-Owen and Cubbin 2002).

Overall, the evidence of variations in clinical activity and outcomes, together with the work of Cochrane (1973) and the Cochrane Collaboration (Maynard and Chalmers 1997), has led to increased questioning of clinical practice and practitioners. While policy-makers are seeking to improve performance management, they face the challenges that: (a) existing workforces are not utilized efficiently so the case for increased investment in personnel may be dubious; and (b) the relationships between any such increased investment and health outcomes need careful evaluation. It is possible that increased stocks of specialist doctors in some countries will have little effect on mortality outcomes, while increased stocks of primary care physicians and nurses may improve population health. However, this will require careful econometric investigation (Mark et al. 2004) and improved measurement of 'success' in terms of patient outcomes in order to ensure that health care capacity is not wasted and additional investments in care are targeted on the basis of demonstrable cost–effectiveness (Kind and Williams 2004).

Types of incentives

Implicit incentives

Table 8.1 outlines one approach to differentiate the different types of incentives. There are two types of implicit incentives, internal and external, both based on trust. Thus, medical practitioners (doctors, nurses or other health care professions) are educated and trained with an obligation to the duty of care for their patients, as epitomized by the Hippocratic oath, which requires that medical practitioners do their patients no harm: 'I will apply dietetic measures for the benefit of the sick according to my ability and judgement; I will keep them from harm and injustice. I will neither give a deadly drug to anybody who asked for it, nor will I make a suggestion to this effect' (Hippocrates 1849). The delivery of health care has been based on trust for the thousands of years since Hippocrates. Trust is 'a firm belief in the honesty, veracity, justice and strength' of the practitioner. One attraction of trust is that potentially it is more cost-effective than the alternative, namely detailed and explicit contracting and policing of the activity and performance of doctors.

The use of trust as a determinant of exchange has some important implications for the operation of competitive markets. The usual economic paradigm is that markets are an efficient means of ensuring that consumer welfare is enhanced by the free exchange of goods and services in networks of buyers and sellers. This is exemplified by the political rhetoric of Reagan, Thatcher, Bush and Blair and by Adam Smith's most famous book, *The Wealth of Nations*, which these politicians like to quote approvingly: 'It is not from the benevolence of the butcher, the brewer and the baker, that we expect our dinner, but from their regard to their own self-interest. We address ourselves not to their humanity but to their self-love, and never talk to them of their necessities but to their advantages' (Smith 1776). However, Smith contradicted this familiar advocacy of self-interest and the hidden hand of the market to enhance economic growth in an earlier book:

> Those general rules of conduct when they are fixed in our mind by habitual reflection, are of great use in correcting the misrepresentations of self love concerning what is fit and proper to be done in our particular situation . . . The regard of those general rules of conduct is what is properly called a sense of duty, a principle of greatest consequence in human life, and the only principle by which the bulk of mankind are capable of directing their actions. (Smith 1757)

Table 8.1 Types of incentives in medical practice

	Implicit	*Explicit*
Internal	Trust: Hippocratic oath	Regulation (e.g. by professional organizations and purchaser agencies)
External	Trust of consumers Trust of providers	Payment

Smith recognized that trust and duty dominated exchange between purchasers and providers in many markets. In the market of health care, self-regulation of the medical profession has been the traditional method of ensuring efficient and ethical practice.

Improving implicit incentives

The concern about the efficiency of the supply side of the market is eroding trust, something seen increasingly among purchasers in many health care markets. Confucius argued, 'without trust, we cannot stand'. O'Neill (2002) developed this argument more recently: 'Each of us and every profession and every institution needs trust. We need it because we have to be able to rely on others acting as they say they will, and because we need others to accept that we will act as we say we will.' The erosion of trust between health care purchasers and medical practitioners has led to increased investment in performance management as a means of ensuring higher levels of consumer protection and the most efficient use of scarce resources (Maynard and Bloor 2003a).

Thus, in the United Kingdom, demand for increased accountability from the medical profession and the NHS resulted in the development of an onerous and costly system of regulation, inspection, target setting and audit, covering both public and private organizations in health and social care. The government under Margaret Thatcher tried to develop medical audit and job plans for hospital consultants, with limited success. The current Labour government has reintroduced job plans, complemented by annual consultant appraisal and a system of revalidation of fitness to practise for all doctors on a five-year cycle. This government has also created NICE to establish evidence-based standards of practice and the Health Care Commission (formerly the Commission for Health Improvement), which audits organizational quality and performance in both public and private sectors.

However, policies such as these require considerable improvements in the collection of data and their use in management by clinicians and non-clinicians. This task needs to differentiate between the measurement and management of activity, failure (in particular mortality) and success (improvements in health-related quality of life). Yet while considerable resources are invested in the collection of administrative data about clinical activity, particularly in health care systems with fee-for-service payment systems for clinicians, often such data are used only by researchers (Wennberg et al. 1987; Bloor and Maynard 2002; Fisher and Wennberg 2003; Bloor et al. 2004).

The measurement and management of clinical performance is complicated by methodological issues such as those related to small numbers and adjustment for case mix severity, such as in the use of mortality data at the level of individual practitioners. While sophisticated methods such as data linkage, linking hospital utilization with death certificate information, are making the exploration of long-term survival increasingly feasible (Roberts and Goldacre 2003), at least in those countries where they are not prevented by data protection laws, the focus remains on indicators of failure rather than success in improving

the health status of patients. The routine measurement of success, or improvements in the functional health status of patients, remains unusual. The BUPA example mentioned earlier demonstrates the feasibility and challenges and also shows that the cost is modest (about €5 per patient). Yet despite long-term advocacy of the use of such measures no public health care system has invested in the collection of such data (Kind and Williams 2004).

Even in those health care systems where data about health care activity are available, they are often unused and require augmenting. Required improvements include the systematic collection, in a common format, of activity data for each practitioner in both their public and their private roles. Also needed is careful definition of the units of measurement, with agreement to ensure that the work of ambulatory and hospital-based doctors is well described.

Clinicians' self-interest in terms of delivering demonstrably effective and efficient health care to patients should encourage them systematically to collect data about their comparative process and outcome characteristics. They and their managerial colleagues need data to answer four fundamental resource allocation questions.

- What is produced in terms of activity and outcome (in particular patient health improvement)?
- How much is produced relative to their peers in terms of activity and outcome, and where there is evidence of economies of scale, do practitioners produce levels of activity consistent with good outcomes?
- How is care produced? What criteria and evidence are used to adopt new and abandon old technologies?
- To whom is care delivered: who gets care by social-income class?

A stimulus for change is increased use of this information by professional and regulatory agencies. Thus the Royal College of Physicians of London (www.rcplondon.ac.uk) has introduced a health informatics section on its web site, advocating validation of hospital activity data by members, as well as promoting an evolving capacity for them to access, check and use their data.

Creating clinicians' professional 'ownership' of such data is essential and regulating agencies can provide incentives. For instance, the Department of Health in the United Kingdom uses star ratings for the performance of English hospitals, one element of which is an improvement in the validity of Hospital Episode Statistics (HES) data. The Audit Commission, an independent regulatory agency, is also pressing for improved data quality (Audit Commission 2004).

The evolution of job plans that set out annual objectives and how they will be achieved commits medical practitioners to annual appraisals, particularly in the hospital sector. Both appraisals and job plans are slowly becoming more explicit and more quantitative. Based largely on these annual appraisals the General Medical Council will review revalidation of fitness to practise at five-year intervals.

Overall, however, progress in developing governance and performance management for doctors is slow and uneven. Practitioners throughout Europe still use the justification of clinical freedom to slow the development and use of essential quantitative information.

Trust and duty are internal and implicit incentives that are complemented by consumer confidence, an implicit incentive that is external to medical practice but significant in terms of its support of professionals' belief that they are trusted. Despite evidence about the sometimes inefficient and inadequate nature of health care provision, levels of public trust remain high, thereby making reform more difficult. Attempts to improve consumer information and enhance informed choice of practitioners and practice interventions seem to have muted consumer attitudes and behaviour (Marshall et al. 2000). In contrast, the erosion of trust in health care purchasers is a primary cause of the development of more interventionist explicit incentive systems.

Explicit incentives

Regulatory controls

Similar to implicit incentives, *explicit* incentives may also be distinguished as internal and external types (Table 8.1). The former are included in the rules and regulations of professional groups; for instance, trade unions such as professional medical associations. These are internal in the sense that they are based on an expectation of good professional behaviour once a practitioner is registered as fit to practise. Typically in Europe, such regulatory bodies tend to be poorly informed about the behaviour and performance of their members and relatively inactive. There are signs that, with the development of systematic reaccreditation over the career of the health professional, these systems of explicit regulation will be externalized. However, this has rarely been the case in the past as regulatory 'capture' has tended to ensure passivity and internalization of the profession groups (Stigler 1971). (This is discussed further in Chapter 10.)

Financial incentives

Basic economic analysis of payment systems predicts that if firms manipulate the level and structure of wages, workers can be induced to supply the desired quantity and quality of activity (Elliott 1991). There is a continuum of payment structures, ranging from time rates where workers are paid per unit of time they work to piece rates where remuneration is related to units of output. Often time and piece rates are combined. In health care, the principal methods of payment are salary (time rates), fee-for-service (piece rates) and capitation (i.e. being paid for each person on the practitioner's list of patients) (Table 8.2).

Information asymmetry in health care markets sustains the agency relationship mentioned previously, enabling physicians to induce demand for their services although this pursuit of income may lead to the provision of inappropriate care. However, this inefficiency may be masked by clinicians' tendency to believe that 'more means better'. Excess activity may be part of a well-intentioned desire to do their best for the patients but also may be a wasteful attempt to reduce uncertainty around their diagnosis and treatment. It

Table 8.2 Provider payment systems

Payment type	Definition	Incentive effects				Incentive to target the poor	Controls cost of doctor employment
		Incentive to increase activity	Incentive to decrease activity	Incentive to shift patients' cost to others			
Fee-for-service	Payment for each medical act	Yes	No	No		Maybe[a]	No
Salary	Payment per unit of time input (e.g. per month)	No	Yes	Yes		No	Yes
Capitation	Payment per patient for care within a given period (e.g. a year)	No	Yes	Yes		No	Yes

[a] If fee-for-service payments for treating poor patients exceed those for treating the middle classes.

is difficult to distinguish between the drive for increased income and the desire for more information. However, different payment methods may provide a means to move activity in a way that promotes the wider interests of the health system. The effects of the three principal methods of paying doctors and other health care professionals are summarized in Table 8.2.

A fee-for-service system is a direct inducement to increase activity. It encourages physicians to see more patients and perform more complex procedures, depending on the relative reward structure of the fee schedule. However, this work effort may not be appropriate. The challenges are to cap the resultant expenditure inflation and ensure that only efficient care is delivered to patients. Fee-for-service payments can create fragmentation and inefficient practice. Specialists in the United Kingdom are paid in this way for vasectomies; the policy was introduced in the late 1970s and resulted in increased activity. Yet while the procedure does not need to be performed by a highly trained surgeon it continues to be so, because of the incentive structure. Once such a fee is introduced it is difficult to remove.

Fee systems may induce unnecessary activity and, in poorly managed systems where efficient self-regulation and budget caps are absent, can distort activity and expenditure. Some countries, such as Germany, therefore use fee-for-service with a budget cap. While this can control expenditure, it does not manage activity efficiently and in particular does not prevent the delivery of care with little or no health benefit to the patient. It is also important to note that in a fee-for-service system what is not incentivized is marginalized. Physicians tend to respond to relative fee levels and where discretion exists may emphasize those activities that generate the best income return.

Capitation payments, unlike fee-for-service, do not induce overactivity but may create underactivity. Physicians may strive to maintain the quality of care in order to attract and retain patients. However, this incentive may be muted, as there appears to be low mobility of patients in such systems, in terms of switching between practitioners. Capitation may induce cost shifting from primary to secondary care, and from face-to-face contact to use of pharmaceuticals, where the prescription is a recognized way of terminating a visit. Capitation may also give rise to a cream-skimming effect, as practitioners seek to select the healthier patients who are easiest to treat.

Capitation salary payments facilitate the maintenance of expenditure control, as both rewards and their volumes are known and finite. Like capitation, salary systems of payment may induce undertreatment and the shifting of costs. For example, British hospital specialists may shift costs by using junior staff and nurses to carry out complex tasks.

Often doctors' payment systems are mixed. For instance, since the creation of the NHS most GPs have been paid largely by capitation. Thus, on average, capitated GPs receive about 60% of their payment according to the number and age of patients registered with them. The rest of their pay comes from fee-for-service (e.g. immunizations) and a salary element (e.g. seniority pay). However, by 2004 over 35% of GPs had shifted to an entirely salaried basis, in part because of the scope for more flexible working patterns for those with family responsibilities. American managed care organizations use various 'blended' or mixed systems of physician payments.

Overall, capitation and salary systems give policy-makers expenditure control but no leverage over microeconomic activity levels. Fee-for-service may create expenditure inflation by incentivizing activity, with no guarantee that this is either appropriate or efficient. Such financial incentives can induce important actions and inactions (Table 8.2), which require careful measurement and management.

In addition to mixed payment systems using salary, capitation and fee-for-service elements, additional performance-related pay mechanisms could be used. Burgess and Metcalf (1999) showed that incentive pay systems are less evident in the British public sector than in the private sector. Performance-related pay is used more often where output can be measured more easily; where output is difficult to measure, more general systems of merit-based payment tend to be used. One example of this is the merit or distinction pay system for British hospital consultants, under which often high awards are allocated on the basis of largely subjective judgements of distinction rather than systematic measurement of individual activity, the activity's congruence with corporate goals and comparative appraisal of patient outcomes.

Another important element in motivating practitioners is the career pay scale. As Burgess and Metcalf (1999) remarked, 'Many individuals who do not receive any performance-related bonus are nevertheless strongly motivated by the possibility of either promotion within the organization or a better job offer from an outside firm.' A remarkable characteristic of physician payment systems, in the United Kingdom and elsewhere, is their compression. In the United Kingdom consultants (specialists) are appointed in their early thirties, often due to supply shortages, and placed high on the short incremental scale. GPs can face similar problems of salaries being relatively flat across their lifetime in practice. However, there is minimal empirical evidence testing models of the salary structures' impact on lifetime earnings; evidence is contradictory for private sector workers and non-existent for public sector workers (Burgess and Metcalf 1999).

Overview

Significant changes in the use of incentives in recent years have involved a redefinition of implicit incentives and alterations in explicit incentives.

Implicit incentives, in particular the tradition of the Hippocratic oath and consumers' trust, remain significant determinants of professional behaviour. The independent clinician is trained to exploit the evidence base and deliver clinically effective care to patients. In turn, the patients trust the doctor to deliver care appropriate to their clinical needs.

The recent complication in these trust relationships is the greater role of the purchaser, whether private insurer, social insurer or government agency. As 'guardians of the patients' wallets' and in the light of documented inefficiencies in health care delivery, increasingly they question their trust in health care providers. As a consequence, purchasers are transforming themselves from passive 'price-takers' into aggressive, or at least increasingly questioning, 'price-makers'; developing their regulatory roles and using financial incentives more innovatively and vigorously. This increasing move away from trust and implicit

incentives towards regulation and financial explicit incentives has two foci: (a) defining performance targets and managing their achievement better; and (b) using mixed or blended systems of financial rewards to induce practitioners to pursue performance targets.

The definition of performance indicators continues to be dominated by limited measures of access and activity, such as waiting times, lengths of stay and the relative activity of clinicians. As discussed in the previous section, there is a marginal shift of emphasis on to the measurement of failures (e.g. practitioners' relative mortality rates, levels of hospital readmission and infection, medical error rates and failure to deliver proven, cost-effective patient care), but little or no development of health-related quality of life measures. When measured in terms of patient-reported health-related quality of life and managed by clinicians (particularly by learning from 'six sigma' safety-engineering techniques, which focus on the tails of distributives), performance can facilitate the adoption of better practices and the erosion of inadequate care.

The other type of explicit incentive, financial rewards, is being used increasingly to motivate change and more efficient practices by clinicians. The policy focus is on mixed systems of remuneration with, for instance, Germany moving away from pure fee-for-service in ambulatory care and the United Kingdom becoming more dependent on fee-for-service (Maynard and Bloor 2003b; Busse 2004).

Conclusions

> There are many mechanisms for paying physicians, some are good and some are bad. The three worst are fee for service, capitation and salary. (Robinson 2001)

This chapter highlights the potential dangers of naive use of financial incentives for health care professionals and organizations in the health care sector. Blended or mixed systems of incentives are emerging in the United Kingdom and the United States. France is seeking to reform the fee-for-service system used in ambulatory care, as it is seen as expensive and wasteful (Wait 2005). Germany is considering the use of capitation and salaried systems to reduce activity. The United Kingdom is developing fee-for-service to increase activity in a system cocooned by salary and capitation incentive systems that have contained expenditure but do not facilitate the micro-management of clinical activity and outcomes.

Whichever systems of incentives are used, financial and non-financial, there will be opportunistic behaviour, or gaming. Evans (1984), a Canadian health economist, argues that physicians' payment systems need to be changed every three years as, by then, they are undermined by gaming.

All incentive systems need careful construction and the blending of implicit and explicit contracts to achieve macroeconomic expenditure control and microeconomic management of activity and patient outcomes. Their management requires careful investment in information systems that produce measurement that is owned and validated by medical practitioners. In most health

care systems it is imperative to link financial incentives to the creation of such information systems; management by clinicians and non-clinicians is impossible without valid measurement of activity and outcomes that is linked across patient episodes and the 'fragments' of the health and social care system. Management is impossible without measurement, but measurement requires careful management.

The continuous international experimentation with organizational and individual incentives requires careful rigorous evaluation. It is remarkable how few robust studies are available in this important policy area. For example, Gosden's systematic reviews of primary care incentives (Gosden et al. 2001) and Bloor's (2003) review of hospital care incentives identified thousands of publications but fewer than half a dozen studies that met scientific standards.

Incentives create action and inaction in all health care systems. Tailoring the responses of clinicians to social goals is not as much a primitive art as an almost absent-minded activity of policy-makers. Consequently it is unsurprising that long-standing, well-researched inefficiencies survive internationally. It is time to experiment systematically with mixed incentive systems (and with evaluation) to improve resource allocation, rather than condone the restrictive practices of trade unions that do not serve the patients' interests.

References

Arrow, K. (1963) Uncertainty and the welfare economics of medical care. *American Economic Review*, **53**: 941–73.

Audit Commission (2004) *Information and data quality in the NHS*. London, Audit Commission.

Blomquist, A. (1991) The doctor as double agent: information asymmetry, health insurance and medical care. *Journal of Health Economics*, **10**: 411–32.

Bloor, K. (2003) An analysis of the performance of NHS consultants in England. PhD thesis, University of York, York.

Bloor, K. and Maynard, A. (2002) Consultants: managing them means measuring them. *Health Service Journal*, **112**: 10–11.

Bloor, K., Maynard, A. and Freemantle, N. (2004) Variation in activity rates of consultant surgeons and the influence of reward structures in the English NHS. *Journal of Health Services Research and Policy*, **9**(2): 76–84.

Burgess, S. and Metcalf, P. (1999) *The use of incentive schemes in public and private sector: evidence from British establishments*. Bristol, Leverhulme Centre for Market and Public Organisations (CMPO Working Paper Series 00/15).

Busse, R. (2004) Disease management program in Germany's statutory health insurance system. *Health Affairs*, **23**(3): 56–67.

Cochrane, A.L. (1973) *Effectiveness and efficiency*. London, Nuffield Provincial Hospital Trust.

Dranove, D. et al. (2002) Is more information better? The effects of report cards on health care providers. National Bureau for Economic Research (working paper 8697, January).

Elliott, R. (1991) *Labour economics: a comparative text*. Maidenhead, McGraw-Hill.

Evans, R.G. (1984) *Strained mercy: the economics of Canadian health care*. Toronto, Butterworth.

Fisher, E. (2003) Is more always better? *New England Journal of Medicine*, **349**: 166507.

Fisher, E.S. and Wennberg, D.E. (2003) The implications of regional variations in Medicare spending, two parts. *Annals of Internal Medicine*, **138**: 273–87, 288–98.

Gosden, T. et al. (2001) Impact of payment method on behaviour of primary care physicians: a systematic review. *Journal of Health Services Research and Policy*, **6**(1): 44–55.

Hippocrates (1849) *The oath written by Hippocrates* (trans. F.C. Adams). London, n.p.

Jones, A. and van Doorlaer, E. (2004) Income-related inequity in health and health care in the European Union. *Health Economics*, **13**(7): 605–8.

Kind, P. and Williams, A. (2004) Measuring success in health care: the time has come to do it properly. *Health Policy Matters*, 9 (www.york.ac.uk/healthsciences/pubs/hpmindex.htm).

Kohn, L., Corrigan, J.M. and Donaldson, M.S. (1999) *To err is human: building a safer health care system*. Washington, DC, Institute of Medicine, National Academy Press.

McPherson, K. et al. (1982) Small area variations in the use of common surgical procedures: an international comparison of New England, England and Norway. *New England Journal of Medicine*, **307**: 1310–14.

Mark, B.A. et al. (2004) A longitudinal examination of hospital registered nurse staffing and quality of care. *Health Services Research*, **39**(2): 279–300.

Marshall, M.N. et al. (2000) *Dying to know: public release of information about quality in health care*. London, Nuffield Trust.

Maynard, A. and Bloor, K. (2003a) Trust and performance management in the medical market place. *Journal of the Royal Society of Medicine*, **96**: 532–9.

Maynard, A. and Bloor, K. (2003b) Do those who pay the piper call the tune? *Health Policy Matters*, 8 (www.york.ac.uk/healthsciences/pubs/hpmindex.htm).

Maynard, A. and Chalmers, I (1997) *Non-random reflection on health services research: 25 years after A.L. Cochrane's Effectiveness and Efficiency*. London, British Medical Association Press.

Nolte, E. and McKee, M. (2004) *Does health care save lives? Avoidable mortality revisited*. London, Nuffield Trust.

O'Neill, O. (2002) *A question of trust. BBC Reith Lectures 2002*. Cambridge, Cambridge University Press.

Pittet, D. and Boyce, J.M. (2001) Hand hygiene and patient care: pursuing the Semmelweis legacy. *Lancet Infectious Diseases*, **1**: 9–20.

Roberts, S.E. and Goldacre, M. (2003) Case fatality rates after admission to a hospital with stroke: linked database study. *British Medical Journal*, **326**: 193–4.

Robinson, J. (2001) Theory and practice in the design of physician payment incentives. *Milbank Memorial Fund Quarterly*, **79**: 2.

Smith, A. (1757) *A theory of moral sentiments*. Oxford, Oxford University Press (1976).

Smith, A. (1776) *An inquiry into the nature and causes of the wealth of nations*. Oxford, Oxford University Press (1976).

Stigler, G.J. (1971) The theory of economic regulation. *Bell Journal of Economics and Management Science*, **2**(1): 3–21.

Vallance-Owen, A. and Cubbin, S. (2002) Monitoring national clinical outcomes: a challenging programme. *British Journal of Health Care Management*, **8**(11): 412–16.

Vincent, C., Neale, G. and Woloshynowyck, M. (2001) Adverse events in British hospitals: a preliminary retrospective record review. *British Medical Journal*, **322**: 517–19.

Wait, S. (2005) Case study: France. *In*: Dubois, C.-A., McKee, M. and Nolte, E., eds, *Human resources for health in Europe*. Copenhagen, European Observatory on Health Systems and Policies.

Wennberg, J.E. et al. (2004) Use of hospitals, physician visits and hospice care during the last six months of life among cohorts loyal to highly respected hospitals in the USA. *British Medical Journal*, **328**: 607–10.

Wennberg, J.E., Freeman, J.L. and Culp, W.J. (1987) Are hospital services rationed in New Haven or over-utilised in Boston? *Lancet*, **1**: 1185–8.

Wennberg, J.E. and Gittelsohn, A. (1973) Small area variations in health care delivery: a population information system can guide planning and regulatory decision making. *Science*, **182**: 1102–8.

Wennberg, J.E. et al. (1989) Hospital use and mortality among Medicare beneficiaries in Boston and New Haven. *New England Journal of Medicine*, **321**: 1168–73.

Wilson, R.M., Runciman, W.B. and Gibberd, R.W. (1995) The quality in Australian health care study. *Medical Journal of Australia*, **163**: 458–71.

Yates, J. (1995) *Private eye, heart and hip: surgical consultants, the National Health Service and private medicine*. Edinburgh, Churchill Livingstone.

Yates, J. (1987) *Why are we waiting: an analysis of hospital lists*. Oxford, Oxford University Press.

nine

Enhancing working conditions

*Sigrún Gunnarsdóttir and
Anne Marie Rafferty*

Introduction

Research in the manufacturing and retail sectors has demonstrated a link between human resource management (HRM) practices and productivity. Researchers have demonstrated that organizations that promote practices that encourage workers' abilities, motivation and opportunities achieve better outcomes. Within the health sector similar links have been proposed and used to explain variation in health outcomes and performance between organizations (West et al. 2002). The precise mechanisms responsible for improved outcomes differ. West et al. proposed a model of employee appraisal, training and teamworking to account for variation in outcomes; specifically, sophistication in appraisal and teamworking were associated with lower mortality rates. American research has identified other HRM factors as being important in explaining variation; namely nurse staffing levels and nurses' educational preparation (Aiken et al. 2002b, 2003). There appears to be a growing consensus that certain HRM practices that incorporate commitment to ensure adequate staffing, investment in training, teamwork, employee autonomy and empowerment are associated with enhanced organizational outcomes and performance.

The purpose of this chapter is to present some key sources of evidence on the relationship between the quality of working life and its impact upon outcomes for health care workers and patients, where possible. We have deployed a model derived from British research, which links human resource inputs with organizational and patient outcomes, to structure the chapter. In their staff survey for the United Kingdom Healthcare Commission, Michie and West (2002) propose a tripartite model that explores the relationship between the context of work, management of people, staff attitudes and organizational performance. We begin by considering the impact of the work context in terms of workload

and climate, management of people in terms of management and leadership, and staff attitudes. We conclude with the challenges associated with creating healthy environments at work.

Our review focuses mainly on nursing, using it as a probe to track the topics and themes within the evidence. We have adopted this approach largely for pragmatic reasons. First, although the majority of studies focus on nursing, nurses form the largest part of the health care workforce and therefore are likely to influence the experience and quality of care for patients in many significant ways. While there is disagreement about what combination of factors constitutes a perfect system for the quality of working conditions and how this should be defined, there is an emerging consensus on such measures' general effects on outcomes.

In the literature there is still a lively debate between competing perspectives on how such measures operate in practice. One of these is the difference between contingent and universalist models of HRM (Guest et al. 2004). The universalist perspective argues that there are a number of human resource practices that, if adopted, will always result in superior performance whatever the context, i.e. the intensity with which human resource practices are adopted has greater effect than organizational fit (Huselid and Becker 1997). In contrast, the contingency model argues that a distinct combination will work only under specified conditions or with specific groups of staff. We argue that this applies not only to groups of staff, but to different health systems and resource environments in which health care is delivered. There is a need for research that focuses upon a multiprofessional agenda and/or explores the extent to which the attributes and benefits of high-quality working environments are shared across all groups of workers or favour one group more than another.

The next section maps out the key factors in the research literature that are thought to impact on better quality working conditions and environments and their various effects on outcomes. The literature is voluminous and complex, often revealing large areas of overlap in topic but little consistency in the use of terminology. We present the map of topics and terms to reveal the topography of the research landscape.

Desirable designs

Much of the research literature on the design features of 'healthy' and high-performing organizations is based on observed associations. It is strong on identifying the defining characteristics of those organizations and their desirable qualities. Much less is known about the causal mechanisms and how the process of organizational transformation through the introduction of appropriate interventions can best be understood. We know that designing a healthy work organization in health care can deliver a range of organizational benefits in terms of patient outcomes, finance and a healthy workforce. In order to foster a healthy workforce the workplace must minimize hazards, employ ergonomic design and provide working conditions that enhance job satisfaction and well-being (Sainfort et al. 2001). A healthy organization can be viewed as one where people are perceived to be nurtured and developed as assets, commonly referred

to as high in human capital (Noer 1998). A successful organization is characterized by excellence, innovation, resilience and optimism, with leaders intent on listening and committed to ethical values and open discussion, and where the labour–management relations are marked by mutual responsibility, flexibility and the belief in doing meaningful work (Rosen 1998).

Interest in healthy working environments has been stimulated not only by the competitive nature of the health care labour markets mediated through the process of mobility and migration but also by the alleged adverse effects of restructuring operations involving different degrees of re-engineering. Such restructuring is recognized as a common phenomenon worldwide, often involving the reduction of staff numbers as a response to reduced funding. Although clearly not a universal symptom of all health systems, where it does occur it is regarded as leading to increased stress among staff and management, with attendant risks for the quality of the patient care provided. Commentators have noted that enhancing the health of the working environment in health care requires due attention to workloads, staffing, adequate administration support, professional relations, autonomy and organizational climate when designing the system (Laschinger and Havens 1997; Aiken et al. 2002a).

Evidence on the well-being of health care workers indicates that stress and job dissatisfaction are increasing among doctors, nurses and other health care groups. These have been linked with poorer quality clinical care (Arnetz 1999; Aiken et al. 2001). Research has also shown that health service workers experience more psychological distress than the general population (Harrison and Loiselle 2002). However, this requires attention to the contexts in which such studies are conducted. The most recent survey of staff in the British NHS provides some grounds for optimism, as the study indicates that the quality of working life is improving and the majority of NHS staff report being happy with their jobs and with their managers (Department of Health 2004).

Much of the research reflects the priorities and practices of high-income countries. We argue in support of the contingency model that there is likely to be a hierarchy of HRM interventions that apply to different countries with different health care systems, resource levels and financial management regimes. In considering the material generated by the case studies undertaken for this volume, it is clear that many health systems are not in a position to implement even a proportion, let alone all, of the measures that could lead to optimal performance. Some are struggling with very basic resource issues around remuneration rates and weak professional organization overall. Issues involving burnout and resilience may assume greater importance in countries and systems that have been under consistently higher levels of stress and pressure over time.

Radical restructuring of health economies in CEE and the consequent disruption arising from the breakdown of public revenues and taxes, for example, have impacted adversely on the health of the populations and health care workers more generally (Afford 2003). At the macro level, decentralization, privatization and restructuring of primary care have changed the payment and provision arrangements for care. Job security has suffered as CEE countries in transition attempt to harmonize their practices with those of the EU (Afford 2003). Assertions that staffing levels are excessive and that the motivation and quality of staff are central to the success of reforms are not matched by careful consideration of

the reform strategies' impact on staff and patient outcomes. Unemployment is known to enhance risks of ill health and must be considered in those countries where the policy objective is to move from less human- to more capital-intensive forms of service delivery. This is a significant feature of the climate of fear in which health care is often delivered (Afford 2003). Indeed, the fear of unemployment in some countries has led to staff working excessively long hours to cover workloads and a culture of 'presenteeism': turning up for work when ill to avoid the risk of being laid off.

The limits to policy transfer between countries mean that often policies require tailoring in an iterative, reflective and mutually accommodating manner, taking account of cultural specificity.

Quality of work environment

Although threats from physical environmental hazards at work are ever present, in health care the social and psychological aspects of the working environment pose some of the greatest challenges to improving the health and quality of work life for health care workers. A healthy physical work environment is one without distracting and unpleasant working conditions, such as noise, slipperiness, cold, heat, inadequate lighting and odour, that prevents unnecessarily taxing bodily postures and movements and that enables the performance of tasks without unnecessary effort. Ergonomic conditions should provide employees with optimal conditions to carry out the tasks for which they have been trained (Schabracq and Cooper 1996). These circumstances are more likely to be seen where there is: scope to exercise control over work and to demonstrate the ability to use one's skills; stimulating work; latitude to take decisions as appropriate; interaction with others; and a supportive climate (Marmot and Wilkinson 2000).

Alongside the social factors, psychological factors at work have been found to be significant contributors to (especially cardiovascular) health, as demonstrated by one of the leading organizational studies that generated the demand–control–support model (Karasek and Theorell 1990). Changes in the physical settings in which health care are delivered, such as the use of telematics, may generate new and unintended stresses and thus hazards for workers' health. Increasing the pace of health care delivery in the face of demands for greater productivity, with stresses induced by driving up standards within a performance culture, can impact on different levels of workers in different ways. Bullying and harassment by managers, for example, can be exacerbated by a culture based on the pursuit of unattainable targets (Institute for Employment Studies 2004).

Health and social care workers compared

The demographic structure and composition of the workforce can impact on the quality of working life. For example, women are much more likely to be part-time workers, especially in countries such as the Netherlands and the

United Kingdom. This has significant implications for accessing training and for the process of cascading information within the workplace (European Commission 2004), and social care workers face a number of specific risks compared to workers in other sectors. One study on work and health in the EU reported that the number of workers in health and social care who reported that their health was at risk (32%) was two-thirds that of construction workers (49%), a group recognized to be at high risk (European Commission 2004). Health and social care workers had among the highest rates of sickness absence (European Commission 2004). One reason is that these workers are among the most likely to undertake shift and night work, exceeded only by the hotel and catering industries. They also report moderately high levels of exposure to direct risk of injury (8%) but have among the highest reported levels of satisfaction concerning their information about the risks they face at work.

Health and social care workers have some of the highest reported levels of musculoskeletal problems, especially backache (40%), and a perceived risk of skin problems, respiratory problems or allergies attributable to work. Health and social care workers had the highest reported incidence of physical violence and intimidation (European Commission 2004), as well as moderately high levels of sexual discrimination and unwanted sexual attention. The EU has sought to ensure minimum safeguards and standards for working conditions, such as the WTD (European Union 1993).

Context: workload and climate

Health care facilities are treating patients who stay for shorter periods, are more ill and receive technologically more intensive health care, at the same time as staff numbers are being reduced. Accordingly, health care personnel, particularly those working long hours or rotating shifts, are at greater risk of poor psychological well-being, ill health and job dissatisfaction (Petterson and Arnetz 1998). High workload and inappropriate staffing mixes are among the factors contributing to adverse events and increased readmission rates, with evidence that overstretched nurses pose a serious threat to patient safety (Aiken et al. 2002b).

An increasing pace of organizational change in some countries also contributes to increased workload and the potential for stress. There is evidence that major downsizing is associated with an increase in ill health and sickness absence among the employees who keep their jobs (Vahtera and Kivimaki 2004). As the Karasek (1979) model suggests, job control and social support at work offer increasingly important means for health care workers to buffer high demands. Professional autonomy and the social aspects of the health care work environment are of prime importance but it is likely that a managerial hierarchy is at work creating the conditions for quality. Efforts to create a better work environment must include better staffing decisions, better communication and teamwork and safe working environments that facilitate healthy choices, supported by adequate resources (Baumann and Brien-Pallas 2001). Staffing, support, intelligent use of feedback systems to manage creatively and redeploy staff, size and stability are all important. Some of the key contextual factors associated with

creating the conditions for quality in the working environment are summarized in Table 9.1.

The psychosocial work environment

The Karasek model of demand and control at work proposes that psychological strain does not result from a single aspect of the work environment. Instead, it is the combined effects of the demands of work situations and the scope of decision-making available to the worker for meeting the demand. According to this model, exposure to an adverse psychosocial environment characterized by high job demands and low control leads to sustained stress, with long-term consequences for health. In contrast, high degrees of autonomy and control, reasonable levels of demands and social support from managers and colleagues give rise to job satisfaction and well-being. Karasek's findings have been confirmed by other research showing a relationship between high strain, stress, low control and job dissatisfaction (Petterson and Arnetz 1998). High job demands are associated with increased risk of psychiatric disorders for both men and women, whereas a high level of social support protects mental health in both men and women (Stansfeld et al. 1997). On the other hand, self-rated health, depression, anxiety, chronic fatigue and reported absenteeism are associated with low control and low levels of social support at work (Godin and Kittel 2004).

The demand, control and support theory can be used to structure a dialogue between managers, unions and employees and offers a valuable framework for

Table 9.1 Work context and conditions for quality

Dimension	Conditions for quality for staff and patients
Organizational climate	Motivating climate Service climate Safety climate Cross-disciplinary collaboration Organizational trust
Senior management leadership	Powerful Visionary Supportive Value-driven Builds trust, collaboration, commitment and open communication
Working hours	Adequate periods of rest Maximum limit for working hours Limited duration for periods of night work Appropriate protection for shift workers
Work–life balance	Family friendliness Possibility to work flexible hours Options to vary own work schedule Balance in demand and control at work

designing a healthy work environment, underpinning a positive work–life balance. Job control, demand, pace and hierarchical relations are all important.

In a recent European survey of health and work in different employment sectors, health and social care workers had the highest reported levels of unforeseen interruptions at work (European Commission 2004). However, this is counterbalanced by moderately high levels of discretion in choosing or changing the order of tasks. Health and social care workers also constituted the highest percentage (37%) of workers reporting their health as being at risk due to stress, irritability or anxiety attributable to work (European Commission 2004). While they appear to have confidence that their skills match the demands of their jobs (82%), their reported rates of stress, depression or anxiety caused, or made worse, by work are second only to those working in education (European Commission 2004). Overall, a moderate number of health and social care workers reported a long-standing health problem or disability attributable to a work-related disease (European Commission 2004).

Social connectedness in organizations

Social connectedness affects our lives in the most profound way. The support of colleagues and superiors has an important impact on the quality of life at work. Social support and social cohesion are related to the concept of social capital. This is defined as representing the degree of social cohesion that exists in a community, referring to the processes that: give rise to networks, norms and social trust; facilitate coordination and cooperation for mutual benefit (Putnam 2000); and act as 'networks together with shared norms, values and understandings that facilitate co-operation within or among groups' (OECD 2001). Social capital is a relational concept shared by a group, is produced by societal investments of time and effort and is a product of inherited culture and norms of behaviour. The term social capital is related further to constructs such as collective efficacy, psychological sense of community, neighbourhood cohesion, community competence and trust; all of which may be viewed as both sources and outcomes of social capital (Lochner et al. 2003).

Social capital can play an important role in communities and organizations where collaboration, shared information and networking are encouraged. One can posit that social capital is a resource that reflects the character of social relations within organizations. It can facilitate successful collective action and be looked on as the glue that binds employees to one another and creates bonds of loyalty and commitment between employers and employees. When an organization is strong in social capital its members share resilience and trust, linking the organization and its employees. The promotion of stability and sociability is one of the methods that can build and maintain social capital within organizations, while short-term arrangements, performance-based pay for individuals and downsizing may be associated with loss of social capital (Leana and Van Buren 2000).

Communication and teamwork

Collaboration, information sharing and networking are fundamental components of working life. Multidisciplinary teams are increasingly used to widen the range of skills and thereby enhance quality of care. Blending diverse values, abilities and perceived authority in the light of differences in history and professionalism can make teamwork a challenging, yet rewarding, task for professionals and leaders (Rice 2000). However, multidisciplinary teamwork is a complex and multifaceted process and it has been suggested that it may be more useful to focus on the characteristics of interpersonal behaviours that facilitate effective interaction and decision-making, rather than retaining a restricted focus on team behaviour. Teams need leaders to pull their members together, provide them with a common purpose and develop their skills, expectations and patterns of learning (Firth-Cozens and Mowbray 2001). The importance of these issues is highlighted by a recent review by the Institute of Medicine (2004) that identified health care professionals' need for better training to promote and support interdisciplinary collaboration and teamwork.

Management and leadership

The dynamics of the health care environment demand powerful, visionary and supportive leaders to help organizations through times of change and meet new demands for long-term success. Successful organizations have a leadership style that is value driven and builds trust, collaboration, motivation and commitment (Pendleton and King 2002; De-Geest et al. 2003). Leadership is not passive but results from a working relationship between the leader and group members, where behaviour and situations are important. A leader's empowering behaviour influences employees' perceptions of formal and informal power and is related to job satisfaction and performance (Morrison and Jones 1997). The theory of organizational empowerment implies that health care leaders must understand the dynamics of the system in which they are working, and the connections between actions and consequences, demonstrate commitment to their team, establish fair rules and ensure that others perceive their actions to be trustworthy. Health leaders must create open channels of communication and actively empower and enable others to take action towards achieving the shared vision (Stein and Kanter 1993).

The difference between management and leadership is understood thus: management controls people by pushing them in the right direction; leadership motivates them by satisfying basic human needs. Systems and structures should facilitate the completion of routine jobs, day after day, while achieving grand visions and occasional bursts of energy when required. Motivation and inspiration energize people to satisfy their needs for achievement, a sense of belonging, recognition, self-esteem, control over their life and the ability to live up to their ideals (Kotter 1998). Recognizing, rewarding and celebrating accomplishment is a critical leadership skill and perhaps the most underused motivational tool. Recognition of achievement is important when implementing change; it

brings the change cycle to its logical conclusion and motivates people to attempt change in the future (Kanter 2000).

Transformational leadership processes inspire a shared vision and enable others to act. Such leaders motivate others to do more than they originally intended or even thought possible, while helping to handle stress better by transforming personal concerns into efforts and providing innovative solutions. On the other hand, transactional leaders depend on rules to maintain and control the system and are less likely to help followers to cope with stressful situations. Transformational leaders achieve superior results by employing one or more of the following four components: idealized influence, inspiration, intellectual stimulation and individualized consideration. These processes correlate with job satisfaction, reduced levels of burnout, productivity and organizational commitment (Bass 1998), and are positively related to empowerment (Morrison and Jones 1997).

Health care is a knowledge-intensive process in which learning is an important resource. Freedom and facilitative working conditions are essential for the efficient performance of creative knowledge workers (Drucker 1999). In order to accomplish this, leaders must build organizations that help people to strengthen their competence, creativity and commitment, so that they are excited about their work, take pride in their accomplishments and facilitate their colleagues to do the same (Rosen 1998). Various strategies can be implemented to promote the conditions for quality in the workplace, some of which are summarized in Table 9.2.

Motivation

Motivation is a cyclical process involving efforts to satisfy unmet needs. These needs are related to different aspects of human nature, such as self-actualization, self-esteem, social belonging, safety and security and physiological needs (Longest and Rakick 2002). A confusing diversity of theories has been developed to explain this concept but a widely used definition is the factors influencing individuals to attend to and act upon information and knowledge. Motivation is a key determinant of the individual health care worker's performance, but is only one of many variables affecting performance. Physical and mental abilities, the nature of the work environment and appropriate equipment and pleasant surroundings facilitate high levels of performance. However, acceptable levels of performance will be achieved only if managers can motivate people to work towards achieving organizational objectives (Longest and Rakick 2002).

The term 'psychological contract' refers to the link between organizational objectives and personal motivation. This is usually unwritten and unspoken but represents a set of mutual expectations and belief that a person's work will fulfil his or her needs for self-actualization, achievement, recognition and personal relationships in the workplace. When organizational changes occur, psychological contracts come to the fore and increasingly are seen as short- rather than long-term relationships between the organization and the employee. Short-term contracts, in which individuals are asked to accept risk and uncertainty,

Table 9.2 Management of people and conditions for quality

Dimension	Conditions for quality for staff and patients
Support from superior	Create listening posts Open communication Articulate shared goals Build coalitions Recognition Deliver confidence Enable staff to participate in decision-making
Job design	Adequate workload Control over work Ability to use skills Appropriate decision in latitude Interaction with others
Teamworking	Shared goals Leadership Clear structure Shared information Collaboration Mutual respect Trust
Personal development plans	Adequate career development Access to continued education Access to training programmes Access to formal and informal education

may lead to an increased sense of powerlessness, loss of trust and diminution of loyalty towards the organization (Brooks 1999; Beardwell and Holden 2001).

Empowerment

Empowerment is a mantra of management and a central concept in contemporary health promotion. It is regarded as both a means and an end in itself (Wallerstein 1999). Empowerment is an intrinsic motivating factor, often construed as being reflected in four factors reflecting an individual's orientation to his or her work role: meaning, competence, self-determination and impact (Conger and Kanungo 1988). Structural empowerment is a theory that is particularly relevant here. This maintains that those work environments that provide access to information, resources and support, with the opportunity to learn and develop, enable employees to accomplish their work more effectively (Kanter 1979).

Individuals' jobs provide formal position power, while the extent of their network of relationships in the organization reflects informal power. Formal power comes from jobs that afford flexibility and visibility and are relevant to

key organizational processes. Informal power evolves from a person's network of alliances with sponsors, peers and subordinates both within and outside the organization. The extent of formal and informal power influences the degree of access to empowerment structures. Nurses' perceptions of access to empowerment structures at work have been identified as being associated with mental ill health, ineffectiveness and three aspects of burnout: level of emotional exhaustion, depersonalization and personal accomplishment (Hatcher and Laschinger 1996).

Shared governance has been advocated as a successful means to empower health care professionals, characterized by a dynamic process that gives health care workers greater authority, control over their work and active participation in the decision-making process. Empowerment is facilitated by a leader who constructs an organizational structure that fits the organizational culture and persists after the individual leader leaves the organization. This process requires the leader to have deep insight coupled with a high level of commitment, moving away from hierarchical, command and control relationships (Porter-O'Grady 2001).

There is also evidence that shared governance has a positive effect on outcomes for the organization, its staff and its patients. There is evidence that it increases job satisfaction, thus reducing costs through reduced recruitment and improved productivity (O'May and Buchan 1999).

Autonomy

Professional autonomy is closely linked to a range of other concepts, such as self-governance, capacity, competence, decision-making, critical reflection, freedom and self-control. It correlates with educational level (Ballou 1998). By definition, worker autonomy means the freedom to act on what one knows (Kramer and Schmalenberg 1993). It is closely linked with self-esteem and the earning of respect (Marmot 2003; Sennett 2003) and contributes to the well-being and performance of health care professionals (Kramer and Schmalenberg 2003).

But autonomy does not mean the ability to do anything one wishes. It implies that discretion is used to pursue the interests of the patient within a framework of professional accountability (Wade 1999). There is evidence that nurse autonomy, linked to control over resources, effective nurse–doctor teamwork and the scope for decision-making, is associated with nurse-assessed quality of care and satisfaction (Rafferty and Ball 2001). However, changes in the delivery of health care can (positively and negatively) affect professional autonomy, and thus staff and patient outcomes (Williams and Konrad 2001).

Trust

Trust is a precious but fragile commodity, susceptible to erosion at times of rapid change. Organizational turmoil creates the risk of disengagement and dysfunctional behaviour, characterized by impaired communication and decreased

respect for others (Kanter 2003), with adverse consequences for quality of care. Organizational trust requires confidence in the words and actions of other people.

Leaders and managers at all levels are key stewards of organizational trust, through their ability to influence others' concerns and values (Firth-Cozens 2004). Building the trust and commitment necessary for organizational success requires the creation of listening posts, open lines of communication, shared, articulate goals, the building of coalitions and acknowledgement of others. Leaders face the task of building collaborative relationships based on trust, listening to staff and enabling them to participate in decision-making (Kanter 2003). Trust is especially important for patients, who should be confident that any errors will be dealt with sensitively and fairly (Firth-Cozens 2004).

A supportive working environment

The working environment should ensure job satisfaction and a manageable workload, avoid the risk of burnout and minimize staff turnover (Table 9.3).

Job satisfaction

There is growing evidence of the association between health care workers' job satisfaction and the outcome of health care. Stress and illness contribute to poor

Table 9.3 Factors supporting positive attributes in health professionals

Dimension	Supporting factors
Job satisfaction	Support from superiors Communication with peers Autonomy
Avoidance of burnout	Support from colleagues Adequate demands Autonomy Control over practice
Reduced intention to leave	Job commitment Supportive climate at work Strong senior management Teamwork Control over practice Access to resources
Manageable work pressure	Balanced demand and control at work Social support at work Flexible hours Influence over own work schedule

clinical judgement, risking harm to patients; stressed workers are vulnerable to injury and have a higher absentee rate (Marmot and Feeney 1995). A review of psychological well-being and job satisfaction's contribution to performance concluded that 'happy' workers perform better (Judge and Bono 2001). Job satisfaction is defined as a pleasurable or positive emotional state resulting from the appraisal of one's job or job experience (Locke 1976). Job satisfaction among nurses has been reported to be low in Canada, Germany, the United Kingdom and the United States (Aiken et al. 2001) but high in Sweden (Petterson and Arnetz 1998). Interventions to improve job satisfaction include policies designed to increase the scope to influence decisions, promoting participatory management, enhancing cooperation between staff and ensuring the availability of resources (Aiken et al. 2001).

Burnout

Burnout is a term used to describe emotional exhaustion in the face of a demanding environment that gives rise to negative attitudes to one's job and to those with whom one works, whether patients or colleagues, leading to a non-productive working relationship (Maslach and Glodberg 1998). Key characteristics of burnout are overwhelming exhaustion, frustration, anger and cynicism (Leiter and Maslach 2001). The emergence of burnout can be linked to factors related to the concept of organizational empowerment (Laschinger 1996) and the demand–control–support model (Karasek and Theorell 2000). Consequently, it reflects both individual and organizational factors.

Maslach has developed a multidimensional model of burnout, operationalized to create an instrument to measure it, based on three core dimensions: emotional exhaustion, depersonalization and reduced personal accomplishment (Maslach and Jackson 1996). Studies among nurses and doctors that have used the Maslach framework have linked burnout to lack of social support from colleagues, high work demands and inadequate autonomy and control over practice (Jamal and Baba 2000).

One of the first steps in reducing the risk of burnout is to be aware of the importance of managing stress in the workplace. This involves designing working environments that balance workload and social support at all levels, reducing job demands and increasing control, drawing on the demand–control–support model (Karasek and Theorell 1990). Career counselling and mentorship systems can also contribute, with some evidence to support the use of individual cognitive–behavioural techniques (Schaufeli and Buunk 1996).

Resilience and hardiness

The concepts of resilience and hardiness have been related to well-being at work, particularly among health care workers experiencing high stress levels. Although individual characteristics, they are shaped, positively or negatively, by the work environment. At an individual level, resilience can be defined as a dynamic process of adaptation to a risk setting (Olsson and Bond 2003). The

concept of resilience is related to constructs that conceptualize aspects of psychological well-being such as a sense of coherence, locus of control, self-efficacy, hardiness and learned resourcefulness. Hardiness is defined as personality characteristics comprising the dimensions of commitment, control and challenge. Commitment is the capacity to be involved in activities such as work, family and interpersonal relationships. Control is the degree to which individuals believe they can influence life events. Challenge is the positive anticipation of change, where change is perceived as exciting and contributing to personal growth. A working environment that favours the development of resilience and hardiness fosters the organization's ability to respond to changing circumstances.

Conclusion

As this chapter indicates, great challenges lie ahead for health care providers, managers and policy-makers in Europe. A major study undertaken recently showed how working conditions exert a significant impact upon nurses' intentions to leave their jobs and significant variation in the experience and expression of these factors across different European countries (Hasselhorn et al. 2003). Yet efficiency gains have often been won at the cost of a deterioration in working conditions (Hasselhorn et al. 2003). The intention to leave increased under poor organizational leadership and clinical management, a phenomenon noted particularly in Belgium and the United Kingdom. Significantly, nurses' satisfaction increased with higher status, greater job control and a sense of being valued in the organization. Nurses from Belgium, Germany, Slovakia and the United Kingdom reported higher quality leadership than nurses from Italy and Poland. Social support, from both immediate supervisors and colleagues, was an important predictor of intention to leave, with the lowest values reported from Italy and the highest from the Netherlands. Rates of burnout were high in all countries and job insecurity was greatest in Poland and Slovakia.

Looking ahead, perhaps the single most dramatic factor to impact upon the working environment is the WTD. This has wide-ranging ramifications for the organization and content of the work of all members of the health care team, with implications for the quality of patient care. The major changes required in operating systems have the potential to open up opportunities for experimentation in ways of working but also generate anxiety about sustaining continuity and quality.

Reviews of factors associated with healthier organizations identify the importance of a combination of employee development and training, participation and empowerment, information sharing and appropriate compensation systems. A study (Guest et al. 2000) examining the ways in which human resource practices might impact on performance seeks to advance the debate from whether they have an impact to understanding how they do. We argue that for people to perform above minimal requirements they must have the ability (the requisite knowledge and skills), motivation and opportunity to deploy their skills.

Human resource policies should turn these three elements into action, with

managers having a key role in implementing policy and practice. Employee motivation is a key intervening variable in producing higher performance and highlights the manager's crucial role in motivating staff. However, in order to apply these lessons to different contexts those concerned must take account of a complex range of historical, socioeconomic and political factors, as well as the cultural specifics that impact on countries at different times. Furthermore, given that health care is a highly gendered activity, it is important to monitor access to benefits in the workplace to ensure that everyone can share in them. It is clear from the available evidence that investing in people is a win–win situation for the organization, patients, practitioners and policy-makers alike.

References

Afford, C.W. (2003) *Corrosive reform: failing health systems in Eastern Europe*. Geneva, ILO Socio-Economic Security Programme.

Aiken, L.H., Clarke, S.P. and Sloane, D.M. (2002a) Hospital staffing, organizational support, and quality of care: cross-national findings. *International Journal for Quality in Health Care*, **14**(1): 5–13.

Aiken, L.H. et al. (2001) Nurses' reports on hospital care in five countries. *Health Affairs*, **20**(3): 43–53.

Aiken, L.H. et al. (2002b) Hospital nurse staffing and patient mortality, nurse burnout and job dissatisfaction. *Journal of the American Medical Association*, **288**: 1987–93.

Aiken, L.H. et al. (2003) Educational levels of hospital nurses and surgical patient mortality. *Journal of the American Medical Association*, **290**(12): 1617–23.

Arnetz, B. (1999) Staff perception of the impact of health care transformation on quality of care. *International Journal for Quality in Health Care*, **11**(4): 345–51.

Ballou, K.A. (1998) Commonalties and contradictions in research on human resource management and performance. Paper presented to the Academy of Management Conference, Seattle, August 2003.

Bass, B.M. (1998) *Transformational leadership*. Totowa, NJ, Lawrence Erlbaum Associates.

Baumann, A. and Brien-Pallas, L.O. (2001) *Commitment and care: the benefits of a healthy workplace for nurses, their patients and the system. A policy synthesis*. Canadian Health Services Research Foundation, The Change Foundation.

Beardwell, I. and Holden, L. (2001) *Human resource management. A contemporary approach*. Harlow, Pearson Education.

Brooks, I. (1999) *Organisational behaviour. Individuals, groups and the organisation*. London, Financial Times Pitman Publishing.

Conger, J. and Kanungo, R. (1988) The empowerment process: integrating theory and practice. *Academy of Management Journal*, **13**(3): 471–82.

De-Geest, S. et al. (2003) Transformational leadership: worthwhile investment! *European Journal of Cardiovascular Nursing*, **2**: 3–5.

Department of Health (2004) *NHS National Staff Survey 2003*. London, Department of Health and Commission for Health Improvement.

Drucker, P.F. (1999) *Management challenges for the 21st century*. New York, Harper Business.

European Commission (2004) *Work and health in the EU. A statistical portrait. Data 1994–2002. Eurostat. Theme 3. Population and social conditions*. Luxembourg, Office for Official Publications of the European Communities Health.

European Union (1993) Council Directive 93/104/EC of 23 November 1993 concerning certain aspects of the organisation of working time. *Official Journal of the European Communities*, L307, 13.**12**: 18.

Firth-Cozens, J. (2004) Organisational trust: the keystone to patient safety. *Quality and Safety in Health Care*, **13**(1): 56–61.

Firth-Cozens, J. and Mowbray, D. (2001) Leadership and the quality of care. *Quality in Health Care*, **10**(suppl. II): i3–i7.

Godin, I. and Kittel, F. (2004) Differential economic stability and psychosocial stress at work: associations with psychosomatic complaints and absenteeism. *Social Science and Medicine*, **58**: 1543–53.

Guest, D., Conway, N. and Dewe, P. (2004) Using sequential tree analysis to search for 'bundles' of HR practices. *Human Resources Management Journal*, **14**: 1.

Guest, D. et al. (2000) *Employee relations, HRM and business performance: an analysis of the 1998 Workplace Employee Relations Survey*. London, Institute of Personnel and Development.

Harrison, M. and Loiselle, C. (2002) Hardiness, work support and psychological distress among nursing assistants and registered nurses in Quebec. *Journal of Advanced Nursing*, **38**(6): 584–91.

Hasselhorn, H.M., Tackenberg, P. and Muller, B.H. (2003) *Working conditions and intent to leave the profession among nursing staff in Europe*. Report No. 7. Saltsa, Joint Programme for Working Life Research in Europe.

Hatcher, S. and Laschinger, H.K.S. (1996) Staff nurses' perceptions of job empowerment and level of burnout: a test of Kanter's theory of structural power in organizations. *Canadian Journal of Nursing Administration*, **9**(2): 74–94.

Huselid, M.A. and Becker, B.E. (1997) The impact of high performance work systems. Implementation effectiveness and alignment with strategy on shareholders' wealth. *Academy of Management Best Papers Proceedings*, 144–8.

IES (2004) *Healthy attitudes: quality of working life in the London NHS, 2000–2002*. London, Institute for Employment Studies.

IOM (2004) *Keeping patients safe. Transforming the work environment of nurses*. Washington, DC, National Academics Press, Institute of Medicine of the National Academies.

Jamal, M. and Baba, V.V. (2000) Job stress and burnout among Canadian managers and nurses: an empirical examination. *Canadian Journal of Pubic Health*, **91**(6): 454–8.

Judge, T.A. and Bono, J.E. (2001) Relationship of core self-evaluation traits – self-esteem, generalized self-efficacy, locus of control and emotional stability – with job satisfaction and job performance: a meta-analysis. *Journal of Applied Psychology*, **86**(1): 80–92.

Kanter, R.M. (1979) Power failure in management circuits. *Harvard Business Review*, **57**(4): 65–75.

Kanter, R.M. (2000) The enduring skills of change leaders. *Ivey Business Journal*, **64**(5): 32–6.

Kanter, R.M. (2003) The confidence factor – an overview. *The Edge, Economic and Social Research Council*, **14**: 4–7.

Karasek, R. (1979) Job demands, job decision, latitude and mental strain: implications for job redesign. *Administration Science Quarterly*, **24**: 285–311.

Karasek, R. and Theorell, T. (1990) *Healthy work: stress, productivity and the reconstruction of working life*. New York, Basic Books.

Karasek, R. and Theorell, T. (2000) The demand–control–support CVD. *Occupational Medicine: State of the Art Reviews*, **15**(1): 78–83.

Kotter, J.P. (1998) *John P. Kotter on what leaders really do*. Boston, Harvard Business Review Book.

Kramer, M. and Schmalenberg, C. (1993) Learning from success: autonomy and empowerment. *Nursing Management*, **24**(5): 58–64.

Kramer, M. and Schmalenberg, C. (2003) Magnet hospital staff nurses describe clinical autonomy. *Nursing Outlook*, **51**(1): 13–19.

Laschinger, H. (1996) A theoretical approach to studying work empowerment in nursing:

a review of studies testing Kanter's theory of structural power in organizations. *Nursing Administration Quarterly*, **20**(2): 25–41.

Laschinger, H. and Havens, D.S. (1997) The effect of workplace empowerment on staff nurses' occupational mental health and work effectiveness. *Journal of Nursing Administration*, **27**(6): 42–50.

Leana, C. and Van Buren, H. (2000) Eroding organizational social capital among US firms: the price of job instability. *In*: Burke, R. and Cooper, C., eds, *The organization in crisis: downsizing, restructuring, and privatization*. Oxford, Blackwell.

Leiter, P. and Maslach, C. (2001) Burnout and quality in a sped-up world. *Journal for Quality and Participation*, Summer: 48–51.

Lochner, K. et al. (2003) Social capital and neighborhood mortality rates in Chicago. *Social Science and Medicine*, **56**(8): 1797–805.

Locke, E.A. (1976) The nature and causes of job satisfaction. *In*: Dunnette, M.D., ed., *Handbook of industrial and organizational psychology*. Chicago, Rand McNally College.

Longest, B.B. and Rakick, J.S. (2002) Motivation. *In*: Longest, B.B., Rakich, J.S. and Darr, K., eds, *Managing health services organizations and systems*. Baltimore: Health Professions Press.

Marmot, M. (2003) Self-esteem and health: autonomy, self-esteem, and health are linked. *British Medical Journal*, **327**: 574–5.

Marmot, M. and Feeney, A. (1995) Sickness absence as a measure of health status and functioning: from the UK Whitehall II study. *Journal of Epidemiology and Community Health*,**49**: 124–30.

Marmot, M. and Wilkinson, R.G. (2000) *Social determinants of health*. Oxford, Oxford University Press.

Maslach, C. and Goldberg, J. (1998) Prevention of burnout. *Applied and Preventive Psychology*, **7**: 63–74.

Maslach, C. and Jackson, S.E. (1996) *Maslach Burnout Inventory manual*, 3rd edn. Palo Alto, CA, Consulting Psychologists Press.

Michie, S. and West, M.A. (2002) *Measuring staff management and human resource performance in the NHS*. Document prepared for the Commission for Health Improvement. Birmingham, Aston Business School.

Morrison, R.S. and Jones, L. (1997) The relation between leadership style and empowerment on job satisfaction of nurses. *Journal of Nursing Administration*, **27**(5): 27–34.

Noer, D. (1998) Layoff survivor sickness: what it is and what to do about it. *In*: Gowing, M., Kraft, J. and Quick, J., eds, *The new organization reality. Downsizing, restructuring, and revitalization*. Washington, DC, American Psychological Association.

OECD (2001) *The well-being of nations: the role of human and social capital*. Paris: OECD.

Olsson, C. and Bond, L. (2003) Adolescent resilience: a concept analysis. *Journal of Adolescence*, **26**: 1–11.

O'May, F. and Buchan, J. (1999) Shared governance: a literature review. *International Journal of Nursing Studies*, **36**: 281–300.

Pendleton, D. and King, J.A. (2002) Values and leadership. *British Medical Journal*, **325**: 1352–5.

Petterson, I.L. and Arnetz, B.B. (1998) Psychological stressors and well-being in health care workers: the impact of an intervention program. *Social Science and Medicine*, **47**(11): 1763–72.

Porter-O'Grady, T. (2001) Is shared governance still relevant? *Journal of Nursing Administration*, **31**(10): 468–73.

Putnam, R.D. (2000) *Bowling alone: the collapse and revival of American community*. New York, Simon & Schuster.

Rafferty, A.M. and Ball, J. (2001) Are teamwork and professional autonomy compatible, and do they result in improved hospital care? *Quality in Health Care*, **10**(suppl. II): 32–7.

Rice, A. (2000) Interdisciplinary collaboration in health care: education, practice and research. *National Academies of Practice Forum*, **2**(1): 59–73.

Rosen, R. (1998) Leadership in the new organisation. *In*: Gowing, M., Kraft, J. and Quick, J., eds, *The new organization reality. Downsizing, restructuring, and revitalization.* Washington, DC, American Psychological Association.

Sainfort, F. et al. (2001) Applying quality improvement principles to achieve healthy work organizations. *Joint Commission Journal on Quality Improvement*, **27**: 469–83.

Schabracq, M. and Cooper, C.D. (1996) Work and health psychology: towards a theoretical framework. *In*: Schabracq, M., Cooper, C.D. and Winnubst, J., eds, *Handbook of work and health psychology*. New York, Wiley.

Schaufeli, W. and Buunk, B. (1996) Professional burnout. *In*: Schabracq, M., Cooper, C.D. and Winnubst, J., eds, *Handbook of work and health psychology*. New York, Wiley.

Sennett, R. (2003) *Respect in a world of inequality*. New York, W.W. Norton & Co.

Stansfeld, S.A. et al. (1997) Social support and psychiatric sickness absence: a prospective study of British civil servants. *Psychological Medicine*, **27**: 35–48.

Stein, B. and Kanter, R.M. (1993) Leadership for change: the rest of the story. *Frontiers of Health Service Management*, **10**(2): 28–32.

Vahtera, J. and Kivimaki, M. (2004) Organisational downsizing, sickness absence and mortality: 10-town prospective cohort study. *British Medical Journal*, **328**: 555–9.

Wade, G.H. (1999) Professional nurse autonomy: concept analysis and application to nursing education. *Journal of Advanced Nursing*, **30**(2): 310–18.

Wallerstein, N. (1999) Power between evaluator and community: research relationships within New Mexico's healthier communities. *Social Science and Medicine*, **49**: 39–53.

West, M.A., Borrill, C. and Dawson, J. (2002) The link between the management of employees and patient mortality in acute hospitals. *International Journal of Human Resource Management*, **13**(8): 1299–310.

Williams, E. and Konrad, T. (2001) Understanding physicians' intentions to withdraw from practice: the role of job satisfaction, job stress, mental and physical health. *Health Care Management Review*, **26**(1): 7–19.

chapter ten

Reshaping the regulation of the workforce in European health care systems

Carl-Ardy Dubois, Anna Dixon and Martin McKee

Introduction

The nature of health care as a social and a private good means that it is the subject of intense regulation in most countries (Saltman et al. 2002). Over time, each society has established an array of institutions, laws and rules to regulate the practices of health care workers in the stated interest of protecting the public and ensuring high-quality services. Recently, in the wake of high-profile cases of poor performance and professional misconduct, health policy-makers have increasingly felt the need to strengthen or reform the regulatory mechanisms for the health professions. Yet overregulation can be as great a problem as underregulation, as it inhibits innovation and demotivates professionals.

Regulation is complex, requiring health policy-makers to balance a number of considerations related to the social, political and economic context of health care. This chapter sets out a framework for the analysis of approaches to professional regulation and applies it to the experience of reforming the regulation of doctors in a number of European countries.[1] The chapter aims to identify recent trends in regulatory reforms in order to increase understanding of what constitutes appropriate regulation – that is, how to ensure high standards and effective accountability without adverse effects on efficiency. It is hoped that it will assist policy-makers and regulators to select, from the vast range of options available, an optimal mix of regulatory instruments.[2]

Primarily, the chapter considers regulatory provisions that aim to protect the public from harm and to foster the provision of high-quality and efficient care. It does not deal directly with the regulation of supply, education and labour

relations, as these issues are examined in more detail elsewhere (Chapters 3, 4, 5 and 9). The following section sets out a theoretical framework for examining professional regulation. A number of case studies are presented, and these form the basis for an assessment of the general direction of regulatory reforms and the key strategies that have been used in Europe. These cases suggest that there is a shift towards greater political accountability and micro-regulation. Recent reforms go beyond traditional models based on professional self-regulation. They suggest a continual expansion of regulatory practices, a larger repertoire of policy instruments and increased oversight by external actors.

A framework for analysing regulation in the health labour market

Occupational regulation in health care is nothing new and has been traced back to the earliest records of the healing professions. The legal code of Hammurabi, established in about 2000 BC in Mesopotamia, created a drastic remedy for malpractice: amputation of the surgeon's hand (Hogan 1979; Merry and Crago 2001). Here the primary public purpose of state intervention was to prevent harm from dangerous or unqualified medical practice. From another perspective the Hippocratic oath, originating in Greece in the fifth century BC, was based on the view that medicine is above all a vocation (Jacob 1999). Doctors operate within an ethical tradition and are subject to self-imposed codes of conduct accepted voluntarily by the professions. Regulation of the health care workforce within contemporary societies has evolved to become a complex and polymorphic system with multiple objectives. However, the main dilemmas remain: who should regulate, and how?

Degree of state intervention

Regulation, by its very nature, requires a source of regulatory authority. However, the most appropriate locus of this authority remains the subject of intense debate in the health sector. Consequently professional bodies' degrees of involvement in the regulatory system and the role of external actors, such as state institutions, vary. The extent to which the state intervenes in the practice of medicine can be seen as a continuum from complete professional autonomy and self-determination to direct state control (Figure 10.1). In reality, the state may intervene more in certain aspects of regulation, such as remuneration, than

Figure 10.1 Degree of state intervention in professional regulation.

in others, such as entry criteria, though this has been shown to vary between countries (Moran and Wood 1993).

The view that regulation should be the sole responsibility of the professional group concerned has long been a fundamental aspect of professionalism in medicine (Freidson 1970; Rottenberg 1980). Self-regulation of health professionals is justified on the basis that their services are experience goods and therefore they themselves have more knowledge about the quality and risks of receiving health services than do public authorities and consumers. Because of this information asymmetry between those who practise and those who seek to regulate, professional organizations argue that they are in the best position to ensure quality and prevent public harm.

Another argument in favour of self-regulation is that it is more efficient. Information to set, monitor and enforce standards is more easily acquired. The self-regulators' level of understanding of the professions gives them the flexibility to adapt to changes in practice and make voluntary compliance more likely (Baldwin and Cave 1999). Furthermore, the costs are lower than those that might arise from a more formal legalistic mechanism, and are borne by the profession instead of the government (or taxpayer). Yet the case for self-regulation is not accepted universally.

Economists in particular are wary about the virtues of self-regulation (Chapter 8), and emphasize self-regulation's economic benefits for the professions. As early as 1770, Adam Smith highlighted the ability of crafts to lengthen apprenticeship programmes and limit the number of apprentices per master, thus restraining free competition and ensuring higher earnings for persons in those occupations. Codes of ethics and standards of practice that are designed to ensure that professionals have appropriate competencies, deliver a high-quality service and continue to develop their skills and knowledge are seen as barriers to entry, as they are used to regulate the numbers of practitioners and the conditions under which they can participate in the market (Smith 1970).

More recently, analysis of regulation has observed regulatory capture, whereby the regulator comes to serve the interests of the group regulated rather than those of the public (Gellhorn 1956, 1976; Friedman 1962). *Capture theory* predicts that health professionals will structure regulations to keep out competition and thereby increase their incomes (Moore 1961; Coase 1974; Posner 1974). Such views are also consistent with the rent-seeking interpretation of interest group behaviour in the public choice literature and the economic theory of regulation (Stigler 1971; Becker 1983; Peltzman 1989; Lowenberg and Tinnin 1992; Zhou 1993). These posit that the demand for regulation comes primarily from practitioners looking for protective regulation, such as regulated prices and barriers to entry to the market. As such, regulation originates where supplier interest groups are concentrated and well-organized so that they can lobby effectively to influence the level and content of regulation to their benefit. However, such control may result in regulatory failures, including the creation of monopolies, a scarcity of certain necessary services and inefficiency.

Thus, where regulation is internalized fully by professionals, there is a danger that it will not serve the public interest. External forms of regulation are thus promoted as a means to achieve a better balance between professional and public interests, combat provider monopolies, avoid unjustified restrictions on

competition and prevent restrictions to access. In reality, most self-regulation is supported by a statutory framework – for example, compulsion or licensure powers – with some role for external actors (e.g. governments or statutory bodies).

The extremes of the continuum of state involvement can be characterized by two ideal types: the guild approach and the bureaucratic state approach.

The guild approach

This approach was foreshadowed in the guilds of the Middle Ages, organizations that possessed quasi-governmental authority to regulate their membership, using their monopoly power to decide who could practise, their prices and minimum quality standards (Hollings and Pike-Nase 1997). Although the guilds' authority diminished with the rise of the nation state, national medical societies, established in many countries between the sixteenth and nineteenth centuries, continued to reflect the medieval structures and in many respects still do so today.

Professional associations operate as primary regulatory institutions, benefiting from a triple monopoly: economic (control of recruitment, training and credentialing, protected contractual positions); political (control of the area of expertise, provision of expert guidance for legislators and administrators); and administrative (control of standards of practice, discipline) (Freidson 1994). Their activity emphasizes approaches that regulate new entrants rather than control those already in practice, as reflected in the low number of disciplinary actions in comparison with estimates of the incidence of incompetent practice (Institute of Medicine 1989).

Turf monitoring and turf protection occupy much of the regulatory bodies' energy as the various occupations battle among themselves about which parts of health care fall under their jurisdiction. Historically, professional associations sought to defend their practitioners' interests against irregular healers (Lindemann 1999); today, changes in professional boundaries are viewed as expansions, encroachments and infringements. Such fragmented, competitive and adversarial regulatory activity, based on exclusive occupational domains, is reflected in a high level of compartmentalization of health occupations that leaves little room for collaborative practice.

The bureaucratic state approach

The bureaucratic state approach dates back to the Enlightenment period of the seventeenth and eighteenth centuries, as nation states sought to reduce the powers and privileges of the guilds. This process accelerated in the aftermath of the French Revolution, as most European nations abolished those institutions that were seen as antipathetic to the ideals of egalitarianism and popular sovereignty (Burrage 1990; Bellis 2000).

During the second half of the twentieth century, with the expansion of the welfare state in both western and eastern Europe, this model of regulation

became more commonplace. The steady expansion of bureaucracy is seen as undermining professional sources of power, contributing to the bureaucratization of medicine and proletarianization of health practitioners (Braverman 1974; Larson 1977; Derber 1982). From this bureaucratic state approach, the case for state intervention is set within a welfare maximization framework. The state can legitimately exercise its power as part of its duty to protect the interests of the public as opposed to those of professional elites (Moran 1995). The government takes ultimate responsibility for care delivery and even clinical standards. Bureaucratic mechanisms are used by the state to exert administrative control over professional bodies and even individual practitioners.

Types of regulation

The other main decision for policy-makers is how to regulate. In particular, at what level should regulation be implemented and what tools should be used? The type of regulation can be understood as a continuum from the macro- through the meso- to the micro-level (Figure 10.2).

At one end of the spectrum there are macro forms of regulation. These shape the market for services and the characteristics and conduct of participants (Table 10.1). Regulation of this sort may influence the supply of health workers, control wages and prices, establish levels of services, harmonize qualifications and requirements or set and enforce common standards for practice. Macro-regulation tends to rely on hierarchy (bureaucratic or professional) and a variety of centralized state-run and professional agencies for its implementation. Usually negotiation is centralized (involving the state and organized representatives) and collective decisions are applied to all workers within a defined geographical area (e.g. country, state or region). Regulations are both prescriptive and comprehensive; that is, providing a detailed definition of scope, conditions of practice and codes of conduct under which professionals can be held accountable.

At the other end of the spectrum, micro-regulation focuses on the delivery of services and their outcomes. Regulatory influences are exerted primarily through devolved institutions or independent agencies such as insurance funds, consumer organizations or audit agencies. Instruments such as quality-based contracting are used to create incentives for practitioners to improve their

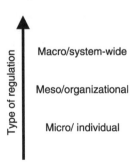

Figure 10.2   Types of regulation.

Table 10.1 Summary of macro- versus micro-regulation

	Macro-regulation	*Micro-regulation*
Purpose	Control of market structure, characteristics and conduct of participants	Management of delivery of services and outcome
Areas of action	Inputs and prices	Outputs and outcomes
Instruments	Numerus clausus Fee schedule Minimum qualifications Standards of practice	League tables Quality-based contracting Continuous quality improvement Risk management Benchmarking, quality circles and standardized treatment procedures
Nature and scope	Prescriptive and comprehensive	Flexible and tailored

performance and adopt the most cost-effective and evidence-based practices. Other interventions, such as continuous quality improvement, risk management, benchmarking, quality circles and standardized treatment procedures, are used *within* organizations to influence the practices of individual health workers. In line with the ideas of NPM (Osborne and Gaebler 1992; Bekke et al. 1996), this approach allows a certain degree of flexibility to tailor the regulations to the circumstances of each organization or group. Often micro-regulation is associated with deregulation and an easing of the degree of prescription imposed by regulations; however, it may instead reflect in practice a process of re-regulation with an increased sophistication of regulatory mechanisms.

The next part of this chapter examines the reforms to professional regulation in Norway, France, the United Kingdom and Germany, highlighting the trends moving away from the traditional approaches set out above or changes in the types of regulation employed.

New modes of regulation of the health labour force in Europe

Within Europe, many countries have introduced reforms to the regulatory environment as it applies to the health workforce. Regulation has proved a highly versatile tool. It has been wielded to: influence the supply of health workers; monitor the process of production; facilitate mobility; stimulate changes in practices; increase responsiveness to consumer needs and expectations; and create incentives for improved performance and higher standards of service. Drawing on empirical data generated from five European case studies prepared for this book, this section explores the extent to which these reforms and concurrent changes in the wider health system have impacted on traditional modes of regulation.

The medical profession in Norway: state capture or cooptive polity?

Governance of the Norwegian health care system and of its workers has been shaped by traditional Nordic decision-making practices. Interest groups, organized around functional sectors, are granted privileges of self-governance but are integrated closely with the state and strongly involved in the process of formulating and implementing health policy (Blom-Hansen 2000; Peters 2000). In this context, the Norwegian medical profession has been able to take advantage of its institutional integration into the state machinery to dominate health care policy and safeguard its self-regulation privileges (Erichsen 1995). Physicians obtained hegemonic positions in shaping health care through their right of veto over policy changes, dominance of formal decision-making arenas and positions in many critical posts in the health bureaucracy.

Even now, the medical profession maintains authority over the context and content of its work and, to a certain extent, health policy-making as a whole. While a substantial part of state authority has been devolved to independent regulatory agencies as part of the structural devolution that took place during the 1990s (Christensen and Lægreid 2001a, b), physicians have remained dominant in the new health care supervisory agencies. For example, at national level the Norwegian Board of Health, an independent technical agency with lead responsibility for the supervision of health services, is heavily dominated by physicians and works in collaboration with 19 county medical officers. At local level, physicians are given primary responsibility for supervising health services and monitoring counties' and municipalities' compliance with national health policy (Feruholmen and Magnussen 2000).

However, recent reforms indicate that the medical profession's efforts to capture the power of the state, so as to maintain its influence over health policy-making, are increasingly counterbalanced by the Norwegian state's concurrent attempts to increase its influence over medical activity through cooptation of the professional elites.

Current developments suggest an active process of reshaping what has been called the 'professional state', creating a new balance of power between the medical profession and the state. Following recent changes in the institutional context, the medical profession has developed a more detached relationship with the state, as reflected in the Norwegian Medical Association's restricted participation in formal policy-making bodies and a reduction in physicians' power of veto. Other examples include recent initiatives involving decentralization and internal market experiments that have created new forms of external influence over medical activity and have coopted professional elites into state structures that control and regulate their peers on behalf of governments at both national and local levels.

Since 1984, municipal councils have been responsible for financing and providing primary health care. By 2001, most GPs (74%) were operating as contractors directly accountable to municipal offices (van den Noord et al. 1998). Consequently, the Norwegian strategy to enhance the quality of health care envisages a leading role for the political and administrative leaders of counties and municipalities (Norwegian Board of Health 2002). In addition, the

Norwegian Directorate for Health and Social Affairs and the Norwegian Centre for Health Technology Assessment (SMM) are developing medical guidelines, quality indicators, medical databases, strategic planning and performance-related budgeting tools; all formal instruments that are designed to reinforce political control over health care professionals.

Thus, although regulation of the Norwegian medical profession still reflects some key features of traditional Scandinavian corporatism, it appears that a reshaping of the corporate order is under way, creating new opportunities for public authorities to oversee professional activity, enforce improvement in quality standards and, more broadly, increase the state's influence over the health policy process.

The case of la médecine libérale in France: self-regulation or a lost legacy?

Despite the long-standing tradition of central state control that characterizes French polity, the French health care system is viewed as one of the most liberal in the world in terms of the autonomy enjoyed by patients and health professionals, particularly physicians (Poullier and Sandier 2000). Under the French model of liberal medicine secured by the *Charte médicale* of 1927, private practice is dominant in ambulatory care and private practitioners are free to set up practice wherever they choose. Doctors' prescriptions are neither monitored nor constrained. Professional status is based primarily on reputation. Physicians are granted considerable autonomy over the content of their work. There is a strong emphasis on professional confidentiality so that physicians are considered to be answerable primarily to their patients and themselves for the quality of their services (Rodwin 1981).

Implicit in this model is the view that self-governance is the preferred regulatory approach and that professional institutions should retain control over key aspects of health care work. Consequently, professional bodies have retained mandates for monitoring the performance and disciplining their members. Efforts to restrict the choice of patients and providers have been strongly and, to a certain extent, successfully resisted. One example is the recent failure to establish GPs as gatekeepers to secondary care (fewer than 1% of doctors signed up to the scheme). However, a closer look at the evolution of the regulation of health professions in France over recent decades suggests a dilution of the legacy of liberal medicine because of significant developments.

First, the French state has been able to tighten its grip over the activity of the health professions through the development of various forms of control and regulation operating at the macro level (Wilsford 1987). Since 1971, the French state has had direct control over the supply of health personnel through a numerus clausus. Through control of education funding, the government has the ability to create national training schemes for the health professions, establish quality norms for educational institutions and influence the location of training and the distribution of specialists in each specialty and region.

Another source of state control comes from contractual agreements between professional trade unions and the government. These agreements, initiated after

the Second World War, define the financial resources available for health care and the maximum fees that physicians may be reimbursed by the sickness funds (Maria and Ostrowski 2003). Since the 1996 Juppé reforms, the French Parliament has held the ultimate responsibility for determining the rate of increase in health care expenditures and setting annual targets for the growth of private practice medical fees and prescriptions.

Second, more recent efforts to improve the efficiency and quality of medical services have targeted the heart of the liberal practice itself, sanctioning prescribing practices and the behaviour of individual professionals at the micro level. The 1996 Juppé Plan introduced provisions for both collective and individual sanctions against overspending physicians. Similar objectives were pursued through mandatory universal practice guidelines known as *références médicales opposables*. These new tools explicitly sought to rationalize medical practices, standardize patient care and limit the unnecessary prescription of redundant and costly drugs, tests and procedures (Durand-Zaleski et al. 1997; Durieux et al. 2000).

New state-controlled bodies have been given new responsibilities for evaluating professional practice and quality assessment. For instance, ANAES (a government agency with statutory authority) has been given a clear mandate to establish the state of knowledge on diagnostic and therapeutic procedures, issue guidelines for clinical practice and provide technical recommendations to sickness funds. ANAES provides support and guidance to the 22 regional associations of independent doctors founded in 1993 to contribute to the improvement of health care quality and evaluate the practice of physicians.

The clinical practice of general practitioners is coming under increasing scrutiny (Maria and Ostrowski 2003). This role has been devolved to counsellor doctors *(médecins-conseils)* employed directly by the medical division of CNAMTS (National Health Insurance Fund for Salaried Employees), who have the right of access to all medical records and data held by local sickness funds. Although access to patient information remains a sensitive issue, the consolidation of all patient reimbursement claims in a single electronic database is proving to be an invaluable tool that enables the counsellor doctors to scrutinize patterns of clinical practice (Or 2002).

In summary, while the medical profession still holds tightly to the principles of liberal medicine, the introduction of a number of new policy tools at both macro and micro levels during successive reforms has extended the state's power and its capacity to exert control while eroding professional independence.

The reform of self-regulation in the United Kingdom: professionally led regulation or managerial dominance?

In contrast to many continental European countries, professions in the United Kingdom have historically developed independently of the state. In line with the guild approach mentioned above, the state-sanctioned model of self-regulation enshrined in the Medical Act of 1858 left the professions considerable authority to set standards for training and practice, control entry to the profession and monitor and enforce standards of practice (Irvine 1997). Responsibility for

ensuring that doctors were performing effectively was the exclusive responsibility of the General Medical Council (GMC) and the Royal Colleges (DoH 1999) until the 1990s.

However, the 1990s saw the emergence of more articulate consumerism in health care, a widespread perception of substantial inefficiencies in the use of health care resources and high-profile examples of clinical practice failures. These created both political and professional momentum for reform of professional regulation (BRI Inquiry Secretariat 1999). In the wake of the Bristol and Shipman cases (the former involving failure to act in response to high death rates among babies undergoing cardiac surgery, the latter a general practitioner convicted of murdering patients using overdoses of morphine), even the survival of the GMC with its system of medical self-regulation was questioned, creating a sense of urgency among medical profession leaders to tackle the perceived failures of self-regulation (CMO Review Group 1995; BMA et al. 1998; Klein 1998; Stacey 2000). A model of professionally led regulation was proposed as an alternative to self-regulation. This still places a strong emphasis on professional bodies' role in setting standards and assuring competency.

New mechanisms are being introduced with the goal of ensuring better monitoring of professional activity. For example, the GMC is developing methods for assessing the performance of allegedly poorly performing doctors (Southgate and Dauphinee 1998) and has introduced a requirement that physicians disclose evidence of inadequate medical practice. The introduction of revalidation for medical practitioners requires all registered doctors to demonstrate periodically that they are up-to-date and fit to practise in their chosen field (Catto 2003). In addition, a number of professional bodies have recently changed their structures and composition, increasing the proportion of lay representatives in order to integrate non-medical input into their decision-making process, making them more transparent and more accountable to the public (Hatch 2001).

Concurrently with these professional initiatives, governance of the health professions has become a highly politicized issue, prompting a wide range of initiatives by successive governments since the late 1980s. The White Paper *Working for Patients* (DoH 1989) introduced the internal market in the British health system; it signalled a greater role for managers in assessing the quality of health care services, a role previously reserved almost exclusively for clinicians. Contracts, and thus the distribution of funds, gave managers potentially strong levers to make professionals take account of specific purchaser or client demands. To some extent, clinical autonomy became circumscribed within the parameters of contracts, although in practice the inherent ambiguities of health care meant that the more ambitious managerial expectations were never fulfilled (McKee and Clarke 1995). More recently, *The New NHS, Modern, Dependable*, published in 1997, warned that self-regulation could be sustainable only if it became open to public scrutiny and responsive to changing service demands. To support such changes, the Council for the Regulation of Healthcare Professionals (rebranded as the Council for Healthcare Regulatory Excellence) has been established in order to coordinate approaches across the various professional bodies and build a common framework that explicitly allows for robust public scrutiny.

In addition to these various structural levers, clinical governance has given

managers statutory responsibilities for the quality of health care delivered by their organizations, together with the legitimacy and authority to monitor clinical services at the micro level. There have been attempts to involve groups of clinicians in management, so that managerial and fiscal discipline can be imposed on clinicians through more subtle clinical–managerial channels (Ferlie 1999). NHS targets, waiting lists, guidelines and protocols have stood out as valuable instruments to control clinical practice and have enabled managers to nibble at the edge of clinical decision-making through micro-management. Such developments have been underpinned by the creation of a number of new national standards agencies, such as NICE and the Health Care Commission, devoted to promoting the performance of health care providers and ensuring quality.

Thus, the reform of professional regulation in the United Kingdom clearly reflects a tension between professional efforts to perpetuate the patterns of self-governance within new arrangements and government attempts to develop a more actively managed, externally regulated system. While the government is using the NHS's strong structural levers and a series of new regulatory agencies to constrain clinical autonomy and achieve its policy objectives, professional elites are seeking actively to consolidate public confidence in self-regulation.

Restructuring German legal corporatism: new corporate order or another version of self-governance?

Regulation of the health care workforce in Germany has traditionally reflected the country's dominant policy style of legal corporatism, with extensive cooperation between governments and various associations granted official standing by law (Offe 1981; Lehmbruch and Schmitter 1982; Dyson 1992; Aguilar 1993; Dryzek et al. 2002). In this system of interest mediation, large organized interests are granted formal sanction by the state and thus official status as legitimate participants in the decision-making process. In exchange for this monopoly, they commit to coordinate their actions and to contribute to the common public interest through the cooperation of their members (Dyson 1980; Jepperson 2000). Above all, the state's role is focused on providing a unified legal framework (set out in Social Code Book V) (Busse and Reisberg 2000). Within this broad framework, the corporatist actors benefit from significant constitutional autonomy and authority both to regulate the behaviour of their members and to shape the organization of health care (Altenstetter 1987; Burau 1999). In many respects, a guild-like approach is evident in this system. Within the statutory health insurance scheme, professional associations operate as the main regulatory, administrative and financing bodies, acting as a buffer between individual professionals and the statutory funds, shielding the funds from direct surveillance of professional activity (Godt 1987; Busse and Reisberg 2000).

Responsibility for professional accreditation in ambulatory care is devolved to the regional associations of ambulatory care physicians, who also negotiate with sickness funds, private insurance companies and voluntary and public agencies. Their monopolistic and cartel-promoting behaviour is reflected in the sharp division between inpatient care and ambulatory care. Ambulatory care

has remained a monopoly of the associations of ambulatory physicians and, until 1993, hospitals (except university hospitals) were not allowed to provide even ambulatory surgery.

Outside the scope of the statutory health insurance system, professional chambers assume certain exclusive regulatory functions, notably in specialist training, continuing education, licensing, access to professional practice, development and enforcement of professional standards.

As in the United Kingdom, German professional bodies have been more proactive recently, taking steps to strengthen and modernize their self-regulatory mechanisms (Birkner 1998). For example, since 1993 the National Association of SHI-Accredited Physicians (physicians working in the ambulatory sector) has launched new quality assurance projects, developed quality control charts and promoted 'quality circles' (more than 1000 peer-based quality groups) (Gerlach et al. 1998). The *Arbeitsgemeinschaft zur Förderung der Qualitätssicherung in Medizin* (Working Group for the Advancement of Quality Assurance in Medicine), founded by the German Medical Association and the National Association of SHI-Accredited Physicians, has been operating as a clearing house for standards and practice guidelines.

This picture adds weight to the argument that the German health care system relies heavily on traditional self-regulation to govern the functioning of its professional elements and that many recent initiatives initiated by the professions seek primarily to secure public confidence in the guild system. However, after more than a century of strong professional autonomy, the German state has re-emerged as a major actor in health policy-making (Hinrichs 1995; Burau 1999; Altenstetter 2001). A series of cost-containment measures, introduced from the 1970s onwards, challenges the financial autonomy of doctors, their freedom to prescribe and their control of key areas of health policy. Capping mechanisms, such as a strict global prescribing budget and lump sum prospective budgets for sickness funds' payments to physicians' associations, were introduced despite vociferous and coordinated opposition by physicians.

In the early 1990s, a requirement that any overspend in the new drug budgets or in the global remuneration envelope be repaid by doctors was introduced (Busse and Howorth 1999). As physicians' associations became liable for overspending, they were forced to scrutinize more closely the practice profiles of their members, measured by such criteria as the number of drugs prescribed, office visits, laboratory tests per case and rates of certain surgical procedures. A number of additional structural changes, including limitation of the number and type of physicians who can practise in different regions of Germany, a reduction in the number of medical students, rationalization of the very fragmented system of sickness funds and the introduction of elements of managed competition, appear to confirm the prospect for further political and managerial encroachment on professional power and autonomy.

Furthermore, while quality issues traditionally were the domain of individual clinicians or professional organizations, actors external to the professional bodies (such as the Federal Committee of Sickness Fund Physicians, a body where doctors are in the minority) have been involved increasingly in the development and enforcement of clinical guidelines, medical audit and quality assurance (Busse and Reisberg 2000).

In summary, professional regulation in Germany is shifting from a system of self-governance towards one that secures a greater role for the state. The overall picture suggests a drive towards a more technocratic model of regulation led by external actors, and the use of more policy instruments by both professional bodies and government, including new micro-management tools such as diagnosis related groups (DRGs), computerized practice profiles, clinical practice guidelines and quality assurance systems.

Changing models of professional regulation

For more than a century, the self-regulation of professionals in health care has provided a powerful tool, at least in western Europe, to guarantee minimum standards of health care delivery, ensure appropriate levels of technical and ethical practice and hold providers accountable when they slip below accepted standards. Statutory self-regulation has required health professions to develop a complex infrastructure that serves to keep professional services acceptable to society. It has also granted the medical profession legitimacy for authoritative advocacy on behalf of patients and autonomy to determine the clinical content of their practice at micro level and the terms of their practice at macro level.

Over recent years, the traditional mechanisms of self-regulation have been challenged by a number of well-publicized concerns about: clinical competence; growing evidence of unexplained variations in medical practice; pressure groups' increasing willingness to publicize information about sub-standard services; evidence of poor outcomes despite increasing expenditures; and changing attitudes within medicine itself. The evidence drawn from the case studies indicates that regulatory reforms broadly are driving changes in two ways.

The growth of public accountability

Increased politicization of the health care decision-making process has resulted in calls for closer public scrutiny of professional activities, the emergence of new externalized forms of control and the development of new reporting lines – upwards to governmental or independent regulatory agencies and downwards to consumers and citizens. The guild approach, evident in the various forms of corporatism in European health systems such as those of Germany and the United Kingdom, has come under attack. Other social actors, not only governments but also managers, parliaments and the general public, have assumed increased responsibility for overseeing professional activity and defining the framework of self-regulation. Many initiatives from governments, payers and consumers have focused on recasting the relationship with medicine in order to reduce its tight grip on policy, overcome its resistance to outside scrutiny and impose various forms of political and/or managerial control over medical care. Professional elites coopted into state structures in Norway, medical associations in Germany, counsellor doctors recruited by the sickness funds in France and clinicians with managerial functions in the United Kingdom have been used as channels for ensuring compliance with governmental and managerial

requirements. In many cases, self-regulatory organizations have been prompted to sacrifice voluntarily some aspects of their collective power in order to safeguard control over the core content of their work.

The perceived regulatory failure of professionally dominated self-regulation, as well as overly bureaucratic state regulation, has led to a growth in alternative forms of public accountability, either through more diverse representation on professional bodies (e.g. from other professions, consumer and patient groups or the state) or through the state establishing quasi-independent public bodies that are seen to be less bureaucratic. In all four countries examined, conventional approaches are being displaced in favour of a concept of regulation that is more pluralistic, drawing upon more diffuse sources of power and a greater diversity in the basis of control. A wide range of formal, externalized regulatory controls is used to ensure that health practitioners account for their performance to a range of stakeholders, including consumers, government agents, citizens' representatives, professional bodies, auditors, purchasers of care and regional and local health authorities.

The regional authorities in Norway, ANAES and the CNAMTS in France, the Federal Committee of Sickness Fund Physicians in Germany and NICE in the United Kingdom exemplify institutions that have been given prerogatives to hold health professionals accountable for their practices. These add to efforts developed in many recent reforms, particularly where there have been experiments with internal markets, to provide consumers and purchasers with the option to choose providers on the basis of their performance (Hibbard and Weeks 1989; Hannan et al. 1994; Edgman-Levitan and Cleary 1996; Lansky 1998; Rosenthal et al. 1998; Schneider and Epstein 1998).

The criticisms of self-regulation have provoked responses from the professions themselves. In the United Kingdom they have initiated reforms to offer reassurance that self-regulation fits the modern context of health care delivery. Such developments have suggested the emergence of a new guild, in which strategic elites within the health professions are attempting to maintain professional control over health care and forestall further managerial encroachment on professional activity by being more proactive and taking initiatives to modernize self-regulation (Tuohy 1976, 1988; Freidson 1994). Increasing lay representation on professional bodies and the changing composition of governance structures, as seen in the recent reforms of the GMC in the United Kingdom, are indicative of this trend.

To a certain extent, all these developments have altered the relationship between medicine and other health occupations such as nursing. Subordination to medicine is being replaced by direct accountability to the public, the government and the legislatures, and by direct access to the policy-making process (Chapter 4).

The shift from macro- to micro-regulation

Recent reforms of health care systems in Europe have shown a clear trend towards new regimes of regulation characterized by an increased emphasis on micro-efficiency and the application of a range of technical tools. The traditional

regulatory tools, favoured by both the bureaucratic state and professional bodies, which have featured mostly a concern for macro-managerial control, are being supplemented with a new generation of policy instruments: *références médicales opposables* in France, quality indicators in Norway, performance indicators in the United Kingdom and practice profiles in Germany.

The formalization and codification of performance standards is a key feature of recent regulatory reforms in the United Kingdom, reflected in the increasing use of business plans, contracts for service delivery and performance indicators and targets. Measures that target costs are complemented by micro-measures that affect clinical practice more directly in France and Germany. In all the countries examined there is an emphasis on the provision of information in the form of league tables, consumer reports, score cards, public performance reports, provider/practice profiles, billing patterns, utilization reviews and quality monitoring systems. These are used to: enforce individual practitioners' compliance with specific performance standards; monitor clinical services; foster provider organizations' and individual practitioners' accountability for their performance; and ensure that all stakeholders have adequate access to information on providers' performance. Such developments have been fostered by a number of technological developments, such as computerized databases, electronic systems for reimbursement and smart cards, all of which make it possible to scrutinize professional practice more closely.

The professions have been involved in this process and have sought actively to initiate innovative measures aimed at rationalizing and modernizing self-regulation. Guidelines, protocols, case mix measures, techniques of evidence-based medicine and other actions to systematize professional practice are promoted as tools that the professions can develop to ensure higher standards of care and protect patients from the consequences of poor practice. Medical audit and other forms of peer review, the development of measurable and auditable outcome indicators, often published as league tables or report cards (Marshall et al. 2003), and scrutiny of professional practice are introduced in order to facilitate early detection and correction of inappropriate care.

Reflecting a move from a reactive regime to a more proactive environment, continuing professional development and competence monitoring are promoted as ways to ensure that professionals regularly demonstrate evidence of their competence. This approach seeks to empower regulatory bodies not only to deal with a few high-profile cases where performance is clearly unacceptable, but also to reduce the tail of underperforming practitioners. Within this model, a significant element of professional control is exerted through local systems of monitoring but within a national framework of self-regulation. Local peers become the primary scrutinizers of professional practice (Sheaff et al. 2004). Although these professionally led measures have been incremental in nature, seeking jealously to safeguard many of the privileges of self-regulation, they have reflected a trend that is similar to the development of technical control mechanisms.

Thus, the evidence seems to suggest a dual process. First, the source of authority for control is shifting from traditional bureaucratic mechanisms and professional bodies towards a broader range of regulatory agencies, which operate at all levels of the health system and aim to enlarge health care workers' scope

of accountability. Second, there is the emergence of new policy instruments that operate mostly at micro level, introduced by both professional and governmental agencies to optimize the control of professional activity.

Conclusion

Over recent decades developments in public administration, in both theory and practice, have challenged the two traditional ideal types of regulation: the guild and the state bureaucratic approaches. New models of regulation are emerging. No longer able to rely on their traditional privileged and trusted status, increasingly professionals have had to find rational and instrumental means to secure their position and ensure the continuation of the present balance of responsibilities for accountability, regulation and the management of professional activities. The principles of new public management, such as decentralization and consumer involvement, have had an important influence on government activity in many sectors and altered the respective roles of government and public service providers. Such trends are also apparent within regulatory structures, with greater diversification of regulatory bodies and delegation of regulatory authority. Changes can also be seen with the growth of lay involvement.

Despite self-regulation's failure to ensure public protection, no reform has attempted to replace it entirely with alternative regulatory forms. The aim of the reforms has instead been to consolidate, complement or renew the prevailing professional and bureaucratic mechanisms. Despite the powerful rhetoric in favour of deregulation, more often the reality has been expansion of the regulatory system through the adoption of new instruments, development of new channels of control and creation of new regulatory agencies, rather than a removal of professional regulatory authority.

Although these trends in regulatory reforms show some consistency between countries, not all countries are at the same stage of recasting their regulatory system. The post-communist countries of CEE are still at an early phase in rebuilding their professional institutions. Similarly, the pace of reform, the choice of regulatory tools and how they are implemented are constrained by the unique institutional history and the distinct corporate structure of each country.

Notes

1 Within the scope of this chapter it is not possible to consider the regulation of all health professionals, such as dentists, nurses, pharmacists, allied health professionals or indeed some of the so-called complementary and alternative medical practitioners. Given the historical precedence of professional regulation for doctors, it is likely that many of the trends identified will apply to other health professionals in due course.

2 Regulatory instruments are defined here as procedural and substantive forms of public action that are used to influence the behaviour and functioning of health care personnel or to modify the production of health services (see Eliadis and Hill 2001).

References

Aguilar, S. (1993) Corporatist and statist regimes in environmental policy: Germany and Spain. *Environmental Politics*, **2**: 223–47.

Altenstetter, C. (1987) An end to a consensus on health care in the Federal Republic of Germany? *Journal of Health Politics, Policy and Law*, **12**(3): 505–36.

Altenstetter, C. (2001) Health care reform in Germany in comparative perspective, with special attention to funding and reimbursement issues of medical and hospital services. Paper prepared for delivery at the 29th ECPR Joint Sessions of Workshops, Grenoble, France, 6–11 April.

Baldwin, R. and Cave, M. (1999) *Understanding regulation: theory, strategy and practice.* Oxford, Oxford University Press.

Becker, G.S. (1983) A theory of competition among pressure groups for political influence. *Quarterly Journal of Economics*, **98**: 371–400.

Bekke, H., Perry, J. and Toonen, T. (1996) *Civil service systems in comparative perspective.* Bloomington, Indiana University Press.

Bellis, C. (2000) Professions in society. *Australian Actuarial Journal*, **6**(1): 1–33.

Birkner, B.R. (1998) Country report. National quality of care activities in Germany. *International Journal for Quality in Health Care*, **10**: 451–4.

Blom-Hansen, J. (2000) Still corporatism in Scandinavia? A survey of recent empirical finding. *Scandinavian Political Studies*, **23**(2): 157–81.

Braverman, H. (1974) *Labor and monopoly capital: the degradation of work in the twentieth century.* New York, Monthly Review Press.

BRI Inquiry Secretariat (1999) *BRI inquiry paper on commissioning, purchasing, contracting and quality of care in the NHS internal market.* London, BRI Inquiry Secretariat.

British Medical Association, Academy of Medical Royal Colleges and Joint Consultants Committee (1998) *Making self-regulation work at the local level.* London, BMA.

Burau, V. (1999) Health care reform and the medical profession – the case of Germany. Paper presented at the 27th ECPR Joint Sessions in Mannheim, 26–31 March.

Burrage, M. (1990) Beyond a subset: the professional aspirations of manual workers in France, the United States and Britain. *In*: Burrage, M. and Torhstendahl, R., eds, *Professions in theory and history.* London, Sage.

Busse, R. and Howorth, C. (1999) Cost containment in Germany: twenty years' experience. *In*: Le Grand, M.E. and Le Grand, J., eds, *Health care and cost containment in the European Union.* Aldershot, Ashgate.

Busse, R. and Reisberg, A. (2000) *Health care systems in transition: Germany.* Copenhagen, European Observatory on Health Systems and Policies.

Catto, G. (2003) Improving professional competence – the way ahead? *International Journal of Quality Health Care*, **15**: 375–6.

Christensen, T. and Lægreid, P. (2001a) *New public management: the transformation of ideas and practice.* Aldershot, Ashgate.

Christensen, T. and Lægreid, P. (2001b) Coping with modern leadership roles – the problematic redefinition of public companies. Paper presented at the 2001 Meeting of the IPSA Section of the Structure of Governance, 29–31 March, University of Oklahoma, Norman.

CMO Review Group (1995) *Maintaining medical excellence.* London, Department of Health.

Coase, R.H. (1974) The choice of the institutional framework: a comment. *Journal of Law and Economics*, **17**(2): 493–6.

Department of Health (1989) *Working for patients.* London, HMSO.

Department of Health (1997) *The new NHS, modern, dependable.* London, The Stationery Office.

Department of Health (1999) *Supporting doctors, protecting patients*. London: Department of Health (www.doh.gov.uk/cmoconsult.htm).

Derber, C. (1982) Towards a new theory of professionals as workers: advanced capitalism and post-industrial labor. *In*: Derber, C., ed., *Professionals as workers: mental labor in advanced capitalism*. Boston, G. K. Hail.

Dryzek, J.S. et al. (2002) Environmental transformation of the state: the USA, Norway, Germany and the UK. *Political Studies*, **50**(4): 659–82.

Durand-Zaleski, I., Colin, C. and Blum-Boisgard, C. (1997) An attempt to save money by using mandatory practice guidelines in France. *British Medical Journal*, **315**: 943–6.

Durieux, P. et al. (2000) From clinical recommendations to mandatory practice: the intro-duction of regulatory practice guidelines in the French health care system. *International Journal of Technology Assessment in Health Care*, **16**(4): 969–75.

Dyson, K. (1980) *The state tradition in western Europe: a study of an idea and institution*. Oxford, Oxford University Press.

Dyson, K. (1992) *The politics of German regulation*. Aldershot, Dartmouth.

Edgman-Levitan, S. and Cleary, P.D. (1996) What information do consumers want and need? *Health Affairs*, **15**: 42–56.

Eliadis, F.P. and Hill, M. (2001) *Instrument choice in global democracies*. Concept paper. Ottawa, Policy Research Initiative.

Erichsen, V. (1995) Health care reform in Norway: the end of the profession state? *Journal of Health Politics, Policy and Law*, **20**: 719–37.

Ferlie, E. (1999) Organisation and management: archetype change in the organisation and management of health care? *In*: Dargie, C., ed., *Policy futures for UK health: technical series*. London, Nuffield Trust.

Feruholmen, C. and Magnussen, J. (2000) *Health care systems in transition: Norway*. Copenhagen, European Observatory on Health Systems and Policies.

Freidson, E. (1970) *Profession of medicine: a study of the sociology of applied knowledge*. New York, Harper and Row.

Freidson, E. (1994) *Professionalism reborn: theory, prophecy and policy*. Chicago, University of Chicago Press.

Friedman, M. (1962) *Capitalism and freedom*. Chicago, University of Chicago Press.

Gellhorn, W. (1956) *Individual freedom and governmental restraints*. Baton Rouge, Louisiana State University Press.

Gellhorn, W. (1976) The abuse of occupational licensing. *University of Chicago Law Review*, **44**: 6–27.

Gerlach, F.M., Beyer, M. and Römer, A. (1998) Quality circles in ambulatory care: state of development and future perspective in Germany. *International Journal for Quality in Health Care*, **10**: 35–42.

Godt, P.J. (1987) Confrontation, consent and corporatism: state strategies and the medical profession in France, Great Britain and West Germany. *Journal of Health Politics, Policy and Law*, **12**(3): 459–80.

Hannan, E.L. et al. (1994) Improving the outcomes of coronary artery bypass surgery in New York State. *Journal of the American Medical Association*, **271**: 761–6.

Hatch, D. (2001) Professionally led regulation in medicine. *British Journal of Ophthalmology*, **85**(5): 513–15.

Hibbard, J.H. and Weeks, E.C. (1989) Does the dissemination of comparative data on physician fees affect consumer use of services? *Medical Care*, **27**: 1167–74.

Hinrichs, K. (1995) The impact of German health insurance reforms on redistribution and the culture of solidarity. *Journal of Health Politics, Policy and Law*, **20**(3): 653–87.

Hogan, D. (1979) *The regulation of psychotherapists. Volume I: A study in the philosophy and practice of professional regulation*. Cambridge, MA, Ballinger.

Hollings, R.L. and Pike-Nase, C. (1997) *Professional and occupational licensure in the United States*. Westport, CT, Greenwood Press.

Institute of Medicine (1989) *Allied health services: avoiding crises*. Washington, DC, National Academy Press.

Irvine, D. (1997) The performance of doctors: professionalism and self-regulation in a changing world. *British Medical Journal*, **314**: 1540–2.

Jacob, J.M. (1999) *Doctors and rules: a sociology of professional values*, 2nd edn. London, Transaction Publishers.

Jepperson, R.L. (2000) *Institutional logics: on the constitutive dimensions of the modern nation-state polities*. Florence, Robert Schuman Centre for Advanced Studies, European University Institute.

Klein, R. (1998) Competence, professional self-regulation and public interest. *British Medical Journal*, **316**: 1740–2.

Lansky, D. (1998) Measuring what matters to the public. *Health Affairs*, **17**: 40–1.

Larson, M.S. (1977) *The rise of professionalism*. Berkeley, University of California Press.

Lehmbruch, G. and Schmitter, P. (1982) *Patterns of corporatist policy-making*. London, Sage.

Lindemann, M. (1999) *Medicine and society in early modern Europe*. Cambridge, Cambridge University Press.

Lowenberg, A.D. and Tinnin, T.D. (1992) Professional versus consumer interests in regulation: the case of the US child care industry. *Applied Economics*, **24**: 571–80.

McKee, C.M. and Clarke, A. (1995) Guidelines, enthusiasms, uncertainty and the limits to purchasing. *British Medical Journal*, **310**: 101–4.

Maria, S. and Ostrowski, T. (2003) *The organisation, financing and quality monitoring in general practice: a comparative study between England, France and Poland*. EUROPHAMILI /AESCULAPIUS professional study. Nottingham, University of Nottingham.

Marshall, M.N. et al. (2003) Public reporting on quality in the United States and the United Kingdom. *Health Affairs (Millwood)*, **22**(3): 134–48.

Merry, M.D. and Crago, M.G. (2001) The past, present and future of health care quality: urgent need for innovative, external review processes to protect patients. *Physician Executive*, **27**(5): 30–5.

Moore, T.G. (1961) A theory of professional licensing. *Journal of Law and Economics*, **4**: 93–117.

Moran, M. (1995) Explaining change in the NHS: corporatism, closure and democratic capitalism. *Public Policy and Administration*, **10**(2): 21–33.

Moran, M. and Wood, B. (1993) *States, regulation and the medical profession*. Buckingham, Open University Press.

Norwegian Board of Health (2002) *Quality in health care: the role of government in supervision and monitoring in Norway*. Oslo, Norwegian Board of Health.

Offe, C. (1981) The attribution of public status to interest groups: observations on the West German case. *In*: Berger, S., ed., *Organizing interests in western Europe*. Cambridge, MA, MIT Press.

Or, Z. (2002) *Improving the performance of health care systems: from measures to action (A review of experiences in four OECD countries)*. Paris, OECD.

Osborne, D. and Gaebler, T. (1992) *Reinventing government: how the entrepreneurial spirit is transforming the public sector*. New York, Addison-Wesley.

Peltzman, S. (1989) The economic theory of regulation after a decade of deregulation. *Brookings Papers: Microeconomics*, 1–41.

Peters, G. (2000) Administrative traditions. *In*: TWB Group, eds, *Administrative and civil service reform* (www1.worldbank.org/publicsector/civilservice/traditions.htm), accessed April 2004.

Posner, R. (1974) Theories of economic regulation. *Bell Journal of Economics*, **5**: 335–58.

Poullier, J.-P. and Sandier, S. (2000) France. *Journal of Health Politics, Policy and Law*, **25**(5): 899–905.

Rodwin, V.G. (1981) The marriage of national health insurance and la medecine libérale in France: a costly union. *Milbank Memorial Fund Quarterly: Health and Society*, **59**(1): 16–43.

Rosenthal, G.E. et al. (1998) Using hospital performance data in quality improvement: the Cleveland health quality choice experience. *Joint Commission Journal on Quality Improvement*, **24**: 347–60.

Rottenberg, S. (1980) Introduction. *In*: Rottenberg, S., ed., *Occupational licensure and regulation*. Washington, DC, American Enterprise Institute for Public Policy Research.

Saltman, R.B., Busse, R. and Mossialos, E. (2002) *Regulating entrepreneurial behaviour in European health care systems*. Buckingham, Open University Press.

Schneider, E.C. and Epstein, A.M. (1998) Use of public performance reports: a survey of patients undergoing cardiac surgery. *Journal of the American Medical Association*, **279**: 1638–42.

Sheaff, R. et al. (2004) Governmentality by network in English primary health care. *Social Policy and Administration*, **38**(1): 89–103.

Smith, A. (1970) *The wealth of nations, Books I–III* (first published 1776). Harmondsworth, Pelican.

Southgate, L. and Dauphinee, D. (1998) Continuing medical education, maintaining standards in British and Canadian medicine: the developing role of the regulatory body. *British Medical Journal*, **316**: 697–700.

Stacey, M. (2000) The General Medical Council and professional self-regulation. *In*: Gladstone, D., ed., *Regulating doctors*. London, Institute for the Study of Civil Society, St Edmundsbury Press.

Stigler, G.J. (1971) The theory of economic regulation. *Bell Journal of Economics*, **2**: 3–21.

Tuohy, C. (1976) Medical politics after Medicare: the Ontario case. *Canadian Public Policy*, **2**(2): 192–210.

Tuohy, C. (1988) Medicine and the state in Canada: the extra-billing issue in perspective. *Canadian Journal of Political Science*, **21**(2): 267–96.

Van den Noord, P., Hagen, T. and Iversen, T. (1998) *The Norwegian health care system*. Paris, OECD.

Wilsford, D. (1987) The cohesion and fragmentation of organized medicine in France and the United States. *Journal of Health Politics, Policy and Law*, **12**(3): 481–503.

Zhou, X. (1993) Occupational power, state capacities and the diffusion of licensing in the American states: 1890 to 1950. *American Sociological Review*, **58**: 536–52.

eleven

The challenges of transition in CEE and the NIS of the former USSR

Carl Afford and Suszy Lessof

This chapter examines the specific issues facing the health care workforce in CEE and the NIS of the former USSR. It explores the historical and political context that has framed transition and the resultant challenges that continue to affect the way health professionals operate. It reviews key health system reforms, highlighting their impact on health personnel, and examines the specific challenges facing those countries as they continue to engineer the transition(s) from Soviet-style models of planning, education and training, and as they rethink professional roles and management approaches. It highlights the difficulties inherent in transferring some of the models described elsewhere in this volume to those countries that are still tackling the consequences of profound transformation.

A common inheritance and the challenges of change

The countries of CEE and the NIS of the former USSR are immensely diverse, yet their health systems shared many common features before the transition of the early 1990s (Afford 2003).

The Semashko model: an attempt to create equity through standardization

Before 1989, variants of the Soviet Semashko model dominated the region. The model was based on the principle that access to preventive, curative and rehabilitative services should be free at the point of use. Care was delivered

through extensive networks of health posts, ambulatory polyclinics and hospitals. The system was skewed towards secondary care, with a dominant role for hospitals and a proliferation of outpatient specialists working alongside poorly trained generalists in the primary care setting. A focus on infectious diseases and epidemic preparedness prompted the establishment of large numbers of hospital beds and inpatient facilities.

Parallel health services were a common feature in much of the region, with large enterprises and many ministries providing (mostly ambulatory) health care through the workplace. Mainstream services were financed from general government revenues that flowed through structures administered by central and local government. Government resources were allocated to regions and institutions in line with comprehensive norms based on population numbers. The number of hospital beds and staff deemed necessary for a local population was relatively high compared to much of western Europe (Saltman and Figueras 1997). To a large extent this reflected the fact that labour was cheap and easily available (Rainnie et al. 2000) but capital was scarce.

The system's stated aim was to be fair, but attempts to adjust resources according to differences across regions were insufficient to offset geographical inequalities. Indeed, such inequity was compounded by annual budgets that were increased by historical increments on the basis of past practice, thereby perpetuating inefficiencies. There was little scope for adjusting the flow of funds, responding to local conditions or introducing incentives that would encourage efficiency or innovation (although senior managers did develop an extensive repertoire of opportunistic behaviours to offset the vagaries of central planning).

Pervasive influence of government and the vulnerability it fostered

The dominance of central government was felt not merely in the way that it determined the level of resources devoted to health and the scale and nature of services provided. The Semashko model also dictated strict guidelines on:

- workforce planning, the numbers in training and in any given speciality;
- the content of education and training;
- the scale and nature of continuing education;
- pay;
- working conditions.

Features rooted in Soviet economics and social policy exerted a powerful influence on health sector employees. Levels of pay reflected the fact that the health system was defined as non-productive and employees received relatively low pay compared to industrial workers. Even today, health sector salaries in Lithuania amount to only 83% of average national income. In the Russian Federation, nurses' basic pay is well below the official poverty line. This has dented morale and helped to foster a culture of informal, gratitude or under-the-table payments from patients, subverting attempts to introduce rational incentives into provider payments and widening workplace inequalities (Padaiga et al. 2005).

During the Soviet period employment was effectively compulsory and the workplace was the key means of distributing benefits (including health care). Labour markets were based on the notion of an individual salary providing only the marginal cash needs of an individual worker. Family needs were catered for by the state, which provided, among other benefits, housing, child care, health and leisure services. Cash transfers, which commodified labour, were kept to a minimum (Standing 1996). While this approach was able to meet the broad needs (if not the aspirations) of the population, it made transition to market structures extraordinarily difficult. When the system did transform, low wages combined with pressures for price liberalization and restructuring from international financial institutions (IFI) to make real pay particularly vulnerable. Cash income was devalued by inflation and in-kind benefits were drastically reduced, with staff receiving minimal compensation for the loss. The guarantee that the state would (at least) meet the population's physiological needs collapsed and workers were left deserted by the state (Standing 2002), with a monetary income that was never intended to support individual, let alone family, existence. The situation became intolerable for many who, because work had been compulsory, had scarcely any benefit system on which they could rely, independent of the workplace (Standing 1997).

Attitudes and expectations: implications for transition societies

The common inheritance of CEE and the NIS of the former USSR can also be traced through more intangible elements, such as the expectations of health service users and staff. Communist societies provided comprehensive services but there was a significant gap between what was meant to happen and the way things actually worked. The system did little to develop people's sense of responsibility for their own health. Nor did it foster an awareness of (or effort towards) efficiency, although many employees were dedicated to their patients and used enterprising strategies to make the system function. Health posts and hospitals often fell well below acceptable standards. In parts of the region many smaller rural facilities were without mains water, sewerage or a secure electricity supply (McKee and Healy 2002). Often pharmaceuticals were unavailable and there were quality problems. Gaps between the formal and informal, the rhetoric and reality, fed into the widespread perception that the state system failed people and could not meet their needs.

Inevitably this led to a desire for real change and a demonstrable shift away from central control, towards greater responsiveness. It was also inevitable that the reforms formulated in response to these pressures were frequently over-ambitious and difficult to implement and sustain. In these circumstances the reforms created huge uncertainties for employees, who often felt acutely threatened by the spectre of radical change (ILO 2001).

CEE and the NIS of the former USSR: diversity that shapes experience

Despite the dominance of the Semashko model outlined above and the commonalities of planned economies, considerable cultural and developmental diversity remained across CEE and the NIS of the former USSR, largely reflecting the history of pre-communist Europe. Thus, the former centres of the Austro-Hungarian Empire approached the introduction/reintroduction of Bismarckian welfare models from a different starting point from, for example, the countries of the Caucasus. There were also profound cultural differences between countries, including attitudes to illness and care, and variations in the level of economic development. Inevitably, these affected (and continue to affect) decisions on the financing and organization of health systems and workforce compensation (Afford 2001).

Grouping countries

No single way of classifying the countries of CEE and the NIS of the former USSR avoids overlap. Nor are sufficient data available to explore in any detail the differences between those subsets of countries that have superficially divergent patterns of human resource development. Still, it is expedient to group countries loosely and according to where they stand in relation to EU membership, levels of GDP and so on.

At the broadest level a distinction can be made between rapid and non-rapid transition countries. This subsumes geographical and economic differences and divides the region roughly into new Member States of the EU plus higher GDP stability pact countries and, separately, the NIS of the former USSR and lower GDP stability pact countries. These broad classifications should be understood in the light of the specific attributes of countries within the two groups. It is also important to recognize that many of the countries in CEE and the NIS of the former USSR experienced major upheavals, including conflicts and civil war. The break-up of the USSR (even where no conflicts erupted) and the division of Czechoslovakia also had far-reaching effects. None the less, and while the division is not clear-cut, the rough distinction between rapid and non-rapid transition countries does help to simplify discussion of a range of human resources issues.

Key transition pressures: implications for the workforce

Economic collapse and public sector retrenchment

Transition posed substantial challenges for countries of CEE and the NIS of the former USSR, with profound consequences for health sector staff. Probably the most telling was the immense economic upheaval that affected the whole region. Industrial output plummeted, established supply and trading links within the COMECON system broke down and spiralling inflation undermined

already weak economies. Stagflation devalued salaries and savings and poverty increased. Without exception aggregate health care funding was reduced across the region. The value of already low health sector pay (often tied to the minimum wage) fell further, physical conditions deteriorated and shortages of pharmaceuticals and other supplies worsened. Furthermore, governments' ability to respond or to negotiate successfully with foreign donors and investors was severely constrained.

Unemployment quickly became entrenched, challenging social provision. People were utterly unprepared because work had been compulsory and unemployment was still seen as stigmatizing. Often the authorities were hostile to those seeking support, few benefits were available and many people simply looked for opportunities outside the formal labour market (and disappeared from employment/unemployment figures). Official data across the region therefore underestimated the scale of the problem, although job cuts and unemployment were not as pronounced in the health sector as elsewhere. Where there was evidence of withdrawal from the labour market by health professionals, or public sector retrenchment, often unemployment was offset by jobs shifting into the private sector (ILO 2001). None the less, as unemployment became commonplace across the region, the perception of insecurity among health sector employees increased, colouring attitudes to reform.

Breakdown of the structures that shaped working life

Economic collapse coincided with a breakdown in many of the regulatory and legal structures that had shaped health services, resulting in a great deal of uncertainty for health professionals. Most countries re-examined the constitutional basis of health service provision. While fundamental values were generally reasserted, the debates over public versus private provision created anxiety. In addition, discussion of the legal status of health sector workers, the individual's right to practise and liability for medical error increased feelings of insecurity, even though little actually changed.

As overarching legal frameworks were re-examined, the basis of regulation was undermined. The structures that had transmitted and enforced rule systems collapsed, particularly in the NIS of the former USSR where a vacuum was left by Moscow's removal as the ultimate source of authority. The trade unions' role (and legitimacy) of providing oversight withered. Local authorities took on new responsibilities, often without the skills or capacity to respond to these new demands. Institutions became the de facto stewards of health care delivery and direct employers of staff. For some this led, among other things, to gaps in health and safety and the loss of control over working hours, bonuses and recourse for staff grievances (Afford 2003).

Resource constraints, the changing framework of governance and anxiety about the future coincided with a profound decline in health status, increasing the demands on health systems and their staff (Merkel and Karkkainen 2002). The effects of this decline in health status are poorly understood but clearly these pressures were more pronounced in countries that experienced conflict, population displacement and the traumas of ethnic cleansing.

For many the situation improved from the mid to late 1990s, particularly at the macro-level, as increased resources became available in the public sphere. Yet only Hungary, Poland and Slovakia achieved, or almost achieved, their 1989 levels of GDP by the end of the millennium (Dunford and Smith 2000). This created opportunities for development, although the consequences of transition and its impact on human resources persisted where health was not a priority or economies failed to recover (European Commission 2001, 2003). Thus, for example, physical conditions improved in the more successful rapid transition countries like the Czech Republic and Hungary, while poorer countries like Kazakhstan and Ukraine were left with a long-standing lack of capital investment, deteriorating facilities and outdated equipment (Stepanchikova 2001; McKee and Healy 2002; Strózik 2005).

Key reforms: impact on employees

In an attempt to respond to the problems experienced under communism and remedy those triggered by transition, policy-makers across CEE and the NIS of the former USSR sought to introduce a series of reforms during the decade following transition. One of the major factors shaping the debate was a deliberate effort to leave behind the Semashko model and the central control of command economies. Perhaps inevitably there was a preoccupation with market mechanisms and the private sector, coinciding with international pressures to realign public services. There were also deliberate attempts to move towards standards applied within the EU, not only in accession countries but also in those with little medium-term prospect of membership. Governments responded to real and perceived pressures and sought to:

- decentralize;
- adjust funding mechanisms (in particular shifting from tax-based systems to social health insurance);
- privatize and/or introduce market elements;
- reform primary care and use it as a gatekeeper to specialist provision.

The reforms were intended to provide better, more responsive services, to improve efficiency and to enhance population health. However, often implementation proved problematic, hindered by, for example, the neglect of employees and the focus on reducing staff numbers and substituting nurses for doctors. The human resource impacts of these key reforms will be examined in turn.

Decentralization

Decentralization has revolved to a significant extent around a perceived (and often real) need to break with the past. While the degree of authority devolved or delegated to regions or municipalities has varied considerably, there has been no coherent strategy to increase local managerial competence or to address resource shortfalls. In CEE and the NIS of the former USSR early decentralization

dealt a major blow to data collection, fragmenting information and reducing the capacity for coherent human resource planning (Kolehmainen-Aitken 1998). It also exacerbated difficulties such as the indebtedness of local authorities and institutions and contributed to the late payment of wages, particularly in many of the poorer countries of the NIS of the former USSR.

The most radical versions of decentralization saw powers passed to hospital directors, who were given the ability to hire and fire staff and to determine levels of pay and bonuses. This encouraged local initiative but also ended national guarantees on employment rights, jeopardizing protection against arbitrary dismissal and fuelling uncertainty. Several countries devolved powers to newly established physicians' associations. These took on elements of the state's regulatory role, setting standards and exercising quasi-licensing powers. In Poland, for example, statutory associations now license private practitioners and oversee claims of malpractice (Strózik 2005). While this has many positive features, it reflects the emphasis on the doctors' role at the expense of other occupational groups (Kolehmainen-Aitken 1998).

Adjusting funding: social health insurance and out-of-pocket payments

The introduction of social health insurance in many parts of the region, particularly CEE, decentralized the collection and pooling of resources and introduced the concept of purchasing. The creation of insurance funds (alongside or as an alternative to tax) was expected to protect finances allocated to health care and to introduce market mechanisms that would enhance the quality and quantity of services. However, the reality was not always as clear cut. In Poland, for example, separating government and third-party payer functions and channelling salary budgets through sickness funds complicated the workforce's position in pay negotiations. In 1999 the government agreed above-inflation pay rises for nurses without making provision to cover the costs. The sickness funds refused to pay the increases and nurses were left with no obvious redress (Strózik 2005). More generally, the appropriateness of financing health services through payroll deductions remains questionable in countries with extensive informal economies (McKee et al. 2004). Estimates suggest that the shadow economy accounts for as much as 33% of the Estonian labour force and 36% of total GDP in Bulgaria, and that the frequency of informal payments for health services is as high as 60% in Slovakia. The scale of the problem is substantial, undermining health systems' ability to manage the flow of resources and challenging the viability of payroll-based social health insurance.

Notwithstanding such complications, the separation of purchasing and provision has created new roles and opportunities in management (where adequate risk-bearing funds were established), although these have been marred by the fact that the managers and administrators negotiating and handling contracts have often been unprepared for their new roles. In parallel with the introduction of social health insurance, several countries of CEE and the NIS of the former USSR sought to introduce limits to entitlement and to formalize out-of-pocket payments. Typically this has meant introducing formal co-payments

for pharmaceuticals and charging for dentistry. Less often, co-payments have been required for primary care, laboratory tests or services like physiotherapy (as in Croatia and Kyrgyzstan). Very occasionally all routine primary and secondary care for the population outside a predefined special need group has to be paid for wholly out of pocket (Georgia). Ostensibly these payments have been intended to bring funds into the system where governments have failed to do so, to help to tackle under-the-table payments and to enable institutions to pay staff adequately. There is little evidence, however, that they have either increased salaries or decreased gratuities.

Privatization and market mechanisms

A further tranche of reforms has revolved around privatization (Table 11.1). A common initiative has been to privatize the ownership of facilities; for example, through the sale of pharmacies and dental practices. Privatization of service delivery, whereby doctors establish themselves in single-handed or group practices, has been less common (Scheil Adlung 2001). It has none the less created a new category of effectively self-employed professionals who often, in turn, employ support staff (privatizing employment). It is unclear how these changes have affected issues such as regulation, career progression, union representation or pensions.

Table 11.1 Forms of privatization: impacts on the socioeconomic security of staff

Privatization of	Impact on workers' security
Funding	New roles created by insurance system and collection of co-payments. Doctors have some privileges over other occupational groups in negotiating remuneration.
Ownership of facilities	Creation of self-employment (pharmacists/dentists) with all its implications. Direct employment of support staff by private facilities with greater rights to hire and fire, questions about entitlement, transferability of skills, etc.
Service delivery	Encourages independent practitioners with implications as above.
Employment	Employment is fragmented; as new employers emerge so do potential barriers to mobility. Pay differentials may evolve between sectors and institutions, creating inequities. Rights to union membership may be withdrawn in the private sector.
Functions (contracting out)	Pay levels and pension entitlement tend to fall, protection against arbitrary dismissal undermined. Rights to union membership may be withdrawn. Trust relationships jeopardized.

Hospital privatization has been much more restricted and only limited numbers of facilities have shifted to local government or joint ownership or have become not-for-profit ventures. Privatization of functions, such as contracting out of cleaning, catering or computer services (Hall 1998), does not appear to have played a significant role as yet. However, experience elsewhere suggests that the consequences can be negative, depressing staff wages and (pension) benefits (Saltman and Figueras 1997), as well as undermining trust, accountability and access to representation (Hunter 1998).

Primary care

Attempts to develop a stronger primary care sector with a gatekeeping function have been heavily promoted by international agencies such as WHO and the World Bank, in the expectation that they would shift the region away from its dependence on expensive, bed-intensive specialist care and create incentives for quality and efficiency. Considerable investment in training and retraining for doctors has achieved significant successes in Latvia, Lithuania and Poland (Karaskevica and Tragakes 2001).

There has been less investment in providing the appropriate settings for recently trained family doctors to apply their new skills. In the Russian Federation, for example, new general practitioners work in highly unsuitable conditions with little choice but to revert to previous modes of practice. What is more, the awareness that the traditional Soviet form of general practitioner (the *Uchastkovii terapevt*) is outmoded has made it increasingly difficult to recruit at this level, leaving a gap in the workforce that general practice training programmes have failed to fill (Danishevski 2005). This has been exacerbated by the phasing out of feldshers or nurse-practitioners.

Reforms have sought to cut back on specialist provision and the paediatricians, obstetricians and gynaecologists in polyclinics. However, it is still unclear whether the focus on general practice will succeed in changing the system. Indeed, governments and donors do not seem to have fully appreciated the scale of popular resistance to restricted rights of access to specialists, or staff concerns about abandoning established models. Experience in Spain suggests that developing interdisciplinary primary care based approaches is a long-term challenge with no guarantee of success (Lopez-Valcarel et al. 2005). Yet despite these difficulties, doctors and nurses have been presented with new opportunities to develop their skills, forge new career paths and enhance patient care.

EU membership

For the Czech Republic, Estonia, Hungary, Latvia, Lithuania, Poland, Slovakia and Slovenia a further, more recent, round of reforms has been linked directly to the May 2004 enlargement of the EU and their subsequent need to meet the acquis communautaire (European Union 2001). Although, on paper, the EU has limited competency in the health care sector (see Chapter 12), accession has

already had a major impact on health services in the new Member States, albeit tangentially. In particular, the Commission's remit has seen:

- stringent economic measures to control public sector spending;
- regulation of the free movement of goods, including opening markets for pharmaceuticals and medical technologies;
- insistence on the free movement of services, allowing patients to seek health services across the EU (under certain conditions);
- the introduction of restrictions on working hours (see Chapter 12);
- the establishment of free movement of professionals so that health sector staff can seek employment anywhere in the EU.

This last provision has proved to be important for human resources, requiring countries to harmonize medical and nursing training to facilitate mutual recognition of professional qualifications (see Chapter 12). It has prompted a reappraisal of the development of occupations in new Member States, reducing the number of clinical specialties and establishing minimum training periods. It is also influencing training agendas beyond the EU, including countries as distant as Kyrgyzstan that are voluntarily following EU sectoral directives (ILO 2001).

These efforts to remove barriers to movement have prompted widespread concern that the best qualified staff will move from east to west in significant numbers in pursuit of better pay and conditions (European Commission 2001). This is examined in more detail in Chapter 3. However, in brief, where the pay gradient between new and established Member States is sufficiently steep, migration has been shown to be more likely (McKee et al. 2004). This may lead to possible brain drain, with a domino effect in the non-EU countries of eastern Europe. The true scale of movement is yet to be determined but, from early reports, it is not as extensive as feared. Yet the risk of losing staff complicates efforts to manage the production and career progression of staff and to maintain an appropriate balance of specialists and generalists.

The response to transition

It is undeniable that reforms have had a considerable impact on health care delivery but attempts to introduce many changes have been undermined by a lack of resources and capacity. Health care employees' ability and willingness to cope with new approaches have been crucial factors in determining performance. This section examines some of the more specifically 'eastern European' challenges faced by rapid and non-rapid transition countries as they struggle with resource generation, professional roles and management.

Transforming resource generation

A significant part of human resources management has always concerned producing and maintaining a suitably skilled workforce. Furthermore, 'resource generation' (WHO 2000) in the health sector has particular features rooted in

the nature of health as a public good that distinguish it from the production of staff for other sectors. Health's role as a precursor to economic development (WHO 2004) and the information asymmetries between health care professionals and patients, for example, justify state involvement in the production of staff. The governments of CEE and the NIS of the former USSR recognize their role in developing human resources to meet their populations' health care needs better, yet face substantial challenges in reworking traditional approaches.

Planning the workforce

As described above, the employment and production of staff for health services in pre-1989 CEE and the NIS of the former USSR were premised on norms and a commitment to full employment. Medical and nursing schools were geared to produce and replace large numbers of staff while seeking, inevitably, to expand their roles. At the same time, low pay encouraged a labour- rather than capital-intensive approach. Almost all countries have sought since to review the numbers employed so as to reduce the size of the health sector workforce, albeit with differing levels of commitment and success.

From the outset of transition there was a powerful presumption that cuts were needed in the number of doctors and, to a lesser extent, nurses. This was largely attributable to the influence of IFI and others working with new governments to address restructuring and public sector costs. These operated in the belief that the same services could be delivered with fewer staff, reducing both the call on budgets and the risk of doctors escalating costs through surplus (expensive) tests and interventions. Inevitably, there was some scope for reducing medical staff numbers and, as importantly, addressing the balance between doctors and nurses. Equally, there was a strong case for continuing a labour-intensive model in countries where capital investment was severely constrained, labour costs were low and unemployment had enormous social consequences (including reducing access to care) (Afford 2001; O'Brien-Pallas et al. 2001).

Despite government and IFI concern, neither staffing levels nor training places have fallen uniformly across the region (Afford 2001) (Table 11.1). In some cases this demonstrates planners' lack of commitment to cuts (Belarus), in others it simply reflects the difficulties of implementing reforms.

In reality, staff numbers in newly decentralized systems are often determined by local dynamics rather than national plans. Local governments in more affluent areas have been able to fund larger workforces, while heads of powerful institutions have successfully resisted cuts in staff levels. There is also anecdotal evidence that some chief doctors in non-rapid transition countries, specifically in the Caucasus, 'sold' jobs to nurses and physicians: appointing them in return for cash payments that the member of staff recouped by charging patients. While these practices may have been limited, they illustrate the various factors that eroded incentives for implementing cuts and the weak governance in many highly decentralized systems.

Neoclassical economists had expected privatization to lead to enhanced efficiency and staff reductions, but there are few data to confirm or contradict this. However, the private sector has had a discernible (and damaging) impact in

Armenia and Georgia, where private medical and nursing schools that opened immediately after independence have proved almost impossible to regulate. They have produced large numbers of graduates, undermining government efforts to restrict entry into medical schools, illustrating (since students are willing to pay to enter) that medicine is lucrative despite low levels of formal pay. Countries such as Lithuania and Poland have been able to maintain tight controls over policy and practice and have cut staff production radically, sometimes enough to raise concerns about nurse shortages.

The introduction of social health insurance has also had a limited impact on staff numbers, even though strategic purchasing has been seen as an ideal mechanism for translating health system objectives into clear specifications of service (and thus staffing) needs. Estonia provides an example of an insurance fund using selective purchasing to bring about effective rationalization of facilities and staffing levels (Palu and Kadakmaa 2001). However, in most instances, the contracts that have been established have had no noticeable impact on staffing. In part this may be because recent reforms have had little opportunity to mature and exert real strategic influence. However, it is also the case that many countries, such as Kyrgyzstan and Latvia, supplement insurance funding with direct budgetary flows from government to institutions. Often these are earmarked for salaries and reduce the leverage of the contracting process.

The pervasive lack of adequate data is a further obstacle to reorienting delivery and resource generation to reflect health needs rather than centrally determined norms (O'Brien-Pallas et al. 2001). Some countries, such as Armenia, Georgia and Tajikistan, have seen the complete breakdown of centralized census and reporting systems and now lack reliable population estimates. Many, including the Republic of Moldova and the Russian Federation, face difficulties in distinguishing between currently practising and retired physicians and in providing reliable data on those still in the active workforce, differentiated by specialty or by type or place of practice (public/private, urban/rural, full-time/part-time) (Kolehmainen-Aitken 1998; Padaiga et al. 2005; Strózik 2005). These difficulties are not unique to eastern Europe: France, Malta and Spain report similar difficulties in harmonizing and consolidating data (Azzopardi Muscat and Grech 2005; Lopez-Valcarcel et al. 2005; Wait 2005). However, in eastern Europe the scale of change and the implications of EU enlargement have exacerbated the problem.

Despite these continuing difficulties, examples of successful change reflect a growing commitment to linking provision and staff levels to health needs. There are attempts to build a strategic dimension into contracting (Estonia), to define basic packages of care, making explicit what the country can afford (Bulgaria) and to determine numbers of specialists (Hungary). None the less, it is proving difficult to establish reliable information and to integrate public health and strategic management into planning. Similarly, implementation of effective mechanisms (including payment systems) to reinforce policy directions has been problematic, although these tend to be better developed in the rapid transition countries. As always there are no easy answers for effective workforce planning, particularly given the uncertainty of EU enlargement and the free movement of professionals.

Education and training

Controlling access to education has had mixed success but most countries have taken significant steps to revise the content of undergraduate courses and to modernize. The acquis communautaire played an important role for the new Member States, particularly in nursing education (Zajac 2002). Yet other countries with little prospect of joining the EU also chose to harmonize with EU standards. For example, the Russian Federation signed the Bologna Declaration and is planning to meet EU standards over the next decade. Most countries converted nursing qualifications to degree level and introduced changes to reflect advances in health care and health promotion. Heavy reliance on imported education models and on international support has tended to replace earlier responses to health needs, such as the creation of the role of the feldsher.

Graduate education for specialists has been overhauled, with a focus on developing a general practice/family medicine model of primary care. The difficulties of implementation have been mentioned and these continue to challenge the value and influence (if not the content) of the training. Training for other specialties has also been reviewed, often in the context of a reduction in areas of practice. Syllabuses were revised, usually, but not exclusively, in line with EU experience. Gaps in training remain and there are challenges to address in areas such as mental health, palliative care and care of the elderly, especially in countries such as Romania and Slovakia that do not have strong traditions to draw on. Ensuring that those trained in new approaches are able to apply their skills in practice is equally challenging.

The provision of retraining and continuing education has had some limited success. During the communist era, periodic in-service training was mandatory but widely regarded as of little value. Course attendance triggered increments in seniority/pay but did little to address skills or knowledge. In many countries the systems collapsed at the time of transition and current training programmes are, almost without exception, the product of more recent innovations. Nevertheless, while quality and relevance have improved, significant barriers to access remain. In Latvia and Lithuania staff have had to attend courses in their own time and cover training costs; in Kyrgyzstan staff in rural areas have often had difficulties getting to training centres (Afford 2001). There is still some way to go before consistent and fully funded programmes of continuing education are established and integrated into career development paths and licensing processes, and to protect against the risk that training in the use of new technologies will be driven by industrial rather than strategic objectives.

Management training has progressed yet continues to present a challenge. Across eastern Europe there is the continuing presumption that managers should be doctors. Shifting the culture to allow a greater role for nurse- and business-managers is proving difficult, although training is going some way towards addressing the skills gaps. Public health's role in strategic management has been developed, particularly in Hungary. None the less, public health professionals' role in defining needs and shaping strategy is not yet fully established and there has been little progress in developing training routes for the new, nonmedical roles created by contracting and strategic purchasing. Most

countries in CEE and the NIS of the former USSR, particularly those experiencing slower transition, could benefit from a more explicit commitment to public health as a driver of strategic management and to integrating public health and management training into structured career paths.

Transforming professional roles and job boundaries

Initiatives to restructure health system workforces have inevitably moved beyond a focus on numbers to address the transformation of professional roles in order to improve health system performance. Attempts to redefine primary care as a specialist area and to reduce the number of specialties have been highlighted. In addition, there have been efforts to rebalance nurse- and doctor-led tasks and to adjust the boundaries between their roles. Previously, doctors had almost exclusive responsibility for clinical decision-making, while the role of nurses was poorly developed and subordinate to doctors. Yet the scope for change was largely missed at transition, since a focus on cutting costs by replacing doctors with lower-paid staff overshadowed opportunities to enrich (and enlarge) nursing jobs and create more satisfying roles. Resource constraints exacerbated the position by limiting the scope for investment in change, notably training.

There is very little information on the extent to which nursing roles have altered in practice and little indication of clear patterns emerging. Available evidence indicates that, in general, the number and range of tasks that staff are being asked to take on have grown over recent years (ILO 2001), although employees are often not compensated for additional responsibilities. While there is considerable pressure for job enlargement, the failure to reflect the extra demands of extended roles in terms of pay will inevitably detract from the long-term viability of reforms. Indeed, in Lithuania and the Russian Federation it has already proved difficult to attract nursing students, not least because of low pay and uncertainties about the profession and its prestige (despite Lithuanian efforts to enhance nurses' status) (Danishevski 2005; Padaiga et al. 2005).

Nursing shortages by default leave doctors carrying out what might otherwise be nursing duties for which they may have little training. Difficulties are further exacerbated as health systems seem not to have addressed the need for auxiliary staff to take on less-skilled tasks as nurses take on a greater clinical role. This seems to be reflected across much of the region, with the ratio of nurses to doctors often moving in the wrong direction (Table 11.2), making widespread substitution policies and a shift to a northern European pattern of physician–nurse relationships untenable (Saltman and Figueras 1997). The moderate cost differentials between occupational groups in many countries may limit the incentives for managers to tackle this issue. The quasi-market mechanisms' failure to penalize less efficient providers also undermines pressures to balance the professions better. The imbalance is worrying in the long term, particularly for countries undergoing rapid transition, and may have powerful consequences should physicians' salaries increase.

In both rapid and non-rapid transition countries, resource constraints complicate the challenge of re-engineering roles and job boundaries. A lack of

Table 11.2 Numbers of physicians and nurses per 1000 population 1990–2002, in selected countries

		1990	1993	1996	1999	2002
Armenia	Physicians	3.92	3.34	3.11	3.05	3.40
	Nurses	7.29	6.33	5.43	5.61	4.26
Belarus	Physicians	3.56	4.08	4.29	4.57	4.51
	Nurses	8.27	11.28	11.56	12.19	12.24
Estonia	Physicians	3.50	3.21	3.15	3.22	3.08
	Nurses	7.41	6.42	6.53	6.46	6.39
Georgia	Physicians	4.92	5.00	4.45	4.87	4.40
	Nurses	9.81	10.13	7.00	5.79	4.09
Latvia	Physicians	4.12	3.20	2.99	3.18	2.99
	Nurses	8.60	7.26	6.04	5.27	5.11
Slovenia	Physicians	1.99	2.03	2.13	2.15	2.24
	Nurses	5.61	5.90	6.55	6.93	7.17
Tajikistan	Physicians	2.55	2.18	2.08	2.09	2.03
	Nurses	8.09	7.21	5.58	4.85	4.26
Uzbekistan	Physicians	3.39	3.34	3.17	3.00	2.86
	Nurses	10.46	10.95	10.14	10.14	10.07

Source: WHO Regional Office for Europe, health for all database (2004).

Data do not always capture the shift of staff into self/private sector employment or changes in reporting during the transition period.

funding inevitably reduces a policy-maker's ability to manoeuvre and constrains improvements in working conditions or the provision of new equipment, or indeed the salary increases that might attract and motivate nursing staff. It also undermines efforts to change perceptions and achieve a more equitable relationship between doctors and nurses, particularly in countries where differentials with doctors' pay are widening. The lack of options also inhibits the implementation of new roles for physicians, making it harder to lever change. None the less, in rapid transition countries there have been significant successes in retraining and enhancing human resources. Ironically, this may prove costly for those countries that have achieved most. Certainly, countries that cannot afford to improve conditions for staff will be especially vulnerable to migration within the EU. In non-rapid transition countries there may be a lesser risk of brain drain but a real danger that policy-makers will pursue reforms that push the workforce towards a high-technology, capital-intensive approach that their country can ill afford, crowding out lower cost approaches tailored to national circumstances.

The transition of management and performance

There have been immense changes in management systems in the past 15 years. Before, senior managers in centrally planned economies had only to comply

formally with comprehensive norms, administrative guidelines and report outcomes (informally there were complex sets of parallel relationships and heads of institutions often used entrepreneurial skills to mobilize resources). Decentralization and purchaser–provider splits have transformed these certainties. This poses challenges for individual management roles and skills, as well as for the mechanisms used to manage performance, including quality control, regulation, pay and working conditions.

Performance management

Traditionally, leadership roles fell almost without exception to chief physicians (mostly men). This has changed little – hospitals are run by doctors. Although polyclinics and health posts, which used to come under their control, have often been floated off, they are normally managed by doctors. Typically clinicians also hold the key posts in regional authorities and insurance bodies (many continue to practise medicine part time) (Stepanchikova 2001; Danishevski 2005). The approach has its strengths, building on accumulated experience and skills and avoiding the tensions reported elsewhere. In Spain, for instance, non-medical managers struggle to persuade medical staff of their legitimacy and credibility (Lopez-Valcarcel et al. 2005). None the less, this slows the shift in management culture that training programmes try to foster and does little to convince women (the majority of the health workforce) that they have a future in senior roles. Those completing postgraduate management training face the same difficulties as general practitioners in applying the skills learned in the classroom, with few suitable or well-paid job opportunities (Danishevski 2005). They also have limited scope for creating incentives for staff while informal payments undermine their attempts to influence practice. Crucially, the mechanisms and information tools that might support a strategic overview of health system performance are yet to be firmly established, particularly in non-rapid transition countries.

Although governments continue to regulate and are generally regarded as having a legitimate role in setting and enforcing standards (Saltman 1995), the state's role has been reduced in much of the region. This has devastated many of the structures for managing performance, abandoning authority to the most local level, to underprepared institutions and insurance funds. Progress is being made but significant challenges remain. For example, quality criteria are linked formally to contracts in most social health insurance systems but are not fully institutionalized and enforced, with exceptions such as the Czech Republic and Estonia. This reflects the continuing weakness of third-party payers relative to providers, physicians' reluctance to face infringement of their clinical autonomy or detailed scrutiny of their work (Danishevski 2005) and the lack of effective information systems. Of course, these problems are not peculiar to CEE and the NIS of the former USSR. Western European experience suggests that shifting to evidence-based practice is challenging and that providers' strategies for manipulating reports become increasingly sophisticated as purchasers increase their demands for information.

Similarly, many licensing and accreditation systems are in disarray and do not support purchasers, managers and the state to ensure core standards or

close failing institutions. Although they are more effective in scrutinizing individuals, peer review mechanisms remain underdeveloped and, together with a lack of flexibility in wage scales and resource constraints, prevent managers from creating incentives for change or rewarding staff members who perform well. The use of guidelines, norms and algorithms is also limited, despite (or perhaps because of) the traditional use of treatment protocols (*prikaz*) in the Semashko system. Yet, in Lithuania at least, updated pathways and approaches to record-keeping allow local managers to encourage and monitor changes in practice (Padaiga et al. 2005). Expanding these approaches across rapid transition countries and adapting them to the constraints of non-rapid transition countries offers policy-makers an opportunity to influence quality.

Pay and working conditions

Remuneration is undeniably important in managing performance. There have been efforts to create financial incentives for general practitioners to perform in particular ways, such as using capitation payments to encourage preventive measures (Contandriopoulos et al. 1990). Yet in secondary care there have been fewer initiatives to reward appropriate performance or to encourage care by nurses. Low pay persists, especially among nurses and auxiliaries, and non-cash benefits (such as access to holiday resorts, which managers used to reward staff in the past) no longer exist. Below average income clearly creates genuine anxiety for staff and inevitably interferes with performance (Figure 11.1). Set in the

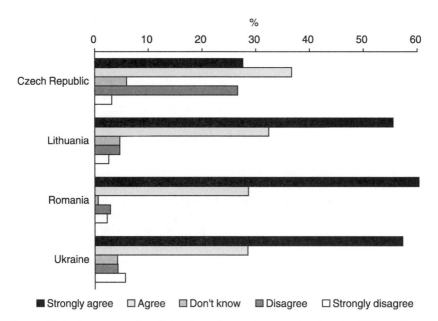

Figure 11.1 Percentage of staff, in selected countries, agreeing that the ability to live on their wages was one of their greatest worries (from *Health care in central and eastern Europe: reform, privatization and employment in four countries 2001*, copyright © 2002 International Labour Organization).

context of living costs, particularly in urban centres, it also restricts staff mobility. Thus, unemployed nurses in rural areas of Poland cannot afford to move to cities where there are nurse shortages (Strózik 2005). Low pay also contributes to a sense that staff are undervalued and undermines the perception that health professionals are respected by society. Experience in France suggests that the wearing away of prestige and respect (or indeed the perception that they have been eroded) undermines staff commitment and motivation (Wait 2005).

Physical conditions are also an important determinant of how staff experience work. Capital investment in health systems has not been a priority anywhere in eastern Europe (European Commission 2001) and the fabric of many facilities has declined. Equipment has not been maintained and shortages of supplies are common. New technology has often been confined to urban settings, with access to training and use restricted to elite staff. Non-rapid transition countries such as Kazakhstan and Turkmenistan, staff in post-conflict settings including Azerbaijan and Georgia and, to a lesser extent, those in remote rural areas in rapid transition countries like Poland face the most profound problems, but wherever conditions are poor, staff morale is undermined and quality is affected (Saltman and Figueras 1997).

Poor pay and conditions have also encouraged the acceptance of under-the-table payments, sometimes on a large scale (Lewis 2000). Thus, in Tajikistan and Ukraine 70% of users expect to pay informally for health services. The practice is common across CEE and the NIS of the former USSR and only the Czech Republic and Slovenia appear exempt from under-the-table payments. While suppliers may induce demand in order to increase earnings (Danishevski 2005), this is often unconscious. Certainly, medical staff have difficulties recognizing some of their own behaviour as problematic. For example, in Armenia doctors regard informal charges as key to subsidizing the treatment of poorer patients, while in Poland 80% of doctors deny receiving informal payments yet 70% acknowledge that they accept presents from patients in gratitude for their services (Strózik 2005).

All the efforts to improve performance outlined above are complex and to work effectively must be fully integrated, properly funded and well managed. This is far from easy given the wider challenges of transition. In addition, the traditional dominance of medical managers and a top-down culture make it more difficult to develop a sense of inclusion or shared ownership of change. Insecurity and doubts about job tenure also contribute to short-term approaches, making employers and staff reluctant to invest in long-term initiatives. Policy commitments to develop training and capacity building and greater efforts to involve all occupations in dialogue will help to achieve progress, but as experience in western Europe shows, there is no single, easy way to transform performance.

Conclusions

A host of challenges confronts human resources in eastern Europe, not least how to achieve acceptable working conditions, adequate wages and appropriate security for all staff. The reforms under way address these issues, although their

primary focus is to reorient health services and their staff so as to enhance efficiency, effectiveness and the responsiveness of care. But a number of current factors obstruct positive developments. Some, such as the antiquated physical infrastructure or resistance to innovation, relate to the historical legacy of communism; others stem from the upheavals of transition. None the less, progress is being made even though few recent initiatives are fully embedded in national health systems as yet.

Certainly, where decentralization was excessive it has been reversed. Similarly, social health insurance schemes have been adapted (and continue to adapt) to address indebtedness, increase their strategic role in matching services to population health needs and promote efficiency and quality. Problems with data persist but these should ease with planned investments in information technology and adherence to international data collection methods. Capacity building at the regional and municipal levels should also begin to pay dividends over time. It is less clear how the issue of under-the-table payments will be resolved, and as long as they are commonplace they will undermine formal priority setting.

The impact of EU enlargement should be positive in the long term for rapid transition countries. It is not possible to model accurately the consequences of increased staff mobility or reduced working hours or to predict the extent to which the expectations of patients and staff will change as integration continues. Nevertheless, if GDPs rise as anticipated and there is a commensurate increase in health spending, problems in the new EU Member States and candidate countries should be overcome, eventually. However, some western European trends (e.g. reduced respect for the medical professions, a more litigious culture) bode ill for human resources in health in eastern Europe.

Even more worrying, perhaps, is the way so many non-rapid transition countries are pursuing western European approaches without considering fully the suitability of standards intended for high-spending countries. The fact that western European style reforms were appropriate for some countries emerging from communism in the 1990s has tended to be taken as evidence that all former communist states should pursue similar approaches to development. Some of the NIS of the former USSR at the opposite end of the spectrum of transition might be better served by looking at policy options being developed in middle-income countries. For them a labour- rather than capital-intensive model, the maintenance of high employment levels and less expensive, lower technology care might be most suitable even when conflicting with initiatives to cut public sector employment. It is to be hoped that countries will examine their options and choose the reforms that are most appropriate for them, those that relate to their own experience and culture, so that they can best reconcile their economic position with the preferences and expectations of their citizens and health sector staff.

References

Afford, C. (2001) *Failing health systems: failing health care workers in eastern Europe*. Geneva, International Labour Organization.

Afford, C. (2003) *Corrosive reform: failing health systems in eastern Europe*. Geneva, International Labour Organization Socio-Economic Security Programme.

Azzopardi Muscat, N. and Grech, N. (2005) Case-study: Malta. *In*: Dubois, C.-A., McKee, M. and Nolte, E., eds, *Human resources for health in Europe*. Copenhagen, European Observatory on Health Systems and Policies.

Contandriopoulos, A.P. et al. (1990) Systèmes de soins et modalités de remuneration. *Sociologie du travail 1. In*: Saltman, R. and Figueras, J., eds, *European health care reform, analysis of current strategies*. Copenhagen, World Health Organization.

Danishevski, K. (2005) Case-study: Russia. *In*: Dubois, C.-A., McKee, M. and Nolte, E., eds, *Human resources for health in Europe*. Copenhagen, European Observatory on Health Systems and Policies.

Dunford, M. and Smith, A. (2000) Catching up or falling behind? Economic performance and regional trajectories in the 'new' Europe. *Economic Geography*, **76**(2).

European Commission (2001) *Economic and financial affairs. Real convergence in candidate countries: past performance and scenarios in the pre-accession economic programmes*. Brussels, European Commission (ECFIN/708/01-EN).

European Commission (2003) *Investing in research: an action plan for Europe*. Commission staff working paper. Brussels, European Commission.

European Union (2001) 19/EC of the European Parliament and of the Council of 14 May 2001 amending Council Directives 89/48/EEC and 92/51/EEC on the general recognition of professional qualifications and the specific Council Directives concerning nurses responsible for general care, dental practitioners, midwives, pharmacists and doctors (www.europa.eu.int/eur-lex/en/lif/dat/2001).

Hall, D. (1998) Cited in: *Workshop on employment and labour practices in health care in central and eastern Europe*. Joint report by the International Labour Organization and Public Services International. Geneva, ILO.

Hunter, D. (1998) Cited in: *Workshop on employment and labour practices in health care in central and eastern Europe*. Joint report by the International Labour Organization and Public Services International. Geneva, ILO.

ILO (2001) *Basic security survey*. Geneva, International Labour Organization.

Karaskevica, J. and Tragakes, E. (2001) *Health care systems in transition – Latvia*. Copenhagen, European Observatory on Healthcare Systems.

Kolehmainen-Aitken, R.L. (1998) Decentralization and human resources: implications and impact. *Human Resources Development Journal*, **2**(1).

Lewis, M. (2000) *Who is paying for health care in eastern Europe and central Asia?* Human Development Sector Unit (ECAR). Washington, DC, World Bank.

Lopez-Valcarcel, B.T., Quintana, C.D.D. and Cocorro, E.R. (2005) Case-study: Spain. *In*: Dubois, C.-A., McKee, M. and Nolte, E., eds, *Human resources for health in Europe*. Copenhagen, European Observatory on Health Systems and Policies.

McKee, M. and Healy, J. (2002) *Hospitals in a changing Europe*. Buckingham, Open University Press.

McKee, M., MacLehose, L. and Nolte, E. (2004) *Health policy and European Union enlargement*. Maidenhead, Open University Press.

Merkel, B. and Karkkainen, K. (2002) Public health aspects of accession. *Eurohealth*, **8**(4): 3–4.

O'Brien-Pallas, L. et al. (2001) Integrating workforce planning, human resources, and service planning. *Human Resources for Health Development Journal*, **5**(Dec/Jan): 1–3.

Padaiga, Z. et al. (2005) Case-study: Lithuania. *In*: Dubois, C.-A., McKee, M. and Nolte, E., eds, *Human resources for health in Europe*. Copenhagen, European Observatory on Health Systems and Policies.

Palu, T. and Kadakmaa, R. (2001) Estonian hospital sector in transition. *Eurohealth*, **7**(3): 61–5.

Rainnie, A., Smith, A. and Swain, A. (2000). Employment and work restructuring in transition. *In*: Smith, A., Rainnie, A. and Swain, A., eds, *Work, employment and transition: restructuring livelihoods in post-communism*. London, Routledge.

Saltman, R. (1995) *Applying planned market logic to developing countries' health systems: an initial exploration*. Forum on Health Sector Reform Discussion Paper No. 4. Geneva, WHO.

Saltman, R. and Figueras, J. (1997) *European health care reform: analysis of current strategies*. Copenhagen, WHO Regional Office for Europe.

Scheil Adlung, X. (2001) *Building social security: the challenge of privatization*. New Brunswick, NJ, Transaction Publishers.

Standing, G. (1996) Social protection in central and eastern Europe: a tale of slipping anchors and torn safety nets. *In*: Esping-Andersen, G., ed., *Welfare states in transition: national adaptations in global economies*. London, Sage.

Standing, G. (1997) The folly of social safety nets: why basic income is needed in eastern Europe. *Social Research*, **64**(4): 1339–79.

Standing, G. (2002) The babble of euphemisms: re-embedding social protection in 'transformed' labour markets. *In*: Smith, A., Rainnie, A. and Swain, A., eds, *Work, employment and transition: restructuring livelihoods in post-communism*. London, Routledge.

Stepanchikova, N. (2001) *Socio-economic status of health care workers in the Russian Federation*. Geneva, ILO.

Strózik, M. (2005) Case-study: Poland. *In*: Dubois, C.-A., McKee, M. and Nolte, E., eds, *Human resources for health in Europe*. Copenhagen, European Observatory on Health Systems and Policies.

Wait, S. (2005) Case-study: France. *In*: Dubois, C.-A., McKee, M. and Nolte, E., eds, *Human resources for health in Europe*. Copenhagen, European Observatory on Health Systems and Policies.

WHO (2000) *The World Health Report 2000. Health systems: improving performance*. Geneva, World Health Organization.

WHO (2004) *Macroeconomics and health: investing in health for economic development*. Report of the Commission on Macroeconomics and Health (www.un.org/esa/coordination/ecosoc/docs/RT.K.MacroeconomicsHealth.pdf).

Zajac, M. (2002) EU accession: implications for Poland's healthcare personnel. *Eurohealth*, **8**(4): 13–14.

twelve

The impact of EU law and policy

Rita Baeten and Yves Jorens

Introduction

The management of HRH in EU countries is increasingly influenced by decisions and legislation at EU level. Examples include the EU directives on professional qualifications and minimum training periods for health care professionals, as well as other EU policies and laws that restrict or support the scope of action by Member States. This chapter examines EU policies' impact on HRH in Member States. We begin by interpreting EU competencies in health care and the objectives of these policies. We then discuss the European legislation relevant to HRH by examining: (a) the legislation on professional qualifications; (b) the European Community (EC) Treaty provision on free movement of services and its applicability to health care provision as defined by the ECJ; (c) the WTD; and (d) some recent developments in EU policy. A cross-cutting section analyses this legislation's impact on each of the key dimensions of HRH, followed by a concluding section. The policy and legal initiatives in this domain are developing rapidly, so it is possible that some of the problems we discuss might have been addressed by the time this book is published. However, our main conclusions remain valid.

EU competencies versus Member State competencies

The organization and financing of health care within the EU is the responsibility of the Member States. The EU has no formal competency in this field (European Commission 1997b), unlike in education where it has some competency to define educational matters but any harmonization of the content of education or vocational training is excluded (European Commission 1997a). Furthermore, the treaties empower the Community to act only in instances where it can be

more effective than an individual Member State in achieving a particular object-ive. Thus, Article 3 (b) of the EC Treaty states that the EU may act: 'only if and in so far as the objectives of the proposed action cannot be sufficiently achieved by the Member States and can therefore, by reason of the scale or effects of the proposed action, be better achieved by the Community'. This principle of subsidiarity has been invoked frequently in relation to initiatives on health care provision and financing.

Member States' responsibilities for the organization and financing of health care include: defining the conditions for access to a health care profession; the scope and nature of professional training; the scope of activities specific to a health profession; a framework for continuing education, monitoring the quality of clinical practice and ensuring the application of ethical standards; the scope and conditions of publicly financed care; the establishment of pricing systems; and the terms of contractual relationships between purchasers and providers of care.

Member States do have to comply with EU law when establishing national regulations. European integration aims to create a single market by removing trade barriers between Member States through the treaties guaranteeing free movement of persons, products, services and capital. These four fundamental freedoms apply to the health care sector as they do to any other. However, the implementation of the principles of the single market is the task of the author-ities responsible for economic affairs and the internal market at both national and EU levels. As a consequence, health policy-makers have little influence on policies that affect the health sector.

There are essentially four ways in which the EU can impact on HRH in Member States, relating mostly, though not exclusively, to legislation.

Secondary legislation specific to the health care sector

The conditions for access to the health care professions have long been regu-lated by the Member States. They aim to protect both patients and licensed health care professionals (De Bijl and Nederveen-van de Kragt 1997). However, the variation in regulations across Member States has the potential to obstruct the free movement of professionals. Indeed, national regulations on structures and conditions for access to health care professions can create de facto barriers for migrant professionals coming from another Member State. The EU has there-fore established a regulatory framework guaranteeing minimum qualifications to be met by health care professionals seeking to assert the right to practise their profession in other EU countries without discrimination. Thus, Article 47 (3) of the EC Treaty specifies that: 'in the case of the medical and allied and pharmaceutical professions, the progressive abolition of restrictions shall be dependent upon coordination of the conditions for their exercise in the various Member States' (European Commission 2002). These professions have been singled out for special treatment because of their role in protecting human health (Lonbay 2000).

Rulings of the ECJ

Treaty provisions can also apply directly to health services, sometimes in ways in which their applicability to the health care sector was not considered when they were drafted. This is seen in a series of recent rulings of the ECJ. The ECJ has declared the provisions on the free movement of services to be applicable to health care provision and to the relationship between health care providers and funders of public health care. Member States had always considered these aspects to be part of their national social protection systems and thus under their individual exclusive competence, exempt from single market rules. Since their applicability to the health care sector was not considered when the treaties were drafted they do not take account of its specific nature. This creates substantial uncertainty, in some cases creating concerns about the sustainability and social characteristics of the systems in Member States.

In the wake of these rulings, since the late 1990s the political bodies of the EU have sought to reclaim issues of health care from the ECJ. However, this has led to contradictory responses that reflect the diffuse responsibility for health within the Commission. On the one hand, the EC launched a proposal for a directive on services in the internal market that considers health care services as being like any other commercial service. On the other hand, there have been attempts to include safeguards in the European constitutional treaty to redress the balance between the internal market objectives and the social objectives of the EU. A so-called *social clause* was introduced in the draft to ensure that internal market legislation would take account of requirements guaranteeing a high level of social protection and protection of human health (European Commission 2004c).

Secondary legislation not specific to the health care sector

European secondary legislation that is not drafted specifically for the health care sector but applies none the less includes EU legislation on the employer–employee relationship, such as the WTD (see below).

Other EU policies

Finally, EU initiatives other than legislation have the potential to influence HRH. For example, during the process of acceding to the EU in 2004, the then candidate countries received support for restructuring their professional training programmes. Some of these initiatives were financed by European funds. Other Member States benefit from investment in skills development in regional programmes also funded by the EU. Recently, Member States have decided to cooperate on health care issues in a structured way, to define common objectives and create common databases and analyses.

Directives on the recognition of professional qualifications

European legislative efforts on the mutual recognition of professional qualifications proceeded in four phases: transitional, sectoral, general and legal. The last of these is being driven by the ECJ. European regulations on the mutual recognition of diplomas still have a number of important gaps, so substantive policies on education, training and professional experience have not yet been finalized. These gaps and shortcomings are being filled by case law. The rules on mutual recognition were introduced originally to facilitate the freedom of establishment, but have since been used progressively to ensure the free movement of services (Mossialos and McKee 2002).

The first phase resulted in 35 transitional directives, aimed at the recognition of professional experience rather than mutual recognition of diplomas. This was followed by the introduction of sectoral directives enabling mutual recognition. Medical and paramedical professions were first regulated by sectoral directives in the 1970s, mainly because the treaty regarded it as a sine qua non for liberalizing services in this sector. The subsequent general directives on the mutual recognition of diplomas are also highly relevant. The first set up a general system for the recognition of higher education diplomas and established a three-year minimum period for professional education and training. This is supplemented by a second general directive. The third and final directive coordinates the previously mentioned 35 transitional directives on the recognition of professional training.

Sectoral directives

Sectoral directives establish minimum periods for educational and training programmes and comprise lists of diplomas that meet those standards in the various Member States. A diploma listed in the directive is automatically recognized in another EU Member State. This enables the competent authority to confine its efforts to determining whether a diploma is included in the sectoral directive without the need to assess the competence or knowledge of the holder of the diploma.

Many of the 14 sectoral directives concern the health care professions, i.e. medical doctor, general care nurse, dentist, midwife, pharmacist and veterinary surgeon (EU 1977, 1978, 1993a). In theory the right diplomas will be recognized automatically. In practice, however, the procedures in place require the applicant to contact the competent authority in the host Member State and, in some countries, to pay administrative charges. The authority has three months to examine the request and, if rejected, the applicant is entitled to appeal against this decision in the national courts.

This system is rather rigid and it is difficult to keep it up to date. In addition, some Member States with high standards of training are concerned about the quality of training in others, particularly since recognition is granted without assessment of the migrant's knowledge and skills. Indeed, it is an explicit principle underpinning the directives that the coordination of legal and administrative provisions is not intended to lead to harmonization of content. However,

there remain considerable differences between Member States regarding the status of professions and length of training. Advisory bodies such as the Advisory Committee on Medical Training were set up to address this issue. Despite rather infrequent meetings and limited financial support, this body has provided influential reports on medical training.

The limited opportunities for updating sectoral directives create considerable concern among those seeking high standards of patient care. The medical profession, perhaps more than any other, requires continuous training to keep abreast of the latest technological innovations and scientific developments. Free movement of health care workers needs to take account of these developments and should adjust the minimum training periods for medical qualifications accordingly. Furthermore, these directives do not take account of changes in some of the medical professions. Thus, the directive for general care nurses ignores the current trend for specialized nurses (e.g. branch nurses). Specialized nurses from Member State A cannot work in Member State B because they do not meet the requirements for designation as a general care nurse set out in this sectoral directive. In addition, they cannot call upon the general directives on mutual recognition because these do not apply if there is a sectoral directive for the relevant profession. Increasingly, therefore, the ECJ has to fill the gaps in European legislation on the mutual recognition of qualifications.

A related concern refers to the minimum requirement for the length of training (in years or hours) as set out in the directives. This is emphasized at the expense of content and scope. Thus, while current procedures ensure that migrant health workers have undergone the minimum period of education and training, they fail to assess the skills and capacity of the person concerned or the continuous updating of their knowledge and skills, and therefore fail to address quality standards. Given current developments in health care, such as advances in technology or rising patient expectations, there is a need to develop further the process of mutual recognition at the European level.

There is also a need to improve the system of exchanging information on professional and personal references. Before granting permission to practise, the doctors' directive allows the host Member State to request a certificate from the state of origin attesting that the requirements of good character or good repute have been met. This also includes knowledge of all necessary information on previous or outstanding sanctions, disciplinary action of a professional or administrative nature against the person concerned, criminal penalties imposed when pursuing his or her profession in the Member State of origin and a certificate of physical and mental health (EU 1993a). However, these provisions are very ambiguous and leave Member States much scope to decide what they should disclose.

The main challenge is the lack of uniformity between the various national regulations regarding preventing and penalizing professional misconduct and the consequent failure to capture these differences in ways that ensure high-quality medical care (Roscam Abbing 1997). As a result, the provisions on the exchange of information between the host Member State and the state of origin were applied insufficiently, incorrectly or not at all. One blatant example concerns a doctor who was barred for life in the Netherlands but set up practice

again in Spain without any problems. In Luxembourg, a migrant doctor was authorized to practise because the authorities were unaware of proceedings that had led to his suspension in his original country (Sheldon 1997).

EU enlargement highlights this issue further, with the enhanced possibilities for attracting health care workers from the new Member States as a means to meet increased need (see Chapters 2 and 3). However, it is important to ensure that this increased mobility does not affect quality.

New Member States have to comply with the acquis communautaire and implement EU standards such as the minimum requirements for education and training outlined earlier. The Treaty of Accession also permits certain acquired rights, as set out in Annex II, 2.C. of the Accession Treaties. Thus, for nationals of new Member States whose formal medical qualifications do not satisfy the minimum training requirements laid down in the corresponding directive, each Member State shall recognize evidence of formal qualification in medicine awarded by those Member States in relation to training that commenced before the date of accession (1 May 2004). This is to be accompanied by a certificate stating that the individual concerned has effectively and lawfully been engaged in the activities in question for at least three consecutive years during the five years prior to the date of issue of the certificate.

Similar provisions apply to nurses. In order to allow nurses who were trained before accession to continue to practise, most new Member States established licensing procedures, including bridging courses and requirements for work experience, to ensure that they comply with minimum European standards (Padaiga et al. 2005; Strózik 2005). Specific provisions have also been developed for people with diplomas, certificates or other qualifications obtained on the territory of the Czech Republic, Slovakia, Estonia, Latvia, Lithuania and Slovenia when they were part of a different country.

In summary, the European regulations on mutual recognition of professional qualifications in the 15 countries belonging to the EU before 2004 failed to ensure uniformity of quality standards and approved medical practice. This is even truer of the enlarged Union. Further action is needed to develop European standards designed to ensure high-quality health care, including standards of care for practising medicine, monitoring doctors' skills and competence, cross-border accreditation and improved exchange of information between Member States.

General directives

The regulations on professional recognition evolved in a piecemeal fashion with numerous parallel provisions, variations and lack of flexibility. This has created a great need for a more flexible and general system of mutual recognition in the various Member States. This general system applies to 'regulated professions', expanded to include 'regulated professions, qualifications and training' by a second general directive. However, this system applies only to people who have the necessary qualifications to exercise a profession in their country of origin. It is not applicable to those who want to continue their studies in another Member State, or to those who want to exercise their

profession in another state but have not yet completed the required training in their state of origin.

Compared to the sectoral system, general directives require the systematic assessment of the qualifications and skills of the applicant and introduce compensation mechanisms (supervised training, adaptation period or aptitude test) if the requirements are not met. In accordance with ECJ case law, professional experience following training has to be taken into account before compensatory measures can be imposed. The general system is therefore flexible and ensures that Member States no longer have to agree on parallel professions, while providing a relatively rapid system of recognition with sound assessment procedures. However, it is clear that this system places a higher burden on the competent authorities assessing candidates prior to recognition or accreditation.

The general system is becoming increasingly important in the health care sector, particularly for paramedical professions, where there is still substantial variation in the regulation of titles, training duration and content and scope of activity across EU countries.

Proposal for a framework directive on the recognition of professional qualifications

In 2002, the European Commission proposed a new framework directive on the recognition of professional qualifications for regulated professions (Commission of the European Communities 2002). It seeks to promote a more flexible market for labour and services and to simplify and consolidate existing regulations, while improving control, clarity and flexibility. It clearly distinguishes between freedom of establishment and the freedom to provide services, which we examine in turn.

Freedom to provide services

The existing directives on professional qualifications require professionals who provide services on a temporary basis abroad to do so according to the same rights and obligations as host country nationals and, in particular, the rules of conduct of a professional or administrative nature. Member States may request only a pro forma registration with a professional organization or body rather than registration with a public social security body that funds health care. The host Member State may require the person concerned to make a prior declaration to the competent authorities concerning the provision of services.

In contrast, the new proposal allows for the temporary provision of services based on the legislation in the country of establishment. A service provider who is legally established in one country and moves to another Member State would thus be allowed to pursue a professional activity for a period of not more than 16 weeks per year under the professional regulation of the Member State where the provider is legally established. The service provider concerned must inform in advance the designated contact point in the country of establishment and is obliged to inform those receiving their services about these arrangements.

Freedom of establishment

The proposed new directive integrates the existing general system for recognition and the sectoral system for certain professions, imposing stricter requirements on the right of establishment.

As noted above, the general system assesses whether individual applicants satisfy the conditions for recognition and provides for compensatory measures. The directive also allows for exemption from compensatory measures on the basis of so-called common platforms; a set of criteria for professional qualification that testify to the holder's competence to practise a certain profession. These are developed by professional associations at European level and are designed to be used for official accreditation by competent authorities in the Member States. It also includes recognition of professional experience; relevant activity practised in another Member State is sometimes regarded as sufficient evidence of skill and competence.

For certain professions, the directive has adopted the sectoral system and the principle of automatic recognition. Thus each Member State shall recognize automatically evidence of diplomas or certificates of professional qualifications that satisfy the minimum training conditions referred to in the proposal. A Member State shall, for the purpose of access to, and pursuit of, professional activity give such evidence the same effect on its territory as the evidence provided by diplomas or certificates of professional qualifications that it itself issues. Specific provisions are established for each profession in relation to training, specific acquired rights and the pursuit of professional activities.

Administrative cooperation and competence to act on recognition of professional qualifications have been simplified and are expected to make the system more flexible. The competent bodies of the country of origin and the host country are required to cooperate closely and assist each other in applying the directive, facilitated by a designated coordinator in each Member State.

The Commission's initial proposal was subject to considerable debate. Professional bodies opposed the drastic reduction in the system of automatic recognition. In contrast to current legislation, which allows for automatic recognition of all medical specialty diplomas present in at least two countries, the new proposal foresees that only specialties common to all Member States will be recognized. The remainder would fall under the general system of recognition by individual assessment and (possible) compensation measures. This reduces the number of automatically recognized specialties from 52 to 17, with the list of those included and excluded appearing quite arbitrary. Furthermore, if one Member State decides to abolish a certain specialty, that specialty will lose its automatic recognition. It was contended that this will not simplify the system because the competent authorities will have to assume the difficult task of comparing medical specialties across countries, requiring strict separation between the general and sectoral system.

There is also concern about the inability to control health care providers who make use of the freedom to provide services without establishment, particularly since they will no longer be bound by the professional rules of the host Member State. To ensure patient safety there are calls for a distinction to be made between the freedom to provide services and establishment and that both be

subject to stricter regulations than those outlined in the current proposal on registration, codes of conduct and disciplinary procedures.

At the time of writing the proposal is still being discussed in the European Parliament and the Council. The proposed amendments following the first reading and the common position in the Council seem to suggest a rather less radical move, with future legislation more like that which is currently in place (Council of the European Union 2004; European Parliament 2004).

Health care providers subjected to the treaty provisions on the free movement of services

The ECJ ruled, in a series of judgements starting with the famous Kohll and Decker rulings in 1998, that health care provision is an economic activity in the sense of article 50 of the EC Treaty (ECJ 1998a, b, 2001, 2003a). This means that the treaty regulations relating to the freedom to provide services also apply to the delivery of health care and its financing by national social protection systems. It applies to systems where health care funding is based on cost reimbursement (as where a patient pays the provider and is reimbursed by a sickness fund), as well as those that provide care based on benefits in kind (where services are provided free at point of use). Consequently, systems for funding health care that are regulated by national governments may not discriminate against foreign care providers unless there are justifiable reasons. Obstacles to the free movement of services may be justified if they threaten the financial sustainability of the social security system or the maintenance of a broad range of health care services accessible to all. However, these restrictions must be based on objective criteria.

The ECJ did not find any justification to inhibit the free movement of ambulatory care services. The costs of non-hospital care provided abroad when the patient has not sought prior authorization must be reimbursed by the patient's home funding body, at the same rate and on the same conditions that apply to domestic care providers, provided these conditions do not discriminate against care provided abroad. In contrast, for hospital care the court ruled that there may be justifiable reasons to restrain free movement because of the importance of planning the distribution of facilities to enable maintenance of a rational, balanced, accessible, affordable and high-quality supply of hospital services.

According to these rulings, health care funding is now subordinated not to the conditions and criteria applicable in the country where the care is provided but to the conditions and criteria applying in the patient's country of origin; these criteria may not discriminate against foreign providers. This can have far-reaching consequences for national health care systems, for the relationship between health care providers and the funders of public health and consequently for Member States' capacity to manage their human resources. We discuss some of these potential consequences below.

Non-discrimination of providers established abroad

Member States and health care purchasers may not discriminate against either providers established in another Member State or care provided abroad; therefore national criteria for funding health care that are inconsistent with those employed in other countries might be considered discriminatory. Thus, the ECJ did not accept a funder's right to refuse to reimburse ambulatory care provided by non-contracted providers abroad even where domestic providers were first obliged to enter into a contractual relationship with health care purchasers. It also accepted that patients have free choice of provider abroad even though this may be limited in their home country.

On the other hand, contracts or collective agreements between public health care purchasers and health care providers define the price and content of care provided and so may establish rules to ensure cost-effective use of funds. Examples include budget ceilings or performance-related payment systems. If health care purchasers have to reimburse services provided by non-contracted ambulatory providers they risk losing these important mechanisms to control the provision of health care abroad.

Although the existing constraints focus primarily on hospital treatment, reimbursement of ambulatory treatment received abroad may also have important implications for planning. Examples include national regulations on access to health care, such as referral systems and patient registration systems. Even if public health care purchasers were allowed to impose some of these requirements on foreign providers, it would be very difficult to do so.

Quality standards

The ECJ stated that conditions for exercising the profession of medicine in Europe were established in a uniform way and should be sufficient to ensure an equivalent quality of health care in the different Member States. This assertion may be questionable (Jorens 2003). As discussed previously, health care providers established in another Member State do not necessarily meet the same quality requirements as providers in the home country. Certain professionals can exercise their profession perfectly legally in Member State A but be refused the right to do so in Member State B (Nickless 2001). Furthermore, health care professionals have to comply with quality requirements defined by the Member States and the funders of health care. These quality standards may include guarantees of continuity of care, record-keeping, regulations on prescription or referral and participation in peer review activities.

In theory, EU law cannot oblige purchasers of public health care to fund a treatment provided abroad that does not meet these conditions. However, according to the ECJ, the free movement of services may not be hindered for reasons of general interest if the objective of the intended requirement is met by comparable requirements in the country where the provider is established. Therefore, Member States will have to take account of existing requirements in the country of establishment and it will be very difficult to prove that the provisions to ensure quality abroad are insufficient to achieve the same objectives.

Risk of reverse discrimination

If rules imposed on domestic providers cannot be enforced on providers established abroad, the question is: to what extent are national regulations tenable when applied to home providers? National providers could feel discriminated against, placing national regulations under pressure. This may lead health care providers to question the justification for their cooperation with the domestic health authorities and refuse to engage in contractual negotiations concerning availability, quality, quantity, price and efficacy of care (Mossialos and Palm 2003).

In Luxembourg, the main result of the Kohll and Decker judgements was that the medical profession perceived the opening of borders and the reimbursement of care provided by non-contracted foreign providers as discrimination. Consequently, discussions concerning the introduction of profiles of medical activity to trace abuse of the system have been blocked. Furthermore, Luxembourg's physicians sought to withdraw from the compulsory system that requires doctors to comply with imposed tariffs. In response, the government was forced to increase reimbursement fees by an average of 6.5% (Kieffer 2003).

The WTD

As noted previously, European legislation that is not specific to the health care sector can also impact quite considerably on health care professionals, who generally are considered to be regular workers rather than a special category. One obvious example is working time.

Directive 93/104/EC concerning certain aspects of the organization of working time (the WTD) defines working time as 'any period during which the worker is working, at the employer's disposal and carrying out his activity or duties, in accordance with national laws and/or practice' (EU 1993b). The WTD establishes minimum requirements for the organization of working time, such as daily rest periods, breaks, weekly rest periods and annual vacations, all with the aim of improving the working conditions of employees in the EU. The original Directive 93/104/EC did not cover some sectors, such as doctors in training, but was amended in 2000 (EU 2000) to include doctors in training. This may lead to considerable problems in health care staffing because of the complexity of the concept of working time in this sector, such as the status of on-call work. Thus, cases brought before the ECJ have led to two important rulings regarding the definition of on-call service.

The first case, SIMAP, concerned Spanish legislation regarding the 'resident on-call' service, following regular working time, with specific reference to primary health care teams (ECJ 2000). The workers concerned were required to be either physically present or available to answer professional calls in the workplace. This additional time on call was not taken into account when determining the maximum amount of working time. The ECJ was asked to pronounce whether doctors' time spent on call, either at or away from the workplace, counts as full working time. More specifically, the question was

whether doctors on call who are on the premises but asleep may be considered to be working.

As noted above, the WTD defines working time as any period during which the worker is working, at the employer's disposal and carrying out his or her activity or duties, in accordance with national laws and/or practice. The ECJ requires that the three conditions must be met to qualify as full working time. It is argued that during periods on call the first two conditions under WTD regulations are fulfilled. Moreover, even if the activity performed varies according to the relevant circumstances, the fact that doctors resident on call are obliged to be present and available at the health centre to provide their services means that they are carrying out their duty in that instance. The ECJ stated that time spent resident on call in primary health care teams must be regarded in its entirety as working time, overtime if appropriate, if they are required to be at the health centre. The situation is somewhat different for doctors who are on call by being contactable at all times without having to be present at the health centre. Even if they are at the disposal of their employer, in that they must be contactable, they may manage their time with fewer constraints and pursue their own interests. Here, only the time spent actually providing primary health care services is regarded as working time.

The more recent Jaeger case also asked whether on-call service in hospitals (*Bereitschaftsdienst*) should be regarded as working time (ECJ 2003b). During on-call service the employee was obliged to be present at a place determined by the employer, at or away from the employer's premises, and to be contactable but at the same time authorized to rest or to spend time otherwise as long as his or her services are not required. The ECJ ruled that if the doctor is required to be physically present at the hospital, time spent on call must be regarded as working time even though the person concerned is permitted to rest at the workplace during periods when services are not required.

The decisive factor is whether those concerned can choose where they are during waiting periods. Those who must be in a designated location, such as a hospital, are subject to appreciably greater constraints. By virtue of their separation from family and the social environment they face constraints on their use of time when their professional services are not required. This interpretation is not altered by the fact that the employer makes a rest room available for use until the service is required. The argument is even stronger for doctors on call in health centres because periods during which their services are not required may be of short duration and/or subject to frequent interruptions or they may be required to monitor the condition of patients placed under their care or to perform tasks of an administrative nature.

The ECJ rulings in the SIMAP and Jaeger cases will have substantial (financial) consequences for national health care systems. They may be required to recruit more health care staff in order to avert exceeding the maximum daily and, especially, weekly working time and ensure sufficient breaks for personnel. WTD prescribes a daily break of at least 11 consecutive hours within 24 hours. A 'sleeping wake service' followed by a normal working day and vice versa may not respect this minimum daily break. The average working time per seven-day period, including overtime, may not exceed 48 hours. This limit can be reached easily. The normal length of work for night shift workers may not

exceed an average of eight hours in any 24-hour period. Problems may arise when 'sleeping wake services' last 12 hours or more.

Although the impact of the case law is not limited to the health sector, its impact is greatest here. In Germany it was calculated that applying the SIMAP and Jaeger cases to the health care sector would require a 24% increase in staff and 15 000–27 000 additional doctors, amounting to an extra cost of €1.75 billion (European Commission 2003). The Netherlands estimated it would need to recruit 10 000 additional workers at an extra cost of €400 million. The United Kingdom believed it would require about 1250 additional health care staff other than doctors and between 6250 and 12 550 additional doctors, at an estimated €550–1130 million. Malta would require double the number of specialists in the highest training grade and up to a third more doctors-in-training (Azzopardi Muscat and Grech 2005).

A transition period was agreed in order to allow Member States time to adapt but the impact of this case law is expected to be even greater with progressive application of the WTD. For the three years after 2004 the number of weekly working hours may not exceed an average of 58; 56 for the following two years; and 52 for any remaining period, which may be no more than three years. The challenge arises because, in many countries, much front-line care is provided by doctors-in-training; as their working patterns change to comply with the WTD the training authorities must find new ways of delivering the training (European Commission 2003).

It is important to note that, prior to the SIMAP ruling, working time was generally interpreted to mean that periods of inactivity during time on call were not defined as working time. Following the SIMAP case some Member States made use of the opt-out arrangement provided in the WTD as a means to alleviate some of the problems created by this case law. The opt-out provision allows individual workers voluntarily to opt out of the 48-hour average weekly working time limit (including on-call time). For the health sector alone, the opt-out clause was adopted in the legislation of several Member States, including Cyprus, France, Germany, Malta, the Netherlands, Slovenia and Spain. Only the United Kingdom implemented the opt-out provision in national legislation as a general possibility for all its workers (European Commission 2003).

Following the considerable problems caused by the interpretation of the ECJ's rulings on on-call service, the European Commission embarked on a consultation with the social partners at EU level (European Commission 2004e) and subsequently adopted a proposal to update key aspects of the WTD. At the time of writing this is being reviewed by Council and the European Parliament (Commission of the European Communities 2004a). The amended proposal suggests that time spent on call but where the individual is not actually working would not be considered working time, while compensatory rest would be provided after 72 hours. An individual opt-out would remain possible but subject to stricter conditions to prevent abuse.

Recent developments (2004)

Directive on services in the internal market

The ECJ rulings on the freedom of provision of health services described above relate to the *passive* provision of services, i.e. where the service recipient moves to the country where the service provider is established. However, as outlined in previous sections, the principle of the free movement of services also implies service providers' right to establish themselves in another Member State or to provide temporary services in a Member State other than the one in which they are established.

In January 2004, the EC submitted a proposal for a directive on services in the internal market that extensively liberalizes the services sector (Commission of the European Communities 2004b). It introduces a general legal framework for services provided for remuneration and explicitly includes health services and services provided by regulated professions, such as the medical profession. It applies in cases when:

- the patient moves to the country where the provider is established to receive care;
- the health care provider travels to the Member State of the patient to provide care;
- care is provided at a distance (e.g. telemedicine).

The proposed directive distinguishes clearly between freedom of establishment, relating to services provided through a fixed establishment for an indefinite period, and free movement of services, concerning services provided on a temporary basis in a Member State other than the Member State of establishment.

Concerning the *free movement of services*, the proposed directive introduces the principle of the country of origin. Thus, health service providers operating legally in one Member State may market their services in others but are not required to comply with corresponding regulations in the host country. Health service providers would no longer be subject to the national regulations of the host country when engaging in cross-border activities. The country of origin is responsible for supervising the provision of services abroad.

Member States may not impose on health service providers established in another Member State an obligation, for example, to inform the competent authorities or to engage in specific contractual arrangements between the provider and the recipient. The future directive on recognition of professional qualifications, described above, is partially exempt from these provisions.

This proposal, if it does become law, could lead to deregulation of the health care sector. Providers could choose to establish themselves in the Member State that imposes the least restrictive conditions on the provision of health care. Subject to the legislation of this Member State, they could then provide care in other Member States and so compete with health care providers who have to comply with more restrictive legal requirements. In turn this could put pressure on regulations in those Member States and cause a downward spiral of deregulation.

A related problem is the country of origin's responsibility for supervision of

health care provision. The corresponding authorities are not required to give an account of their conduct towards the citizens in the host country who receive care. There is thus a lack of motivation and legimitization to control health care provided abroad.

Finally, Member States must ensure that service recipients (i.e. patients) are informed appropriately. This includes information on the legislation applicable in other Member States related to the access to, and exercise of, the (health care) activity. Given the complexity of health care legislation, it will be difficult to explain the systems of 25 countries to patients in a comprehensible way, especially since patients may need this information when they are in vulnerable and dependent positions because they need immediate care.

The chapter on the freedom of establishment obliges Member States to simplify and remove a large number of authorization and licensing procedures and to limit the number of documents required. The proposed directive introduces a major screening exercise, requiring Member States and the European Commission to identify and assess conditions for establishment. Member States must verify that the requirements are non-discriminatory, necessary and proportional; if not, they must be abolished. These include: quantitative or territorial restrictions, particularly restrictions determined on the basis of population distribution or minimum geographical distance between service providers; requirements imposing an obligation for providers to take a specific legal form; requirements stipulating a minimum number of employees; and fixed minimum and/or maximum tariffs with which providers must comply. The conditions listed here thus include national legislation on planning, staff norms in health care institutions, price fixing mechanisms and others, all crucial instruments for the organization and funding of health care systems. When this comes into force, Member States can introduce any new requirements of this kind only if the need arises because of new circumstances. The Commission will examine any new requirements' compatibility with Community law and can oblige abolition.

The proposed directive also defines the conditions under which national social security systems are to reimburse the costs of health care received in other Member States, based on ECJ case law. It lifts bans on advertising for regulated professions, while stipulating that this must respect certain rules and limits.

Overall, the proposal fails to take account of: the specificity of the health care sector, characterized by information asymmetry between provider and patient; the involvement of third-party payers in the definition of prices, content and quality of care; and the complexity of the health care sector, with its complex interplay between so many different actors. The proposal could have a substantial impact on the health care sector, stimulating deregulation and thus restricting the stewardship capacity of Member States as it relates to human resources, regulating and controlling quality, planning, setting rules of conduct and payment and others.

Health care's inclusion in this directive has caused substantial concern. Europe's health ministers expressed their disquiet in a collective letter to the Council administration responsible for the internal market.

European cooperation in health care

Cooperation in health care between Member States is being formalized progressively. Once it was acknowledged that the single market impacted on national health care systems, public authorities responsible for health policy began to accept the need for some EU cooperation in this domain. The EC presented a communication on the application of the 'open method of coordination' to health care and long-term care (European Commission 2004d) and patient mobility (European Commission 2004a). Member States would cooperate to define common objectives and indicators with relevance for HRH, including the following topics:

- collecting information on the movement of health professionals;
- developing a concerted European strategy covering issues such as monitoring, training, recruitment and working conditions;
- addressing regional inequalities in the provision of care;
- earmarking financial and human resources to the regions, services and different types of care, according to need;
- decentralization involving the various actors and making them responsible for the management of resources and the provision of care;
- introducing incentives for providers and patients or measures to promote new treatments that reduce costs while providing the same service;
- reducing staff shortages by investing in basic and continuing training and an improvement of the quality of jobs.

To promote this process of cooperation, the Health and Consumer Protection Directorate General (DG SANCO) of the European Commission, responsible for public health, established the High Level Group on Health Services and Medical Care, bringing together Member State representatives and the Commission (European Commission 2004b). This committee works closely with the Social Protection Committee on these issues.

EU impact on key dimensions of human resources management

This section discusses the findings from the previous sections and analyses the extent to which they may impact on key dimensions of HRH.

European legislation defines the minimum *training* requirements for regulated health care professionals, defined as minimum length of training and, for some professionals, the substantive content. It also defines the regulations for the mutual recognition of health care professionals' diplomas and the conditions they may impose for the establishment of health care professionals in their territory. Member States' discussions defining those minimum standards within the sectoral directives have undoubtedly led to improvements in the quality of training and a certain level of convergence of training programmes across the EU. However, the legislation does not provide for a harmonization of training standards. Nor does it impose conditions for continuing education, which is becoming crucial for the exercise of effective health care in a quickly developing scientific and technological environment. The instruments

employed by the directives concerned are not flexible enough to adapt to new developments in the professionalization and specialization of health care professions. Moreover, the definition of the field of competence of most professions is left to the Member States, indicating that the content of training will differ according to the responsibilities of the professional in each Member State. National authorities are strictly limited in their capacity to impose additional training for the entry into practice of health care professionals from abroad, thus restricting their capacity to adjust for the differences in training.

We have discussed recent developments by which the rules on mutual recognition of diplomas, originally introduced to facilitate the freedom of establishment, are used progressively to ensure the free movement of services. Hence, the legislation is supposed not only to guarantee minimum standards for entry into practice but also to ensure the quality of health care provided. This trend reduces further the national authorities' capacity to guarantee the quality of care.

The impact on *workforce planning* is exemplified by the ECJ rulings that require purchasers of public health care to fund ambulatory care provided in another Member State. As a consequence, the supply of health care workers is de facto extended to provision of care abroad. If the proposed directives on professional qualifications and on the free movement of services are adopted as they stand, Member States may lose further control over the number of health care providers that are active in their territory, and there may be a limit on the ability of health care managers to define the need and supply of health services for their population.

On the other hand, EU law offers the opportunity better to adjust the supply and demand of the health care workforce internationally. The principles of freedom of movement will make it easier to recruit or contract health care professionals from other countries, resulting in a 'win–win' situation if there is oversupply in one Member State and shortage in another. However, where there is a substantial difference in salaries, tariffs or working conditions there is a risk of health care professionals responding to attractive conditions abroad, regardless of the needs in their country of origin. The ten Member States that joined the EU in May 2004 have much lower living and working standards, and therefore there is a genuine risk of such a brain drain (Chapter 3). This has the potential to threaten levels of remuneration in the countries of origin and the financial viability of their public health care systems.

The definition of working conditions at EU level can also impact on national health care workforce planning. We have discussed the impact of the WTD. Many health care workers, mostly junior medical doctors, are employed in hospitals on conditions that do not meet the provisions of the WTD and its interpretation by the ECJ. Its application requires hospitals to recruit more health care staff. This not only has budgetary consequences but also may provoke important supply problems in countries with shortages of health care staff. When balanced with training requirements this may require extensive reconfiguration of services, and some commentators in the United Kingdom have argued that many peripheral hospitals may have to be closed.

EU law can impact on *performance planning*, namely the instruments that ensure that resources are used to achieve optimal health outcome. We described

the lack of appropriate EU-level mechanisms to enforce and control disciplinary measures for health care providers moving within the EU. We also described how the Kohll and Decker rulings may lead to reverse discrimination and might induce pressure to change or abolish national regulations on evaluation and accountability, practice standards, performance monitoring, clawback mechanisms for inappropriate care, etc. The same applies to the recent proposals on services in the internal market and on the recognition of the professional qualifications outlined above. The application of the regulations on the free movement of services also leads to a fragmented approach to service delivery. Health care providers are considered not as part of an interconnected system but as single providers of a service.

Finally, European legislation can also have an impact on *working conditions*. The most obvious example is the WTD, which impacts on the working hours of medical staff, but potentially also on remuneration. We have discussed the possibility of health care professionals from the new Member States moving to countries with higher salaries and better working conditions. This may push the countries of origin to increase salaries and improve working conditions in order to retain their workforce. The increased possibilities of cross-border contracting of health care may also produce financial pressures. Health care providers can opt to enter into contracts with the purchasers that offer the most profitable level of remuneration. The Luxembourg doctors who refused to renew their agreement with the Luxembourg health insurance system until they agreed to considerable increases in compulsory tariffs further illustrates the EU legislation's potential impact on the health care workforce. Finally, the ECJ rulings may lead to the introduction of new methods of remuneration; for instance, countries with a benefit-in-kind system have to reimburse ambulatory care provided abroad on a fee-for-service basis.

Conclusions

This chapter has traced the development of EU legislation and policies that have a potential impact on HRH. We identified European law's important influence on the education and training of health care staff, workforce planning, performance planning and the working conditions of the health care workforce. Despite the fact that the EU has no formal competency in the health care sector, we can conclude that its impact is considerable and growing.

EU legislation elaborated specifically for the health care sector undoubtedly has had some positive impacts on, for example, the quality and standardization of training. However, the driving force behind EU regulations is the creation of the single European market and the removal of trade barriers. These policies are elaborated by those responsible for economic policy, competition and the internal market rather than the authorities responsible for public health. Consequently, public health concerns are not always considered sufficiently when developing these policies. This places the authorities responsible for health care organization and human resources in a defensive position and limits their scope of action. National policies for human resource planning are often bypassed, neutralized or overridden by EU law.

Thus, although EU policies aim to remove trade barriers between Member States, their impact on the internal national organization of the health care systems and human resources management is often more important than their impact on the cross-border movement of professionals and services. On the other hand, Member States are reluctant to hand over some of their responsibilities in order to incorporate the safeguards necessary to ensure effective human resources policies at EU level.

References

Azzopardi Muscat, N. and Grech, N. (2005) Case-study: Malta. *In*: Dubois, C.-A., McKee, M. and Nolte, E., eds, *Human resources for health in Europe*. Copenhagen, European Observatory on Health Systems and Policies.

Commission of the European Communities (2002) *Proposal for a Directive of the European Parliament and of the Council on the recognition of professional qualifications.* COM 2002/119, 2002/0061(COD), 7 March. Brussels, Commission of the European Communities.

Commission of the European Communities (2004a) *Proposal for a Directive of the European Parliament and of the Council amending Directive 2003/88/EC concerning certain aspects of the organisation of working time.* COM 2004/607 final. Brussels, Commission of the European Communities.

Commission of the European Communities (2004b) *Proposal for a Directive of the European Parliament and of the Council on services in the internal market.* COM 2004/2, 13 January. Brussels, Commission of the European Communities.

Council of the European Union (2004) *Proposal for a Directive of the European Parliament and of the Council on the recognition of professional qualifications, political agreement on the Council's common position.* 9716/04, ETS 42, CODEC 753, 27 May. Brussels, Commission of the European Communities.

De Bijl, N. and Nederveen-van de Kragt, I. (1997) Legal safeguards against medical practice by not suitably qualified persons: a comparative study in seven EU countries. *European Journal of Health Law*, **4**: 5–18.

European Commission (1997a) *EC Treaty, Articles 149 and 150*. Amsterdam: European Union.

European Commission (1997b) *EC Treaty, Article 152 paragraph 5*. Amsterdam: European Union.

European Commission (2002) *Official Journal of the European Communities* (www.europa.-eu.int/eur-lex/en/treaties/dat/EC_consol.pdf).

European Commission (2003) *Communication from the Commission to the Council, the European Parliament, the European Economic and Social Committee and the Committee of the Regions concerning the re-examination of Directive 93/104/EC concerning certain aspects of the organisation of working time.* 843 final, 30 December. Brussels, Commission of the European Communities.

European Commission (2004a) *Communication from the Commission. Follow-up to the high level reflection process on patient mobility and healthcare developments in the European Union.* COM 2004/301, 20 April. Brussels, Commission of the European Communities.

European Commission (2004b) *Commission Decision of 20 April 2004, Setting up a high level group on health services and medical care.* C1501. Brussels, Commission of the European Communities.

European Commission (2004c) *Conferences of the representatives of the governments of the Member States. Provisional consolidated version of the Draft Treaty establishing a*

Constitution for Europe. CIG 86/04, art. III-2a, 25 June. Brussels, Commission of the European Communities.

European Commission (2004d) *Communication from the Commission to the Council, the European Parliament, the European Economic and Social Committee and the Committee of the Regions modernising social protection for the development of high-quality, accessible and sustainable health care and long-term care: support for the national strategies using the 'open method of coordination'*. COM 2004/304, 20 April. Brussels, Commission of the European Communities.

European Commission (2004e) *Second phase of consultation of the social partners at Community level concerning the revision of Directive 93/104/EC concerning certain aspects of the organisation of working time*. 19 May. Brussels, Commission of the European Communities.

European Court of Justice (1998a) Case C-158/96, *Raymond Kohll* v. *Union des caisses de maladie*. Judgment of 28 April.

European Court of Justice (1998b) Case C-120/95, *Nicolas Decker* v. *Caisse de maladie des employés privés*. Judgment of 28 April.

European Court of Justice (2000) Case C-303/98, *Sindicato de Medicaos de Asistencia Publica (SIMAP)* v. *Conselleria de Sanidad y Consumo de la Generalidad Valenciana*. Judgment of 3 October.

European Court of Justice (2001) Case C-157/99, *B.S.M. Geraets-Smits* v. *Stichting Ziekenfonds VGZ* and *H.T.M. Peerbooms* v. *Stichting CZ Groep Zorgverzekeringen*. Judgment of 12 July.

European Court of Justice (2003a) Case C-385/99, *V.G. Müller-Fauré* v. *Onderlinge Waarborgmaatschappij OZ Zorgverzekeringen UA* and *E.E.M. Van Riet* v. *Onderlinge Waarborgmaatschappij ZAO Zorgverzekeringen*. Judgment of 13 May.

European Court of Justice (2003b) Case C-151/02, *Request to the Court by the Landesarbeitsgericht Schleswig-Holstein (Germany) in the proceedings pending before that court between the Landeshouptstadt Kiel and Norber Jaeger*. Judgment of 9 October.

European Parliament (2004) *European Parliament Legislative Resolution on the Proposal for a European Parliament and Council Directive on the recognition of professional qualifications* (COM(2002)119-C5-0113/2002–2002/0061(COD)), P5-ORIV(2004)0086 A5-0470/2003, 11 February.

European Union (1977) Council Directive 77/452/EEC of 27 June concerning the mutual recognition of diplomas, certificates and other evidence of the formal qualifications of nurses responsible for general care, including measures to facilitate the effective exercise of the right of establishment and freedom to provide services.

European Union (1978) Council Directive 78/686/EEC of 25 July concerning the mutual recognition of diplomas, certificates and other evidence of the formal qualifications of practitioners of dentistry, including measures to facilitate the effective exercise of the right of establishment and freedom to provide services.

European Union (1993a) Council Directive 93/16/EEC of 5 April to facilitate the free movement of doctors and the mutual recognition of their diplomas, certificates and other evidence of formal qualifications (www.europa.eu.int/eur-lex/en/lif/reg/en_register_062050.html).

European Union (1993b) Council Directive 93/104/EC of 23 November 1993 concerning certain aspects of the organisation of working time. *Official Journal of the European Communities*, L307, 13.12, p. 18.

European Union (2000) Council Directive 2000/34/EC of the European Parliament and of the Council of 22 June, amending Council Directive 93/104/EC concerning certain aspects of the organisation of working time to cover sectors and activities excluded from that Directive.

Jorens, Y. (2003) Europa en het recht op gezondheidzorg: een vrij verkeer van patiënten? (Europe and the law on health care: free movement of patients?) *In*: Janvier, R., van Regenmortel, A. and Vervliet, V., eds, *Actuele problemen van het socialezekerheidsrecht (Current problems in social security law)*. Bruges, die Keure.

Kieffer, R. (2003) L'impact de la jurisprudence Européenne sur la politique sanitaire et sociale au Luxembourg. (The impact of European jurisprudence on health and social politics in Luxembourg). Presentation in Lille, 5 December.

Lonbay, J. (2000) The free movement of health care professionals in the European Community. *In*: Goldberg, R. and Lonbay, J., eds, *Pharmaceutical medicine, biotechnology and European law*. Birmingham, University of Birmingham.

Mossialos, E. and McKee, M. (2002) *EU law and the social character of health care*. Brussels, Peter Lang.

Mossialos, E. and Palm, W. (2003) The European Court of Justice and the free movement of patients in the European Union. *International Social Security Review*, **56**: 2.

Nickless, J.A. (2001) Guarantee of similar standards of medical treatment across the EU: were the European Court of Justice decisions in Kohll and Decker right? *Eurohealth*, **7**(1): 16–18.

Padaiga, Z. et al. (2005) Case-study: Lithuania. *In*: Dubois, C.-A., McKee, M. and Nolte, E., eds, *Human resources for health in Europe*. Copenhagen, European Observatory on Health Systems and Policies.

Roscam Abbing, H.D.C. (1997) Quality of medical practice and professional misconduct in the European Union: invitational symposium on the occasion of the Netherlands' EU Presidency, Amsterdam, 20 January 1997. *European Journal of Health Law*, **7**(3): 33–41.

Sheldon, T. (1997). Proposal to stop bad doctors setting up elsewhere. *British Medical Journal*, **314**: 247.

Strózik, M. (2005) Case-study: Poland. *In*: Dubois, C.-A., McKee, M. and Nolte, E., eds, *Human resources for health in Europe*. Copenhagen, European Observatory on Health Systems and Policies.

thirteen

Moving forward: building a strategic framework for the development of the health care workforce

Carl-Ardy Dubois, Martin McKee and Ellen Nolte

Introduction

Ensuring an appropriate, trained and sustainable workforce is clearly a major issue for European health policy now and in the future. Common to all health systems is a dependence on their workforce to achieve the objective of health improvement. Yet all countries are faced with deep-rooted problems of workforce imbalances and human resource bottlenecks. In part, these are created by poor working environments, skills gaps and the use of inappropriate policy tools that often fail to provide the best incentives or to optimize the performance of the workforce. Even though these difficulties are well recognized, the infrastructure to support health workforce development is inadequate in most European countries or is, at best, composed of a fragmented patchwork of separate units, budgets and programmes, each focusing on an individual group of health workers or a narrow aspect of human resource management. Policy-makers are thus faced with the major challenge of how to identify the appropriate steps to move towards more sustained and effective development of the workforce. Rather than listing prescriptions, this chapter focuses on the building blocks of a strategic framework and highlights some critical points in the process of developing and implementing effective human resource policies in health care.

A strategic framework: three building blocks

A strategic framework is seen here as a policy tool designed to promote a more proactive attitude to health workforce challenges and to ensure that investments in the workforce are sustainable, cohesive, coordinated and linked to a clear and agreed vision of the future health workforce. Elaboration of explicit and long-term strategies to guide the development of human resources in health care may be justified on several grounds. The distinctive nature of many features of the health labour market means that market options are often totally inadequate to achieve appropriate solutions to the problems faced by policy-makers.

Traditional ad hoc and reactive interventions have consistently failed to correct workforce imbalances in health care. It takes years to educate, train and socialize health professionals, so there is unlikely to be a quick fix to many human resource problems in health care. Human resource decisions have long-lasting effects and are often difficult to reverse. This means that, rather than responding reactively to immediate or recurrent crises, a strategic approach offers a better prospect of supporting an evolving health system: assessing what kind of personnel are needed to address population health needs and to select mechanisms that will optimize returns from human resource investments, while ensuring the continuity of the workforce itself.

One important implication is that policy responses to human resource problems must be grounded in a national vision for health and developed from an overall perspective of population health that embraces primary care, acute care, health protection and promotion. Another implication is that workforce development must be conceptualized so as to take account of the contingencies of the broad social, political and economic environments that shape the needs and expectations of the population and of health workers and circumscribe the universe of options available to policy-makers. In addition, given the complex and changing nature of the environment in which the health care workforce exists, policy responses must be designed within a framework that is sufficiently flexible to facilitate learning and to foster innovative and self-sustaining processes of development at all levels of the system.

On the basis of the issues raised in this book, the strategic options that will better prepare the health sector to address the workforce challenges it faces can be considered to fall into three key categories.

Supply strategies

Workforce supply requires a broad range of activities in policy development, planning and management. These activities involve identifying the quantity and type of health workers needed at different levels of the health system to ensure that its goals are met. Forecasting studies and modelling are the tools used most often, reflecting a traditionally strong emphasis on quantitative approaches to human resources. However, the models used have often reached only a low degree of sophistication, failing to take account of the many factors that affect workforce supply. Cyclical shortages and occasional surpluses tend to

provoke short-term reactions, often involving changing student intakes and enhanced recruitment abroad. The need for long-term strategic solutions implies a requirement to develop more sophisticated models of forecasting both demand and supply, based on the generation of more diverse scenarios and integration of a more complete set of variables. Moving to a strategic approach also means recognizing that issues related to health workforce supply are more complex than simply whether there are enough workers.

Closer attention to the changing needs of the population and subsequent changes in the modes of health care delivery call for those involved to address the complex issues of what health workers do and how the composition of the workforce and the current mix of skills must change to reflect new ways of delivering these services. A strategic approach to workforce supply also confronts policy-makers with the task of designing the regulatory, financial and organizational structures that will support development, recruitment, retention and equitable deployment of the workforce and are likely to generate incentives that are consistent with the health system's objectives. A supplementary challenge is to site the issue of supply in the global context, envisioning mechanisms that will be able to overcome constraints associated with international workforce mobility for both source and host countries.

Education and training strategies

Education and training refer to a broad set of activities designed to prepare a skilled health care workforce so that it can meet the requirements of the health care task. One main challenge is to develop an educational system that can respond quickly to continuously changing requirements. A number of significant developments highlighted throughout this book create a sense of urgency about the need to transform the skills and roles of health care providers and the way they are educated so as to keep pace with changing population needs and emerging service delivery modalities. Changes in disease patterns, technological advances, changing settings in which health care is delivered and users' increased involvement in the delivery of services, among other things, have contributed significantly to alterations in the roles and the responsibilities of many health care providers. These have created many skill gaps that must be filled by appropriate training.

The strategic actions required in this area relate primarily to continuous realignment between training programmes, health service needs, evolving roles and work practices. Given the growing evidence that integrated teams and networks offer the best option to address many complex health problems, it makes sense that educational curricula and teaching modalities include provisions that prepare the workforce for these types of working arrangements. If health workers have to embrace a more holistic approach to health interventions, training programmes should also place a greater emphasis on primary care, health promotion, wellness and disease prevention. In a dynamic health care environment that calls for constant learning, a strategic approach to education and training will also look to provide health practitioners with incentives to maintain a high level of skills, knowledge and competencies throughout

their careers. Improvements in health care workers' education and training also raise issues relating to the governance, administration and funding of health education institutions. Strategic challenges facing policy-makers include: the establishment of quality control systems for the education of health professionals; the development of a sustainable educational infrastructure and long-term teaching capabilities; the fostering of collaborative planning between the health sector and education providers; and the implementation of funding mechanisms that are consistent with health policy objectives.

Working environment strategies

Building a strategic framework for the development of the health care workforce also calls for the provision of clear directions to ensure that all health care environments are places where the workforce is valued and supported and has the opportunity to develop while providing high-quality care. If health care reforms are to achieve positive outcomes for patients, employees and organizations, comprehensive strategies rather than piecemeal actions should address the complex set of interconnected issues that relate to job design, performance management, employment relationships, workplace cultures and human resource practices. This implies the development of a practical programme of measures that can improve safety and security, create a supportive workplace culture and ensure that staff become fully committed to their work and motivated to achieve the best outcomes.

Strategic solutions may focus on developing flexible working environments, multiple career pathways and work flows that reflect the changing modes of service delivery and the diversity of the workforce. A strategic approach to improving the working environment also means that organizational changes and health care reforms must consider explicitly the impact on workplaces and employees and should include actions that promote the workforce's participation in the implementation of change.

Approaches to rewarding and remunerating health workers must be consistent with the changes needed in service delivery and based on achieving the dual objectives of patient service delivery and nurturing, motivating and developing employees. While much attention is focused on the activities of the clinical workforce, strategic actions are needed to develop an effective system of governance and leadership in the workplace. Investments in management development must ensure that managerial roles and structures are resourced adequately and that managers are given the ability to manage, with the leverage to ensure optimal use of the available workforce. A supplementary challenge is to build a regulatory environment that supports the highest standards but leaves sufficient room to develop innovative work practices and to make adjustments that reflect local imperatives.

A system-wide approach

Putting together these building blocks involves a whole-system approach that links different domains and enables the development of synergistic actions. As the health personnel system is part of a more complex health system, several systemic features operate as facilitators or constraints to effective human resource development and can be altered only through sector-wide strategic interventions. For instance, addressing workforce challenges in the delivery of primary care services, particularly in the post-communist countries, calls for a radical shift away from a traditional focus on hospital-based services.

These three building blocks demonstrate some of the complexity of human resource management, encompassing multiple domains (supply, education and training, work environment). Within each of these there are multiple levers for policy action that can be used at different levels of the health system. A broad system approach stresses the interconnectedness of development strategies in these different domains and may prevent problems that are more likely to arise with a reductionist focus on a single factor. The complexity of human resource management is such that actions taken in one area may have spillover effects in other areas. Policies relating to education and training are likely to impact on the supply of health personnel. Operations intended to balance the distribution of personnel may have consequences for staff motivation and performance. Segmented interventions that attenuate some symptomatic problems can overlook their root causes and may result in new and unwanted consequences. This means that coordination of policy responses to human resources' challenges is a critical condition to achieve success.

Immediate actions

Moving towards the development of such a strategic framework in European countries requires two immediate actions. The first is to improve the collection and dissemination of information on the health workforce. Relevant, accurate and timely information is the cornerstone of policy-making and workforce development. Yet the availability, comparability, comprehensiveness and timeliness of information on the health care workforce pose a constant obstacle to policy-makers across Europe. Data on health personnel are collected for administrative purposes by different groups using different methods and seldom for the purposes of human resource management. Information on certain topics is particularly limited because these have attracted little attention from policy-makers.

In general, the provision of information related to the hospital sector is the most comprehensive. For many occupations no reliable information is available. While the medical and, to a lesser extent, the nursing professions have been extensively studied, data on the professions allied to medicine remain very limited. There is an urgent need to invest in more systematic collection of workforce data at national, local and regional levels (harmonizing nomenclature, putting in place minimum data sets and processing arrangements, enlarging the focus of what is collected).

For each of the three building blocks mentioned previously, several types of potential intervention are underexploited and warrant increased attention from researchers to fill important gaps in the evidence base. There are gaps in understanding how the substitution of roles and changes in scopes of practice can ensure an optimal use of human resources in line with public needs. There is a lack of knowledge about how various forms of financial and non-financial incentives affect the behaviour of health professionals and how they impact on their motivation and mobility. Despite strong emphasis on the development of new models of care delivery, there is still a lack of research on the implications of the emerging models for professional regulation, scopes of practice, workforce supply and management of performance. These information gaps should be filled concurrently with an active process of shared learning. Information on what works, as well as information about potential solutions to human resource challenges, needs to be shared between organizations and stakeholders at national and international levels.

The second immediate requirement for action is to mobilize actors effectively around the current human resource challenges. Building a strategic vision for the health care workforce is a political process that will succeed only if it is undertaken with the commitment of all key stakeholders. Responsibilities for HRH are dispersed among multiple ministries and a variety of institutions, including local authorities, private companies, not-for-profit organizations, statutory bodies, education and training institutions, representative bodies (unions, professional associations) and insurance funds. Each group has access to some levers that it can use to support or block changes affecting human resources. This means that the success of a strategic vision for HRH is contingent on the extent to which these key stakeholders are involved in, and committed to, the process and its implementation. The challenge for policy-makers is to negotiate a pragmatic path through the divergent values and interests of these various groups. This intersectoral, multistakeholder mobilization and collaboration seems to be an essential prerequisite to develop and implement effectively cohesive actions that cut across different sectors (health, education, planning, civil service, finance), different domains (supply, education and training, work environment) and different governance levels (national, regional, local).

The health labour market has an international and global dimension so this mobilization and collaboration should extend beyond national boundaries. A fortiori in the single European market, European countries may profit from working together on solutions that will not only address their own specific challenges but also ensure that collectively they have taken steps to develop coherent policies that address the various aspects of human resources. European organizations such as the European Commission and WHO Regional Office for Europe can play a major role in maximizing the collection and sharing of data, filling the current research and knowledge gaps and improving coordination of the workforce across national boundaries. Donors supporting international cooperation programmes, particularly in CEE, may also facilitate the recognition of the importance of HRH developments by prioritizing the human resource component in their investments.

Index